The

American Academy

in Rome

1894-1969

The

American Academy in Rome

1894-1969

Lucia Valentine

Alan Valentine

University Press of Virginia

Charlottesville

THE UNIVERSITY PRESS OF VIRGINIA
Copyright © 1973 by the Rector and Visitors
of the University of Virginia

First published 1973

ISBN: 0-8139-0444-7
Library of Congress Catalog Card Number: 72-92663
Printed in the United States of America

Foreword

THIS story of the genesis and growth of the American Academy in Rome by Lucia and Alan Valentine was written to commemorate the seventy-fifth anniversary of the Academy's founding. It is an illuminating and readable account of the most venerable and famous American institution on foreign soil devoted to the pursuit of both the fine arts and humanistic scholarship. The authors wrote it as a labor of love and handsomely presented it to the Academy. Lucia Valentine was in a special sense predestined to be one of the authors for her great-uncle, Charles Follen McKim, was a prime mover in the Academy's origins, founding, and early history and her father, Charles D. Norton, later became a dedicated and influential trustee. To her and to her husband for their many months of hard and devoted work in the Academy's archives in Rome and in New York and for their most generous gift of the finished book the Trustees of the American Academy in Rome are deeply grateful.

To the main text of the book has been added a Dramatis Personae prepared by Alan Valentine which provides useful biographical information on the men and women mentioned in its pages whose thought and action constitute the story of the Academy. Although the Valentines' account ends with the year 1969, in order to indicate the range of talent that the Academy has nurtured and to bring it up to date, the names of fellows from the beginning through the year 1971–72 are listed in an appendix. Another list gives the artists and scholars in residence at the Academy since the trustees established this program in 1947. Finally there is a roster of the Academy's board of trustees as of January 1, 1973, among whom are four interested and able women recently elected; this is the first time in the Academy's history that women have served on the board.

The Trustees of the American Academy in Rome wish to express their thanks to the American Council of Learned Societies for a generous subsidy in support of publication and to two old and firm friends of the Academy who together contributed an equal amount. Finally thanks are due Walter Muir Whitehill, who kindly read the manuscript and brought it to the attention of the University Press of Virginia.

RENSSELAER W. LEE

Princeton, N.J.
September 1972

Acknowledgments

THE necessary brevity of these words belies the depth of our gratitude to Richard and Josephine Kimball, to whom this book owes its existence. When we told them—our first confidants—of our tentative idea of writing a history of the Academy, they immediately offered us not only their approval but the priceless gift of their extensive typed notes and outlines. It was then that we realized that they must have been planning the very project we were proposing and which they were abandoning in our favor. This book cannot take the place of theirs, which without doubt would have been more penetrating, but we can think of no warmer example of generous friendship than their unfailing help, including a close reading of our final draft.

Nor can we adequately record here our debt to Laurance and Isabel Roberts. When we made a six months' exchange of houses in Princeton and Frascati, we found that they had opened to us not only the doors of their charming house (with its famous cook, Maria, formerly of the Academy staff) but, by prearrangement, many other doors to friendships and assistance in Rome.

During our hours at the Academy (to which we were given two ponderous iron keys, one to unlock the garden gate for our car and the other to the library), Dr. Frank Brown, then director of the Academy, offered us the quiet assurance of ready help which exactly met our needs. He stole time from archaeology and administration to check our account of Academy excavations at Cosa and elsewhere, and approved the final draft of that chapter. As to our friend Rensselaer Lee, the interest and support he gave us before becoming the Academy's president was only amplified by that promising event. He too read the typescript as we slowly produced it, and by his encouragement kept us going. Our combined hostess, preceptress, and fact-finder, Mary Williams, was as patient as she was helpful during our frequent invasions of the Academy's New York office in quest of the half-buried past. And our days at the Academy library in Rome were warmed by the graciousness of its librarian Inez Longobardi.

Whatever interest our book may have is obviously enhanced by the unique and hitherto unpublished letters of Miss Amey Aldrich to Mrs. Dwight Morrow, made available to us by Constance Morrow Morgan, and by the correspondence of Rutherford Mead, Charles Dyer Norton, and others, provided by Garrison Norton. We record our gratitude to the Library of Congress for making available to us its collection of the papers of Charles Follen McKim and giving us authority to quote from them. We are also grateful to the New York Public Library for similar helpfulness and authorization regarding material from its collection of McKim letters presented to it by William Maloney, the husband of McKim's daughter Margaret. The trustees of the Academy have also given us complete freedom to quote from the Academy's records in its library in Rome, its files in New York, and its publications. Herbert Kubly has authorized us to quote from his articles on the Academy, and the Houghton Mifflin Company to quote from Adams' *Daniel Chester French* and from Mrs. French's volume of *Memories.* In a few cases we have been unable either to locate or communicate with present holders of copyrights, if any, as in the case of Charles Moore's biographies of Daniel Burnham and Charles McKim, but we have authoritative assurances that in those instances our brief quotations come under the legal heading of "fair use." Many of the quotations not individually cited here were taken from papers of the Academy trustees and are included under their general authorization. If in any instance we have exceeded our privileges we offer apologies.

We cannot name all those who have made our work easier and our days more rewarding, but that does not lessen our gratitude to them for contributions often greater than they could have realized. Finally, we regret that we have been unable to include accounts of all the fellows who deserve notice, since it is on their records that the Academy stands.

LUCIA and ALAN VALENTINE

Contents

The

American Academy

in Rome

1894-1969

I

"The Shack"

ANY account of the American Academy in Rome must start with
the Chicago World's Fair of 1893. It was the spark that fired
the idea of a school for American artists in Europe, an idea long
stirring in many minds but now to find a vigorous champion in one.

The fair* surprised its public. Conceived as a means to promote
the commerce of a growing city, it made a startling and unforeseen
impression on the art of its day. If in the beginning the fair had
been brought to the city for profit, in the end it was remembered
not for fortunes gained but for riches of talent uncovered, and for
the order and harmony of their display. This was largely due to the
fair's remarkable overseer, the Chicago architect Daniel Burnham.

"Make no little plans," Burnham once said. "They have no magic
to stir men's blood." He reached out for the best of America's
talent, and first for the landscape architect Frederick Law Olmsted.
Although the site selected for the fair, a tract of marshy land south
of the city at the end of the lake, had been uninspiring enough,
Olmsted saw possibilities of waterways and landfill that could enhance whatever was to be put upon them. As plans took rough
shape, a shelter was put up for the supervisors. It was built on a
newly made island in a newly dug river that flowed into a "lagoon"
about which the fair was to be centered. "The Shack," as it was
thereafter called by the men who came to use it, was a replica of an
early log cabin, itself to become one of the fair's exhibits. Meanwhile it played a pivotal part in the development of the fair's
masterly plan.

Charles Follen McKim and Richard Howland Hunt, architects;
John La Farge and Frank Millet, painters; Augustus Saint-Gaudens
and Daniel Chester French, sculptors, and many others had been

* The official name of the fair was the World's Columbian Exposition.

drawn into Burnham's net. Night after night, around a roaring fire
in the Shack's stone chimney, artist and craftsman discussed their
problems and contrived solutions. The bold and beautiful result of
their close collaboration is now familiar to students of the period.
But, as the participants were fully aware, more than the beauty of
the World's Fair was born of those evenings.

"Do you realize," exclaimed Saint-Gaudens, "that this is the
greatest meeting of artists since the fifteenth century?"

A Renaissance tour de force was being re-created as architect,
painter, sculptor, landscaper, and builder wrought together in the
classical manner. It was an experience that bit deeply into the minds
of those who shared it; it influenced the course of American art for
decades to come.

No one was more profoundly affected than Charles McKim. He
recognized the influence of the fair on the taste of the day and
caught fire from the way in which it had been designed. The special
skills of each profession had brought to fruition the artistry of the
others. It was a lesson, he felt, that must be passed on to future
generations of American artists. The need for an American school
in Europe, where the principles of collaboration within the classic
discipline were still honored, became of first importance to him.

To understand the form taken by the Academy one must know
something of McKim's background, for he founded it, promoted it,
and for the next dozen years of his life dominated it. It reflected his
personality and his inheritance. Its life was interwoven with his
own; in its early days his convictions became its policies.

He was born of Quaker parentage on October 24, 1847, in the
mellow, rural county of Chester, Pennsylvania. He was a namesake
of Charles Follen, a distinguished refugee from the Rhineland
repressions of 1815, who had become Harvard College's first professor of German. Follen, ardently on the side of the free man, had
worked with McKim's father, a leader of the antislavery movement
in Philadelphia. William Lloyd Garrison was also a friend of Follen, and he too had named a son for him. In a small society so
closely knit by abolitionist bonds, no one was surprised when Mc-
Kim's sister, Lucy, married Wendell Phillips Garrison, another
son of William Lloyd.

McKim's background of simplicity and industry was pleasantly
tempered by the warmth, gaiety, and cultivation of his family.
From this merger of ethic and affection he developed a personal

canon of taste. To McKim there was a morality in the discipline of great art, best illustrated in the finest classical work. He never faltered in his respect for it and insistence upon it, and the Academy he founded bore the stamp of his convictions.

The Garrisons, McKim's sister and brother-in-law, had settled close to New York in Llewellyn Park near Orange, New Jersey. In 1866 McKim and his parents joined the young pair in their small, delicate, Victorian-Gothic house. It was simply furnished except for a few contemporary paintings by Pre-Raphaelite friends in England, which were characteristically valued for their reflection of the Italian Renaissance. McKim was at Harvard in 1866, but the "Park House" where his parents and sister lived was his home and remained his strongest family tie for the rest of his life.

McKim spent only one year at Harvard, during which he became convinced that his talent lay in architecture. In 1867 he secured his father's permission, took and passed examinations for the Beaux Arts, and set off for Paris on the small allowance of $700 a year that his family could barely afford. There he spent three years and managed, even with his limited resources, to travel on the Continent and in England.

He was not wholly happy at the Beaux Arts. He did not share French tastes; he did not, as a Quaker, like French manners; as a disciple of Ruskin he was not in complete sympathy with the content of his education at the atelier. London he liked better than Paris, preferring it, as he strove to explain to his family, for the sense of permanence he found there in the established order and "art of living." But it was Rome that won his heart. The Italians were friendly to the solitary, vague, rather shy, and distinctly frugal American youth. Rome, he concluded quickly and permanently, was the true center of civilization, especially for the artist. It was the great reservoir of past culture, the great place in which to study man's classical heritage. Later travels in northern Italy, Austria, and Germany did nothing to change his opinion.

When the Franco-Prussian war broke out, McKim had to leave Paris for home. By May 1870, at the age of twenty-three, he had a job in New York, where for eight dollars a week he was in charge of working drawings in the office of Henry Hobson Richardson, architect. He had chosen his professional association well. Richardson's work on Trinity Church in Boston brought McKim together with La Farge, Millet, and Saint-Gaudens, all of whom became lifelong friends and all of whom were at his elbow when the American Academy was being founded.

His Beaux Arts training stood him in good stead. Few young American architects had experienced its equal, and few such as he were for hire by the architectural firms of his time. If he stood head and shoulders above most, he never forgot the advantage his European years had given him. In 1878 he went into partnership with William B. Bigelow and William Rutherford Mead. When Bigelow retired in 1879, Stanford White joined the firm which became McKim, Mead, and White.

In 1874 McKim married Annie Bigelow, his first partner's daughter. It was not a good marriage, and they were divorced not long after. In 1885 he married Julia Amory Appleton of Boston, with whom he was deeply happy. When she died two years later her will was found to reflect the cause close to her husband's heart: education abroad for the American artist. She left two-thirds of her small fortune for traveling fellowships in architecture, one for Columbia University, one for Harvard College. The Columbia fellowship was to bear his name; the Harvard fellowship, hers.

The reputation of McKim, Mead, and White was by this time not only well established; it had begun to outdistance its competitors. The firm called on the leading artists of the day to ornament the great public buildings of classical design that had become its hallmark. Work poured in so continuously that McKim, whose health was not robust, was strained to meet the heavy demands on his time and talent.

He was also much sought after by the social world, where he was affectionately known as "Charlie the Charmer." Men and women were drawn to him by the surprising shyness and gentleness that overlaid his eagerness for form and beauty in all things. Though he was a burning enthusiast and dogged protagonist, shyness hampered his public utterances. He became involved; he stammered. "Damn the preambles, get down to facts!" Hunt once roared at him when McKim was trying to persuade a meeting on some matter with which Hunt fully agreed. McKim's letters reveal his diffidence even when begging for his beloved Academy, although the support from those to whom he went showed how well they had listened to this "modest, unobtrusive, hesitant" man. Many men of fortune were his warm friends, but he found difficulty in asking them for money, despite his inheritance of the reformer's zeal that puts cause above self. He preferred to dig into his own far from substantial capital, and did so frequently during the first lean Academy years.

Beneath McKim's diffidence, however, lay a firmness of purpose that Charles Moore's biography reveals in several illuminating passages. Moore wrote:

Of all the friendships that grew out of those mind-expanding days [at the World's Fair] the one that had the greatest influence on Burnham . . . was the companionship of Charles Follen McKim. One trait was common to both men—an indomitable will. Burnham could demand perfection; McKim furnished it. McKim could and often did change Burnham's mind. No one ever changed McKim's because he never expressed it until he got to the essence of the problem. That being settled there could be no change. Constantly McKim would say, "you can compromise anything but the essence."

Moore added:

McKim was not only unchangeable but also insistent and persistent. Once his mind was made up as to the course to be pursued he bent every energy to attain his object. Saint-Gaudens speaks of his "rodent-like determination." So quiet, so seemingly yielding, so courteous to suggestions was he that one was often deceived into thinking that he was about to surrender when in truth he was simply gathering for the attack.

The course upon which McKim fixed his resolution in 1894 was the creation of a school for artists in Europe. The evenings at the Shack were still a fresh memory, although even before their stimulus the idea had been simmering for some time in his ardent imagination. Now it must be turned into a reality. He knew at first hand of only one place abroad where architects might continue their studies: the Beaux Arts in Paris. But he also remembered the eagerness with which his fellow students there had sought the Prix de Rome, despite all that France itself could offer artists. He had envied them the resource of the great French Academy in Rome, which had already been in existence for nearly two hundred and fifty years. Undoubtedly McKim was also aware that Spain had opened an academy in Rome within the decade, that Hungarians of private means had recently established a Roman Academy with a section for fine arts, and that, although not itself a fine arts academy, the German Archaeological Institute in Rome had a classics library of the utmost importance to the student of art history. What other countries could provide for their students, surely America could also afford!

He turned over in his mind the shape the school should take. At first he thought almost wholly in terms of architecture. He envisaged a place where graduate architects might be housed to follow their studies under conditions he was already formulating. It should be, he wrote, "a school of contact and research." It should preserve the finest of the classic tradition by studying only at the finest classical sources. No pursuit of new art canons not firmly rooted in the old should be tolerated. Otherwise, he wrote to Burnham, "you will be likely to get all kinds of Yahoo and Hottentot creations which prevail in the east and still crop out in the west." McKim and Burnham had agreed that "The individual designs . . . our scholars make are not so important as the spirit they will introduce and keep alive amongst us." The school "must send men home who shall become a true leaven in America." And the school must be in Rome. For McKim never wavered in his conviction that Rome was the best place for the student of art. "I am very anxious to see brought about the Roman courses of which we talked," he wrote to Professor William Robert Ware, head of the Department of Architecture at Columbia. And to Edward Gale of the Boston Public Library he wrote: ". . . as between Rome and all other Italian cities, give me Rome. Rome contains for the architect the greatest number of examples."

It was late in March 1894 that McKim began the campaign that must have demanded all his waking hours. He launched the proposal to found a school in Rome for American architects at a dinner on March 31, with his partners Mead and White and three other members of their office, William M. Kendall, Austin W. Lord, and William A. Boring. If a single date for the birth of the Academy were to be sought, this date might well be it. The names of these first participants recur repeatedly and are of great significance in the history of the Academy. Under McKim's infectious fervor and persistent pressure each of these men would become deeply involved, as would many of the collaborators of the days of the Chicago Shack. Letters from McKim kept them *au courant* of the development of the campaign.

McKim already had an adroit scheme for financing the new school. He proposed to induce existing institutions with prize funds for traveling fellowships in the arts to send their beneficiaries to the new "atelier" in Rome, as he then called it, or at least to use the atelier as a base for their sojourn abroad. Thus at one swoop was to be solved the problem of the cost of fellowships during the initial years of the enterprise.

"The plan," he wrote to Saint-Gaudens, "is to take one or two rooms in Rome and to compel the scholarship men, who at present go abroad without limitations, to follow a course resembling that of the French Academy, in the Villa Medici—that is, to occupy their time in close contact with the great examples of Greece and Rome and the early Renaissance."

As a first step, he wrote to Burnham in early April, he had made an appeal to "the architectural schools of America, of which there are four* . . . to consent to award prizes under such a 'School' *Atelier* system of study as may best accomplish the object we have in view." He also approached the trustees of the Lazarus Scholarship of the Metropolitan Museum, the Rotch Travelling Scholarship of Boston, and the Rinehart Fund at the disposal of the Peabody Institute of Baltimore. Leaving nothing to chance, he had also sent letters to friends who might influence the decisions of the trustees of these privately established fellowships. Meanwhile (ran the speculations in his letter to Burnham) the cost of the atelier itself should not be much. Some drawing materials would be needed, a few books of reference, and the salary of one instructor. Altogether these expenditures should amount only to about four thousand dollars a year. The rental of a modest place in Rome would, he thought, be a small cost, though he named no figure. The money could "be raised here [in New York] without trouble, and I do not doubt that I can raise it." In the next sentence he revealed his implicit conviction that the school must be of national character, not a local but an American school. "It is better that [the money] should not represent the interest of a single locality. For this reason I suggest you raise half the amount immediately, if you can, and I will supply the other half."

The letter concluded: ". . . we expect to establish the *Atelier* this year." It had not occurred to his other friends that a scheme of such scope, launched only a few weeks before, could possibly be-

---

* The first school of architecture in America was opened at M.I.T. in 1868. Departments, though not schools, of architecture were established at Cornell in 1871, Syracuse in 1873, Columbia in 1881, and Pennsylvania in 1890.

come a reality within the year. They had reckoned without McKim's spirit and the "rodent-like determination" Saint-Gaudens had seen in him. Only Burnham understood him, and at once sent his own contribution, and promised subscriptions from a dozen Chicago men such as Cyrus McCormick, Marshall Field, Levi Leiter, and Franklin MacVeagh.

Meanwhile McKim, at his own expense and on his own responsibility, laid further plans for the immediate realization of his dream. Earlier that spring he had personally financed a trip for Edward Gale to study in Europe. Gale had just arrived in Rome when Mc-Kim swept him into the undertaking. In April he wrote to Gale of "the fair prospect of establishing an American *Atelier* in Rome . . . by the first of May we should know whether the thing is a fact or not," and he asked Gale to send him what information he could about the French Academy, its method of awarding the Prix de Rome, and its course of study for its fellows, in "as much detail as possible." McKim's friend Elihu Vedder lived in Rome: McKim asked him to investigate and to send him recommendations and addresses of quarters that might be quickly rented. "The location is not essential as long as they be sanitary . . . one or two rooms will fill the bill."

Under such persistence the project moved rapidly forward. The scheme had been first presented in March; in April it enlisted wider support, and in May Boring, then president of the Beaux Arts Society of America, had secured its endorsement by the society, which undertook to circularize the universities in America asking them also to endorse the new "plan of study" in Rome.

What was the "plan of study" to be? What would the scholars be required to show for their year of work abroad? How should their work be directed during that year? To settle the matter, McKim organized a dinner meeting in New York on May 23. In addition to the familiar men of his committee, Ware of Columbia, Warren Laird of the University of Pennsylvania, and Robert S. Peabody, architect and overseer of Harvard, were invited to attend. McKim hoped the architectural departments of those universities, which had scholarships to grant, would assign the grantees to the new school. In view of the fact that no "plan of study" has ever been permanently established at the Academy, it is interesting to read of the first encounter with what has remained a constant issue. The question of how much the fellows should be under supervision in their work (and if so, in what ways?) or allowed *laissez faire* (and if so, how much?) recurs like a theme song through the history of the Academy.

Since by its very nature a curriculum reflects the educational philosophy of those who determine it, it is not surprising to find McKim advocating in 1894 a plan of study to match his own experience. He had been an eager, very youthful student when in Europe, who had needed and sought all the guidance and instruction he could get in his chosen profession. When he went to the Beaux Arts he had been a graduate neither of a college nor of a professional school. He likened the fellows at the new school to himself as a student. That prizewinners who had finished architectural schools and put a year of work in an architectural office behind them might have somewhat different needs and desires did not seem to have occurred to McKim. Fresh from the stimulus of his World's Fair experience, he seemed to be concerned only with hastening the day when the returned fellows of the new school would begin bringing back to America the "leaven" of artistic order and good taste which the classics embodied for him. The way to assure this, he was convinced, was through traditional indoctrination and a fixed curriculum.

He saw the matter simply, clearly, and firmly. When he wrote to Peabody inviting him to the May meeting, he said that the new school should offer a "restricted course under the *Atelier* system." Peabody, an old friend and fellow student of McKim in the Beaux Arts days, could be counted upon to understand what McKim meant by this phrase. He meant that the student should do some designing, but mostly should produce measured drawings and careful renderings of classic works of art, all under the guidance of a critic. To Saint-Gaudens, McKim defined the critic as a "qualified pilot who has been over the ground and who will see to it that they [the scholars] spend their prize money *on the greatest examples* and are not allowed to foolishly spend their prize money over their own immediate selections."

If it then occurred to McKim that the plan of study he envisaged could be seriously questioned—that there could be any real difference of opinion on so tried and tested a method of instruction for architects—he was not shaken in his convictions. At the May meeting he must therefore have been dismayed to have it sharply challenged not only by Ware but also by Peabody. Both men felt that the school should be less an end in itself than a vantage point for the talented, from which they might spread their wings as they would. They advocated that the scholars be given a far looser rein than McKim proposed.

To McKim the issue was crucial, a substantive matter—an "essence"—on which he could not compromise. Yet how was he to have his way when opposed by men who controlled the scholarships vital to his plan? Perhaps he had envisaged such a motion before the meeting, as it was at his prompting that the question was placed in the hands of a new committee for further study. In any case, he quickly set about lining up support for his point of view before the coming meeting in June. He wrote to Hunt: ". . . it is of the utmost importance we should attend . . . in order to assure a committal of sound principles which are likely to be endangered by want of them in the person of our dear friend, William Robert Ware. Do come and lay him out if necessary."

It was not necessary. The care with which McKim had picked distinguished associates, the impetus his hard work had given the project of the school, and the general welcome the project had received from artists and architects had given his ideas an almost irresistible momentum. The prestige of the Committee on the Plan of Study, appointed at the May meeting, was certain to carry weight. It was composed of Hunt, McKim, Saint-Gaudens, Edward Simmons, Allan Marquand, and James A. Garland of New York; Peabody and Martin Brimmer of Boston; Burnham and MacVeagh of Chicago; and George Leighton of St. Louis. It also included the heads of the fine arts and architecture departments of six universities: Charles Eliot Norton of Harvard, Francis Ward Chandler of the Massachusetts Institute of Technology, Laird of Pennsylvania, Charles Babcock of Cornell, Dean Nathan Clifford Ricker of the College of Engineering at the University of Illinois, and, although holding to his reservations, Ware of Columbia. Soon after the committee was appointed, the University of Pennsylvania and Columbia University stated that they would send their prize scholarship men to the new school in Rome, to work under whatever rules and curriculum the committee might determine. The Rotch Travelling Scholarship trustees followed suit.

The climax came at the Century Club meeting on June 12, 1894. All controversy over the precise content of the curriculum was swept aside by the news that "$15,000 had been subscribed, sufficient to defray expense for three years." It was a dazzling sum, and it tipped the scales. Motion followed upon motion to bring the new school into being. Ware was elected chairman; McKim, treasurer; Boring, secretary; and Austin Lord, director of "The American School of Architecture in Rome." Three prizewinning scholars, each endowed with $1,000, were waiting in the wings. All that was now needed was a place in Rome for them to live and work when Lord met them there in the autumn. The spark struck at the World's Fair had been blown into flame.

II

Foundations

IN NOVEMBER 1894 the American School of Architecture in Rome found eight rooms on the upper floor of the Palazzo Torlonia, on the southwest corner of the Via Condotti and the Via Bocca di Leone. Modest in scope, spare in furnishings, and insecurely financed, it was not exactly McKim's idea of a castle in Rome, but it was a beginning.

In contrast to it the French Academy, which had been founded in 1666, was superbly housed in the Villa Medici overlooking the city from the edge of the Pincio. It was, in location and appearance, one of the great landmarks of Rome. Government-supported, ponderous with prestige, it enrolled each year a highly select crop of talented young painters, sculptors, architects, engravers, and composers. Its Prix de Rome had long been the supreme award to the French student artist. The French Academy was McKim's model. If the gap between the fledgling School and its great predecessor seemed impossibly wide, McKim had faith that it would rapidly close and that the American Rome Prize would come to be as coveted by the American artist as was its counterpart in France. The first step toward McKim's goal was a small one, but it had been taken.

The new School boasted a staff of one, a fellowship of three, and a guest student. Austin Lord, its director, had been a Rotch Scholar, had traveled about Europe, and had subsequently served in the offices of McKim, Mead, and White. The tone of McKim's letters to Lord show the confidence of a shared view. The letters also show an understanding between Lord and the Committee of Managers that his post was a temporary one until a more permanent director could be secured. Meanwhile Lord undertook duties that proved to include those of secretary, treasurer, and sometimes, perforce, janitor. For these he received an annual salary of $2,500.

Two of the three scholars were in a sense transplants. Harold VanBuren Magonigle, the current Rotch Scholar, had been in the office of Stanford White from 1888 to 1891. George Bispham Page, University of Pennsylvania Travelling Scholar in Architecture, had been in Europe for a year before a persuasive cable from McKim induced him to continue his studies in Rome. With Page came his friend William C. Noland, who was given the privileges of the School. The third scholar was Seth Justin Temple, who had won the McKim Scholarship from Columbia University.

The scholarships carried modest stipends by more recent standards, but in those days a man could travel for thirty-five dollars from New York to Le Havre or Southampton, or for ninety dollars he could luxuriate on a ship from New York to Naples. In "Hints to Students Travelling Abroad," the *American Architect and Builder* of March 1895 reported that a student could live and travel in Italy for one dollar and thirty-three cents a day: forty cents for railroad fares and ninety-three cents for board and lodging. It added of Rome: "In winter, without fire, living costs seventy five cents a day." Since the annual stipends of the first scholars at the Palazzo Torlonia ranged from five to six hundred dollars, and as the School was no more affluent than its scholars, no one complained, and all survived with memories they cherished. One memory, as recalled by Magonigle, was of the School's opening exercise: "A carpenter made two or three drawing boards and trestles—no stools. A hallway recess accommodated the library which consisted of a copy of Middleton.* On a springlike morning in the late winter the opening exercise took place. Temple was off, but Lord . . . leaned against the doorjamb and began to read from Middleton to Magonigle and Page who held up two sections of the wall. Lack of interest on the part of the pupils caused a stop in the reading, and the cultural course was never resumed."

Some items from the first longhand accounts of 1894 show the modesty of the School's beginnings:

One stove 25.00, one stove 18.00	43.00 lire
Two lamps with shades at 12.00	24.00 lire
Doorplate	4.00 lire
Fee, Parthenon—for ladders	.75 lire

* Presumably John Henry Middleton's *Ancient Rome in 1885.*

Inkwell, straight edge, ink, pens	4.55 lire
Wood 9.00, kindling .50	9.50 lire
Two watering cans	16.00 lire
Tea kettle	11.00 lire
Dust pan	1.40 lire
Shoe brush	1.25 lire
Wash basin	1.75 lire
Two sponges	1.80 lire

The value of the lire in 1894 was a little over eighteen cents.

Rome offered many compensations for spare living. Besides its endless architectural and artistic resources it had much to give young Americans in culture, customs, manners, and new viewpoints. The scholars absorbed this background eagerly. But they also noticed that many Romans looked with coolness on youthful barbarians from the New World. The first rebuff came before the scholars had settled into their one-volume hallway library. The Italian authorities refused to recognize the School officially, declaring the credentials of the director inadequate. Only after a flurry of cables did credentials, almost certainly prepared in the offices of McKim, Mead, and White, arrive in Lord's behalf. An impressive job must have been done; the Italians conceded the official recognition of the School so necessary to its standing and privileges.

During those first months the welfare of Lord and his trio could seldom have been out of McKim's mind. While they were busy measuring, drafting, or sightseeing in Italy and Greece, his correspondence showed his constant preoccupation with the School. There was everything to be done, and done at once. Better quarters must be acquired, the search for a long-term director begun. American professional accrediting boards must give their hallmarks to the School. Its financial status must be made secure, and if possible it should, by a special act of Congress, become a national academy. Appeals must be drafted and the right sponsors for each endeavor found. As 1894 ended and the new year began, these were the things upon which McKim wished to concentrate his forces, but he suddenly found that a more immediate need must be given precedence. The academic policies he had pushed through, and had thought permanently settled, were being seriously challenged, and from a most disturbing source. To meet the threat he must postpone all other considerations.

Until this check in his plans occurred, McKim had been in high spirits. He was elated over Columbia University's recognition and support of the new School. Its officers had agreed to send the McKim Travelling Scholars thereafter to Rome. In addition they had offered to sponsor the competition between the professional schools for the new Rome Prize of $1,500 which the School had placed on its budget for 1895. University backing of this sort greatly enhanced the prestige of the new enterprise—and lifted the spirits of its sponsors. And a highly interesting proposal had come from another distinguished source. Professor Arthur L. Frothingham of Princeton, who with other classics scholars was proposing to organize a school of archaeology in Rome, suggested that it be affiliated with the American School of Architecture. McKim was delighted. "I like his aggressive spirit and belief in the success of the undertaking," he wrote to Ware, "and am in favor of encouraging him in all ways except that of any step which might menace our independence as a school later; in other words our relation to other bodies joining us should be that of landlord and tenant."

But by that time the correspondence between Ware and McKim had lost a little of its former easy mutual confidence. Ware had been very active and helpful in the decision to send Columbia's McKim Scholars to Rome, but he was also a member of the committee to shape the academic policies of the School in Rome to which the scholars would be going. It became evident that he disagreed with McKim on a traditionally prescribed graduate course in architecture. Because of this difference of opinion, he must have raised the question of his fitness to continue to chair the Committee of Managers of the School, for on February 5, 1895, McKim wrote to him: "Please quash any misgivings you may have as regards the chairmanship of the Committee. You are our natural chairman, and are sure of re-election. If there is any 'snarl,' to use you own phraseology, we will disentangle it."

Whether Ware was reassured by this, or hid his reservations, in any case he presided over a meeting on February 7 which supported McKim's academic policies and ideas. McKim wrote exuberantly to Lord:

We had a fine meeting of the Committee yesterday, maintaining the policies of the School and enlarging its scope, with every prospect of financial backing by such men as Mr. Schermerhorn, Mr. Marquand, Mr. MacVeagh, Mr. Brimmer and others. The General Committee of the

School including all members East and West, as well as local, are to meet at the University Club for the purpose of further organization. As the Committee is united on the importance of maintaining a professional school along professional lines, devoted to a definite course for a definite period, while offering such hospitalities as we can to outsiders, though drawing the line strictly between them and regular members of the School, all fear as to the aim and purpose of the School is happily at an end.

McKim was either ignoring opposition he must have sensed, or he was seriously mistaken. Within twenty-four hours of writing to Lord he had a communication from Ware, the nature of which was revealed in McKim's shocked reply: "I read with amazement . . . your intention of resigning the chairmanship of the American School in Rome, and giving your reasons therefore." These he summarized to Hunt as "an astonishing draft of a letter which he [Ware] proposed addressing to you and Mr. Burnham stating his reasons for declining the permanent chairmanship of the School on account of its policy, which he characterized as suicidal and preposterous. His letter is intemperate in tone and interminable in length. . . . Mr. Ware is simply attempting to resist the tide of events which are all against him, and to which he opposed arguments illogical and fictitious."

Ware had continued to feel that the course outlined by the committee might deter mature and gifted graduate students from applying for fellowships, while those that did enroll in the School might become restive and rebellious. McKim, on the other hand, had insisted on the traditional curriculum for architects and a required period of residence in Rome, and believed that for a fellow to "spend any part of [his] time elsewhere than as mapped out in the course, is to spend it among things beautiful but of less consequence, and which if never seen it were better to lose. I know it is hard for young men to believe this; I found it so, and I bitterly regret the loss of time and energy and money and consequent inferior quality of design which my persistence taught me." McKim divided the ten-month term of fellowship between six months in Rome, "dealing principally with early Roman work," and four months elsewhere. Of these, three were to be spent in Greece and Sicily and one in Florence. "The Florentine Renaissance may be regarded as a pendant to the Roman one."

No doubt McKim had correctly assessed the majority opinion of architects of the time as to the proper education for their profession. Neoclassicism and the traditional were at their peak, and the Beaux Arts method of teaching architecture ruled the day. That the tide might turn in coming years McKim did not foresee. He rallied his forces, postponed the scheduled meeting to March 9, and persuaded the friendly Hunt to act as temporary chairman in place of the resigning Ware. His colleagues were not surprised to be bombarded by letters from McKim urging their attendance at the next meeting and soliciting their support. By now McKim's role in shaping the school was understood by most of his associates, for though he had not been in good health and had been obliged to rely on others, he had made the project uniquely his. His driving force, strong opinions, unflagging zeal, and skill in persuasion were more than most men could resist. "I am so mad at McKim," said Frederic Crowninshield, the painter, ". . . everybody loves McKim—but I get so mad at him, the way he ropes me into things and makes me so enthusiastic in spite of myself." McKim's confidence in his own judgment was often unshakable, his methods not infrequently high-handed. But his sincerity, his enthusiasm, and above all his total lack of self-seeking, disarmed his critics.

In letters to associates about the coming meeting in March, McKim spoke rather cavalierly of Ware, who after all had been one of his closest supporters in the early days of organization. When Ware seemed to show signs of modifying his stand, McKim wrote: "Uncle Ware's pangs of conscience have given him trouble." He said that Ware's proposals for greater choice of work by the fellows would make the School a "kind of architectural club where the Secretary would be the dragoman so to speak of tourists in architecture." Nevertheless Ware's standing in the academic world of the arts was high and his influence among architects was great. He had been a leader in organizing and directing departments of architecture, first at the Massachusetts Institute of Technology and then at Columbia. It was he who had been the chief channel of communication between professional schools and the Committee of Managers. It would have been a blow if he had withdrawn his support. McKim genuinely desired his continuance on the Committee.

The meeting on March 9 went off more smoothly than McKim had feared. Ware was present, along with Kendall, Burnham, Boring, Crowninshield, Laird, Saint-Gaudens, McKim, Walter Cook, Edwin

Austin Abbey, and Edward Simmons. They confirmed the principles and policies previously adopted. They set specifics in the content of study that were mandatory for fellows in architecture; other enrolled students were not obliged to follow the course. The fellows were given priority in all the facilities of the School. Ware accepted in good spirit the majority verdict and agreed to remain on the committee, though not as its chairman. McKim had won the controversy. Ware (as might have happened in any case) became less active in Academy affairs. But the two men renewed their friendship and maintained it.

The potential strain of the meeting had been eased by the announcement of an exciting possibility. Word had come that the Villa Aurora might be rented, and its attractions were described to the committee. The Villa was part of the handsome Ludovisi estate on the Pincian Hill near the French Academy—an estate that had once stretched from the Via Veneto to the Via Francesco Crispi. The Villa Aurora hung twenty feet above the Via Ludovisi, with a terrace of 80,000 square feet commanding a magnificent view over Rome. Its garden had been designed by Le Notre; its rooms were richly decorated with plaster ornament in high relief and painted panels in luscious late Renaissance style, and its foyer contained an impressive circular stone staircase dominated by Guercino's painting of Aurora.

On the other hand even McKim, the enthusiast, had to agree that from a practical point of view the Villa was less dazzling. There were few fireplaces to take the chill from marble floors and the damp from high-ceilinged rooms; there was no central heating, and the kitchen was so inadequate that the occupants would have to eat elsewhere. What was more, the rental asked was approximately $3,000 a year, and that was a sum larger than the School's total income. It was therefore agreed to postpone a decision on renting the Villa until more facts were available, and the prospects of raising funds to support this higher standard of living could be explored.

The meeting moved on to other business: the relation of the School to American universities, colleges, and other centers of the fine arts; the posibility of future publications emanating from the School. No doubt there was a report on the Tarnsey Bill to incorporate the School into a national academy. The bill had been drawn up too near the close of the congressional session to be introduced until the next session, but there seemed a good chance of its passage then. Perhaps McKim read aloud from Magonigle's cheerful letter, written in February, which said in part: "We have done a lot of work and I like Rome immensely. We are measuring just now the Arch of Titus and the Palazzo Farnese, and find the Roman School a great advantage. We have comfortable quarters here in the Palazzo Torlonia, with every convenience for work both outside and in."

The election of officers took place quietly. Burnham became president; McKim, vice-president; Boring, secretary; and Schermerhorn, treasurer. The meeting had not been a stormy one after all. In a letter dated March 14, McKim described it to Lord as "a great success—educational policies were unanimously approved." The School would be incorporated within the next few weeks, he added, and some forty competitors were expected for the first Rome Prize.

As for malcontents . . . you can snap your fingers at them. . . . The painters and sculptors are waking up, and . . . our affiliations with the Archeologists are likely to be cemented at no distant date. Indeed it is highly probable that if a successful lease is made of the Ludovisi, the Archeological School will commence operation at once, and within the year perhaps one or both departments of painting and sculpture. Of course these other Schools will be quite independent of ours—conducting their own work separately as we propose to conduct ours—we holding title to the property and they becoming our tenants.

Securing the Villa Aurora was uppermost in the minds of the Committee of Managers. From the moment McKim first learned of it he set his heart on it and went to work in his usual indefatigable fashion. He soon had a stroke of luck. Two highly appropriate subtenants for the Villa proposed themselves. The first, as hopefully anticipated, was the Archaeological Society, which asked for housing for their new venture in Rome, to be called the American School of Classical Studies. The second was the already existing British and American Archaeological Society Library in Rome. The financing of the Villa Aurora would, by these arrangements, be considerably eased. McKim had already given $1,200 from his own pocket to carry the new School through its first months. Now he underwrote, with Hunt, the fifteen thousand lire needed to meet the first year's rental of the Villa Aurora. To recoup McKim and Hunt and to finance the School, Burnham agreed to raise $10,000 in the Chicago area, while Hunt would attempt a similar quota in New York. They hoped that another $5,000 could be secured in Boston. On the strength of these plans and hopes, the American School of Architecture rented the Villa Aurora in April 1895, for three years. In July the School began to move in.

Under the prodding of McKim, the School was legally recognized by the state of New York on April 20, 1895, and its incorporation took place on May 18. Ten shares of capital stock were issued: two apiece to Hunt and McKim and one share each to Burnham, Kendall, Schermerhorn, Boring, James A. Garland, and James B. Dill. Burnham then turned over his presidential office to McKim, and Hunt became chairman of the Managers' Executive Committee.

On September 18, 1895 McKim wrote to his brother-in-law Wendell Garrison: ". . . the foundation of the School in Rome has been an absorbing interest of the past year . . . the progress made to date most gratifying." It was true. The School and its founders could look back over its first year with satisfaction. It had incorporated, issued stock, and completed its legal and administrative organization. It had moved into handsome quarters in Rome that it would share with a library and a school of classical studies. The Rome Prize had been created and was being competed for. The School had survived a year without endowment and had lived through a hand-to-mouth existence. It badly needed financial backing, but help might soon be forthcoming. Each step the School had taken had brought it closer to the position of its great model and new neighbor, the French Academy in Rome.

III

Framework

THE trustees continued to hammer away on the framework of the School. Although McKim was neither its sole creator nor its sole supporter, he can certainly be called its architect. Had he not been so determined, the School might have dwindled away, snuffed out by petty debt. However, it was one thing for the trustees in New York to lay down sweeping outlines for the School, and quite another for the director in Rome to turn policy into prompt reality. With bills to be met, conflicts of personality to be soothed, and austerities to be overcome, Austin Lord found principle and practice hard to reconcile.

There was, for instance, a ruffling of feathers as the two schools, one of architecture and the other of classical studies, tried to settle into the same nest in the fall of 1895. The Villa Aurora did not lend itself gracefully to rearrangement. Its upper floor had become a dormitory for the architects: John Russell Pope, the first winner of the Rome Prize; Will S. Aldrich, the Rotch Scholar; and Percy Ash, the University of Pennsylvania Travelling Scholar. The second floor housed the two directors and their families: Lord and William Gardner Hale, professor of classics at the University of Chicago.

On the ground floor lived Hermon MacNeil, the School's first sculptor. ("If we can only get a painter over there it will be fine, and it must be done," the indomitable McKim had written to Saint-Gaudens when he learned of the new scholarship for sculptors. Never content with immediate gain, he looked only toward the next advance.) MacNeil was the first William H. Rinehart Fellow in Sculpture to be assigned to Rome, with the magnificent stipend of $1,000 a year for three years. After winning the fellowship he had had the temerity to marry, an action strongly deprecated by the Committee of Managers. But the prestige of the award and the sum brought to the School tipped the balance in his favor, and the MacNeils were permitted to live in the Villa during the sculptor's three-year term.

The ground floor also had space for a lecture room, which doubled as a studio for MacNeil, and it had a drafting room for the architects and the library where the classicists worked. The fellows of the School of Classical Studies were William K. Denison of Harvard, Walter Dennison of Michigan, and the Reverend Walter Lowrie of Princeton, fellow of Christian architecture and weekly lecturer on the subject. There were also, during that year, nine students of the classics, with varying academic qualifications and standing. All the classics men had to find housing outside the Villa; everyone, classicists and artists alike, had to take their meals elsewhere. A contractual arrangement with the Café Grecco on the Via Condotti supplied these, as well as the bonus of an association with other artists and students who frequented this most popular café of the quarter.

It was apparent that the School of Architecture, as landlord, had the lion's share of the Villa, and that the School of Classical Studies felt the squeeze. Originally the latter had been encouraged by Professor Ware, before a large annual meeting of classicists in Philadelphia, to join forces with the architects if adequate quarters could be found. The classicists had agreed to do so when the Villa Aurora was rented, but during the summer of 1895 McKim had, in a letter to Frothingham, made it very clear that no members of the Classical School except the director and his family could be housed in the Villa Aurora; there simply was not room. This point should have been understood by all the members of the Classical School before the term began, but if so it did not silence their disappointment. It was not surprising that at the end of the academic year the School of Classical Studies withdrew from the Aurora. No ill will was displayed, but in private Lord expressed relief. He felt that the fine arts men had been patronized by the loftier classics scholars, whom he privately pronounced, "self-important."

In December 1895, before the separation took place, McKim had gone to Rome to see the schools at first hand. He had just recovered from a rather difficult operation, and in any case needed a period of convalescence away from his overloaded office. Though he was obviously keen to go anyway, there was another good reason for doing so. Richard Hunt had died a few months before, placing an added burden of responsibility for the School on McKim. With Burnham in distant Chicago, McKim had been relying heavily on Hunt's counsel. Hunt had been an unfailing source of personal support, moving forward to take command during the rift with Ware over policy; accepting the job of fund raising in New York, and sometimes dipping into his own pocket to pay bills of the School.

McKim found at the Villa Aurora an outwardly pleasant atmosphere, the directors on good terms and the young men optimistically facing the limitations of funds, books, space, and living comforts in the Villa's somewhat chilly grandeur. They were pursuing their work with a confidence their talents justified, and on the whole morale was high. McKim made it higher by giving those about him a sense of being pioneers in a great undertaking. In retrospect Pope wrote of the period: "We were a particularly congenial and happy family, tireless and united in our appreciation of McKim's object in building up an Academy and his reasons for sending us 'beyond the Alps' as he put it. I still look back on Rome as the cream of it all." MacNeil wrote: "With the students we [MacNeil and his wife] formed intimate friendships . . . during the summers we travelled and worked together. . . . We went to all the important cities of Italy and many of them several times." And of his remaining years in the Villa he added: "Our whole period was one of continued joy and enrichment, hard work enlivened by sight-seeing." The classicists were attending lectures on paleography and numismatics at the Vatican, were taking courses at the University of Rome, and were welcomed at the German Institute of Archaeology. Nearly every evening some of the students, classicists and artists alike, went to the Circolo Artistico to draw from life. At all these activities the Americans met young men of other nationalities, among whom was Somerset Maugham, a young Englishman who had just published *Of Human Bondage*.

During his stay of three months in Europe, McKim "loaned" the School $3,500 to pay its current bills. He also did his best to persuade the directors of the two schools that their problems of limited space in the Villa Aurora were unimportant compared with the value of each School to the other. He did not succeed. In May 1896, after McKim had returned to New York, the School of Classical Studies stated in its report: "It became apparent that our School as such could not become an integral part of the Academy inasmuch as the representatives of the other School desired to have only a limited number of Fellows within the Academy building thus excluding from its privileges most of the members of our School." The classicists moved into rooms at Via Gaeta 2. They remained there until 1901, when they established themselves in the Villa Bonghi, Via Vicenza 5, near the Baths of Diocletian.

The two schools were not to be joined for another sixteen years. McKim did not live to see the reunion, but he continued to urge it, convinced that the framework of a national academy of the arts was incomplete without classical studies. He fully appreciated the mutual benefit that could come from sympathetic working relations between art historian and creative artist. When in close proximity, the scholar of each discipline was exposed to the values of the other, to the stimulation of both. And, of course, unification into one academy and one building would offer the advantages of more efficient and economical operation.

During his months in Rome, McKim added another important item of his constantly expanding list of desiderata for the School, which more and more he conceived in terms of an extensive and eclectic academy. The new idea had perhaps been engendered, and had certainly been fortified, by Mrs. Winthrop Chanler, a resident of Rome and leader of American society there. She and McKim found each other congenial spirits. He infected her with his enthusiasm for a great American academy in Rome, and "this remarkable musician," as he called her, left him convinced that music must also be represented. McKim urged his fellow trustees to find funds to initiate at least one fellowship in music. He died before this was accomplished, but when the first fellows in musical composition did come to the Academy, they demonstrated with remarkable speed and success how much they had to contribute to the communal life there.

Meanwhile Saint-Gaudens and La Farge were searching for funds to send a painter to Rome. In the spring of 1896 their efforts were rewarded. The Metropolitan Museum of Art, which administered the Jacob H. Lazarus Scholarship for the study of mural painting, agreed to assign the winner to study at the American School in Rome. Like the Rinehart Scholarship it was to carry a stipend of $1,000 a year for three years, including travel expenses to and from Italy. Each fellow was required to spend at least twenty months in Italy, of which sixteen were to be at the School. McKim promptly used the terms of these scholarships as a lever to raise the stipends of the architectural fellows to the same level and to lengthen their stay from one to three years in Rome. Pope, the first winner of the Rome Prize in Architecture, had received $1,500 for one year (actually ten months) in Rome. The terms of the prize were revised, and notice given that should the School become an academy by act of Congress the winner would receive $1,000 a year for each of three years.

McKim urged this commitment in the spring of 1896 even though prospects for the School looked bleak. But he felt that the School could not afford to stand still and quoted to Boring the Chicago saying: "Everything comes to him who waits, but it comes a good deal quicker to him who hustles while he waits." The School was, however, in serious financial straits. Nearly a third of its income had vanished with its erstwhile tenant. It had always operated on a tight budget, in fact on even less income than the budget predicted.

Desperate letters from Lord punctuated the correspondence between Rome and New York: "As you have not sent the money for current expenses," he had written after the move into Aurora, "I am again cramped to keep affairs going. In fact there is not enough money to pay alterations agreed upon. There is coal and wood to buy." And in May 1896: "I have just returned from Greece after an absence of nearly six weeks, leaving three men in Athens to finish their work on the Acropolis. I have not yet received money from Mr. Burnham as I had expected by this time. These accounts have been standing long due and I hope I shall not be obliged to wait much longer." A week later he wrote to McKim: "No money has come yet from Mr. Burnham and I shall be under the necessity of borrowing again from the bank."

The expenses of the school that first year at the Villa Aurora fell into five categories: Lord's salary of $2,500, rent of $3,000, Rome Prize of $1,500, director's traveling expenses of $500, and the fee for incorporation, $450. An accountant of the firm of McKim, Mead, and White was keeping the books and had set up a budget for 1896–97 of $8,000. It had little practical relevance to actual expenses and revenue. In the past, whenever funds had run short, or whenever McKim had found himself juggling too many balls in the air, he had drawn on his own account and cabled these "loans" to Lord. In 1896 he wrote to Burnham: "I have no time . . . to go about raising money and have had to assume the bills as they came in." He was by no means wealthy and could not continue this practice indefinitely, even if he really regarded his advances as likely to be repaid. In fact he never was repaid. By June 1896 he had given in this way something over $12,000.

A few months later the School came to another turning point. For some time Lord had been urging the trustees to replace him in the post of director, which he had accepted as a temporary break in his career as architect. But no new director had been found, and in the interests of the School he had remained. In the late spring of 1896 he firmly stated that he must retire and that he planned to return to America on August 1. With regret the trustees accepted his mandate and pursued their search for a successor. To bring continuity to the administration of the School, they were looking for a man prepared to serve as its director over a considerable term of years. Some of them hoped the director might also be a man of the world, as Hale wrote to McKim in a letter about Edwin Blashfield the painter. Both Blashfield and his wife, Hale wrote, were "attractive, competent in dealings with the general world—a matter of importance in Rome for many reasons." With these thoughts in mind, the trustees sounded several men besides Blashfield regarding the directorship: Edward Robinson and C. Howard Walker of the Boston Museum of Fine Arts and Robert Peabody, the Boston architect. For one reason or another none of them could accept.

When Lord left Rome in August 1896 no new director had been found, and a financial agent in Rome, Dr. R. J. Nevin, rector of the American Church in Rome, was hastily appointed to oversee the business of the School. On October 31 the agent wrote a sharp and revealing letter to Stanford White which showed the slender threads that held the enterprise together and the extent to which all concerned relied on McKim:

My dear White,

Will you tell your friend McKim that the management of the American Architectural School here is bringing it into disgrace and putting me to great inconvenience? No one has appeared to take Mr. Lord's place; the rent is due a month ago and has not been paid and the Porter has not been paid for some months. I have been summoned to pay 3750 lire rent due Oct. 1st and I have just returned without any available cash. This neglect of the Architectural Committee has put me in a very embarrassing position.

Excuse my sending this to you, but I do not know Mr. McKim's address, or indeed, if he is in New York. Should he be absent, will you kindly notify some other member of the Committee of the bad shape in which affairs have been left here?

Sincerely yours,
R. J. Nevin

The trustees' committee was galvanized into action. It appointed Will S. Aldrich, current Rotch Scholar at the School, to serve as its acting director until a new man could be secured. McKim made yet another loan to meet the most pressing bills. This time he wrote: "I trust this will be the last advance that I shall be called upon personally to make." He turned to the faithful Burnham in Chicago: "Can you send me a check for $1000 to keep our credit good? . . . We must keep the School going somehow until after the Academy meeting in June [1897] when arrangements will be made to take the responsibility from our shoulders." Burnham sent $1,450 from his own pocket.

The ups and downs of those early years had a common characteristic: they were closely watched over by a handful of men knit together in the cause of education in the fine arts. One by one the friends of the Academy came forward at the eleventh hour. The names of some of them appear as donors again and again. In the first lean months of the winter term of 1896–97 another name emerges: Samuel A. B. ("Judge") Abbott. A Bostonian who had been president of the trustees of the Boston Public Library at the time McKim designed its fine new building in 1887, he and McKim had formed a lasting friendship. Abbott had worked hard to enlist the great artists of the day to ornament McKim's building: French, Saint-Gaudens, Abbey, John Singer Sargent, Puvis de Chavannes, and others. McKim wrote that Abbott was responsible for "convincing the city that Painting and Sculpture should be added as a necessity, not a luxury"—no mean feat, as those who have dealt with municipal budgets know. In the summer of 1891 the two men, unattached and single, had traveled together in Europe. When the idea of a school in Rome was broached and pursued, McKim had kept Abbott informed of its progress. In 1894, before the School had actually opened, McKim had suggested to Abbott that he be its first director. "We need somebody over there in [the School's] infancy to push it into National character, which is the chief aim of its existence. . . . We await better times to purchase a habitat on the plans of that of France." Abbott had declined the post.

In 1896 Abbott was spending the winter in Rome. McKim made a strong appeal to him. The time had come when "a home in the sense of the Villa Medici is essential for the further development of the Academy scheme." The Villa Aurora could be purchased. Did Abbott advise buying it? If so, would he begin negotiations? Abbott went to work on the problem, entangling himself inextricably in the future of the School.

During the difficult winter of 1896–97 Aldrich managed the business affairs of the School and gave what counsel he could. Pope, still at the Beaux Arts in Paris, promised to help if needed. W. S. Covell and Louis E. Boynton were the architectural scholars sent by Columbia and Pennsylvania respectively. MacNeil and A. Phimister Proctor were the sculptors. In view of the financial stringency, there was no current Rome Prize fellow. McKim had written Ware in March 1897: "I think it will be advisable to state that it is not intended to offer a scholarship this year [for 1897–98] but that it is hoped the Academy will next year be upon a foundation which will enable it to continue competitions."

McKim frequently referred to the School as "the Academy." The goal was never out of his mind. The School must first be merged into an "Academy platform" supporting fellows in the fine arts and archaeology to be elected annually for three-year terms. Then the Academy must be placed "under the protection of the National Government," and national sponsorship by act of Congress must be made clear to the public in Italy and America by the appointment of the United States Ambassador to Italy as a member, ex officio, of the Academy's board of trustees. It would increase the chances of financial support by individuals and foundations and would ease negotiations with the Italian government, including exemption from taxes in Italy.

At a monthly meeting on June 8, 1897 the trustees by vote dissolved the American School of Architecture in Rome and created the American Academy in Rome, which then assumed the former School's assets and obligations. Sculpture, painting, and architecture were currently represented in the new Academy. Archaeology, they thought, would remain in the Villa Bonghi only until suitable accommodation could be found for it in the newly remodeled Villa Aurora. The policy of the coming year was outlined, and the election of trustees took place. In addition to its officers, the new board included the required representation of painters, sculptors, and architects: painters Blashfield and Crowninshield, sculptors Saint-Gaudens, French, and J. Q. A. Ward, and architects F. W. Chandler and Burnham. The board proceeded to elect five lay members: Charles Hutchinson of Chicago, Dr. William Sturgis Bigelow of Boston, Theodore N. Ely of Philadelphia, Henry Walters of Baltimore, and William C. Whitney of New York. The officers were McKim, president; Schermerhorn, treasurer; and H. Siddons Mowbray, secretary.

Abbott was elected the first director of the new Academy. Having just married a lady who had resided in Rome for the past twenty years, he this time accepted the appointment. He and his wife moved into the Villa Aurora in the fall of 1897, after McKim had coached him on "the nature of his work and his relations to the outside world." The new scholars in 1897–98 were to be Henry Allen Jacobs from Columbia and the first Lazarus Fellow, muralist George W. Breck, who had been in residence since mid-January, 1897.

New York had been hearing more and more about the School in Rome. There had been two exhibitions of the work of its members. The first was held at Columbia in 1896, when McKim had written with pride: "It is most successful and free from amateurishness. As an *envoi de Rome* much of the work compares favorably with that of the Villa Medici." The second exhibition, held in the autumn of 1897 at the Metropolitan Museum, was so successful that it was sent around the country and was shown in Chicago, St. Louis, Philadelphia, Washington, and Boston.

The Academy had also been brought to the attention of social New York in the winter of 1897–98 by an influential committee of distinguished women, not the less formidable because charming. They gave a series of *soirées* for the Academy in order that, in McKim's words, "its cause could be brought home and the interest of the people aroused." Led by Mrs. Victor Sorchan and with Edith Wharton, Mrs. F. W. Vanderbilt, and others lending active support, the first "evening" was held in February 1898 in the house of Edgerton Winthrop. McKim was ill and could not be there. La Farge presided. Blashfield gave an illustrated lecture on the Villa Medici and its younger counterpart, the American Academy in Rome, for which he had prepared, he wrote afterward to McKim, by examining the Winthrop drawing rooms to see where he could best put up a sheet for the slides. He added: ". . . whatever may come of [the lecture] people now know that there is a Roman School and that you have founded it, and when they are approached in the future they will at least understand what it is we are talking about."

Greatly heartened by all this, McKim presented his first annual President's Report to the trustees in December 1898. A school of high professional standard had grown into an Academy: the act of incorporation under the laws of the state of New York had taken place in October 1898. A competent director had been at the head of affairs in Rome for over a term, and the Academy was housed in a place of widely recognized distinction. Both President McKinley and John Hay, secretary of state, were looking with favor on national recognition of the Academy. Thanks to Whitney, Schermerhorn, Walters, and Mrs. Sorchan, half of the $35,000 necessary to maintain the Academy for three years was in the bank. The trustees must now center their efforts upon raising an endowment which would enable the Academy to offer its own fellowships, independent of those from universities and foundations. The Academy would of course continue to offer hospitality and aid to the holders of such scholarships and fellowships.

For the moment it looked as though the most difficult years of the founding were behind. The framework of the Academy of the future stood out clearly for all to see.

IV

Bricks and Mortar

FROM the beginning the Academy had been living largely on windfalls. Whenever these failed, a small band of faithful friends would pay the bills. Walters, Schermerhorn, and Whitney had been generous. So had Mrs. Sorchan, who, besides her own gift, had tried with her friends to gather one-hundred-dollar memberships. An unexpected sum had also come in when the purchase of the Villa Aurora was being considered. To raise the money for it, the trustees had issued bonds which were taken up by themselves and a few other friends. When its title had been found to be imperfect, the purchase of the villa was abandoned, and the holders of the bonds generously gave them back to the Academy. But as fast as these and other sums had come in, the Academy had been obliged to use them for what McKim always called its "bread and butter."

In early 1900 McKim told his friend H. S. Mowbray: "Abbott writes as cheerfully as if he were Baden-Powell at Mafeking. He says rations are very low and that we must come to his rescue on May first. . . . In the absence of funds I have been obliged to cable Abbott to draw on me." The cable read: "Draw one thousand. Better times coming. See letter." The letter from McKim to Abbott read: "We hope you will understand and not lose confidence in us, for we have not forgotten you, nor does a single day go by without worry on your account. It has greatly troubled me, for I have many expenses and calls on my purse, and this year's business has been anything but good. But it is a long lane that has no turning!"

A tentative goal of $750,000 had been set for endowment. The first step toward securing it was the preparation of a persuasive brochure describing the new Academy. Issued toward the end of 1900, it reported that heretofore "the payments to the students, as well as the expenses of carrying on the work of the School, were met by advances of [its organizers] and their personal friends." It spoke with more enthusiasm than accuracy of the Villa Aurora: "No better abode adapted to harbor an artistic fraternity could well be imagined than this Villa, which enjoys the seclusion so essential to profitable study, and yet is in the middle of a city containing masterpieces of all the arts."

Thriftily, the brochure served to give prospective students and others information as well as to raise money. It described the fellowships it proposed to establish. Fellows were to be "unmarried youths" who had won first prizes in competitions approved by the Academy. In Rome they would live in accommodations provided by the Academy; they would travel in Europe according to plans approved by the director, and while on fellowship stipends they would give their time exclusively to the program of the Academy with "complete divorce from commercial considerations." It stated that "all works of the beneficiaries during their terms belong to the Academy" and, as if fearful of female invasion, stressed that the opportunities offered by the Academy were "intended for men only." Probably no American institution to be chartered by Congress breathed a more monastic spirit.

If McKim had been hopeful of better times to come, it was in great measure due to the Academy's friend and trustee, Henry Walters. During the next decade it would often be his timely generosity that put fresh heart into the trustees. When they set the goal of $750,000 in endowment, he immediately offered a conditional pledge to give $62,500 provided the balance was raised in full. He also promptly agreed to serve as a trustee of the endowment fund. McKim wrote to Abbott in May 1900:

It is to be hoped that Mr. [J. Pierpont] Morgan will do likewise. They have made me the unhappy channel of communication with Mr. Morgan, and I have agreed to act so far as to endeavor to enlist his interest. . . . Mr. Walters has authorized me to make the statement that he believes it will be easier to find 15 men who will subscribe $50,000 than a larger number of men a smaller amount. . . . The proposition was therefore yesterday decided upon and will be publicly attempted next week. . . . I have no fancy for the task of interesting Mr. Morgan, and if he declines to be interested my sympathy will be with him.

McKim's biographer Charles Moore recorded that McKim had no personal acquaintance with Morgan but thought he might approach him through Charles Lanier, whom he did know and who was a friend and neighbor of the financier. McKim then wrote to Lanier about the Academy, stressing the hope that it would become a national academy on a par with others in Rome. But with what his biographer called "McKim's timidity and also his thoroughness in preparation," he placed this letter in the hands of Francis R. Appleton (Lanier's son-in-law) to be delivered to Mr. Lanier.

Mr. Morgan consented to be approached. On March 9, 1901, McKim wrote:

My dear Mr. Morgan:

Referring to our conversation at your house a few days since, in relation to the American Academy in Rome and the kind consent to the use of your name, so far as approval of its aims and work are concerned, I write to say that I have, since I saw you, consulted with the Executive Committee of the Academy, as to the best manner in which the Academy might avail itself of this expression of interest on your part—without placing you under further obligation.

In view of the efforts to be made East and West for the purpose of establishing the Academy upon a permanent and National foundation, the Committee feel that your consent to the use of your name as a member of the Board of Trustees would prove of incalculable aid and advantage in securing the the Academy public recognition throughout the country.

I am requested to add that the Committee have been drawn to this conclusion as much by your prominent interest in matters of Art as because of your interest in other directions.

I would hesitate to approach you again so soon had you not invited me to write you further on the subject.

Believe me, yours very truly,
C. F. McKim

McKim waited two weeks for an answer and then wrote:

My dear Appleton:

I know how busy a man Mr. Morgan is and how little claim I have upon him, but through your kind offices he has permitted the matter to go so far that I think he owes an answer—Yes or No—to the Academy Trustees before his departure for the other side.

Mr. Morgan left for Europe without a word, and the old grind of getting bread and butter was resumed.

At this point two men came forward to help the Academy. The

first was Henry Walters. Since the Academy had not been able to
meet the condition attached to his pledge of 1900, he was under
no obligation to make it a gift, but in 1901 he quietly pledged
an unconditional $50,000 to its endowment. The second friend
was Waldo Story, a trustee of the Academy resident in Rome, who
arrived in America late in the summer for a round of visits.
McKim had written to Abbott in Rome: "I do not believe we shall
be able to raise $750,000 at present, but I fully believe we can
raise enough of it to secure the rest, and I sincerely hope that Story
will be willing to interest Pierpont Morgan."

Thomas Waldo Story was a son of William Wetmore Story, a
Massachusetts lawyer-turned-sculptor, whose fabulous rooms in the
Palazzo Barberini had welcomed nearly every important visitor to
Rome for the past forty years. The son, himself a sculptor, had
been a familiar figure at these gatherings. He found it quite natural
to call for help on friends who had for so many years frequented
his parent's hospitable apartment in Rome. He put on a whirlwind
campaign for the Academy's endowment, seeing among others
George W. Elkins and Peter B. Widener in Philadelphia and
Morgan in New York. Morgan asked him bluntly what the Academy
expected of him. Story replied that the Academy trustees hoped
Morgan would allow his name to head the list of those appealing
for funds for the Academy. Morgan commented sensibly that to
head such a list implied he must become a subscriber and that he
doubted the present state of his affairs would permit him to do so.
Story protested that his name on the appeal would not in any way
obligate Morgan to give a penny to the Academy. Morgan said
that on that basis he was willing to let his name head the list. He
asked who had already pledged to give to the Academy. When told
that Walters had promised $50,000, Morgan replied, "That means
that I must promise as much," repeating that he was not ready to
do so. Once more reassured on this point, he agreed to the use of
his name. The appeal was issued to the public in November 1901,
and read:

THE AMERICAN ACADEMY IN ROME

France, Germany and other countries have owed their artistic development for generations to National Academies fostering the Fine Arts,
established by them in Rome.

In view of the success attending the beginnings of the AMERICAN
ACADEMY IN ROME, founded on the same general lines, privately sup-

ported since 1894, incorporated in 1897, and lately endorsed by the State Department* of the National Government.

We, the undersigned believe the time has arrived when this country is ready for its permanent establishment and endowment and that such an institution would prove of incalculable value in building up the national standards of taste.

J. P. Morgan
Henry Walters

At that time no gift came from Morgan, but his name greatly helped the undertaking. The episode also gave a new twist to Morgan's relations with McKim. In February 1902, a few months after Morgan had accepted election to the Academy's board of trustees, he engaged McKim to be the architect of his library and of a house for his daughter on East Thirty-sixth Street near his own house. Through these connections the two men met often and on increasingly easy terms. McKim respected Morgan's slow, thorough appraisal of the Academy before making large gifts to it, and for the next few years he did not ask Morgan for funds.

By April, McKim was able to write in his old hopeful spirits to Mead: "The whole thing has taken a tremendous jump. . . . For the first time, let me tell you, we have enough money in the bank not only to carry us through this year's but also next year's running expenses. . . . Mr. Morgan, in Mr. Lanier's presence the other morning at his home, said his subscription would be 'all right.' "

McKim must have been greatly encouraged for the Academy's future when Walters came forward that spring with another offer, a remarkable one. Abbott and the trustees had become increasingly aware that the Villa Aurora was not wholly adequate as a permanent home for the Academy. Its location was convenient; it had merits and charm, but it was not spacious, and its owner was receiving tempting offers to sell it. At any moment the Academy might find itself homeless. Walters offered to loan the trustees $100,000 to buy the Villa as an investment; the Academy could then remain there so long as it wished, or it could sell the Villa with better chance of profit than of loss. When its title had been

---

* Secretary of State John Hay had expressed his approval of the appointment ex officio of the American ambassador in Italy to the board of trustees of the Academy. George von L. Meyer, McKim's brother-in-law, was the first ambassador to become a trustee, in the autumn of 1900.

found faulty, the trustees' decision not to buy the Villa in no way diminished the feeling of confidence Walters' offer had given them.

Ambassador George von L. Meyer had been asked to hunt out another building for the Academy and in 1904 he found the Villa Mirafiori, located about a mile outside the Porta Pia. At that time it was rented, but in August 1904 McKim hurried to Rome to look at it. He found it well built, more commodious than the Villa Aurora, with ample grounds and a garden shaded by handsome trees, and he concluded that it would be "a proper and quite sufficiently dignified home for the Academy until such time as our work performed shall justify acquiring one of the great estates."

McKim had another reason for pressing the trustees to buy Mirafiori. The bill to make the Academy a national institution was due for a vote in December. McKim thought that acquisition of Mirafiori would strengthen the Academy's case before Congress, and that "the Academy in Mirafiori and the Bill passed making it a National institution cannot fail to make raising the endowment easier."

Once again Henry Walters, that "real patron" as McKim called him, offered to come to the rescue. He proposed to make a loan, without interest, of $130,000 to the Academy to purchase Mirafiori. Although some trustees had reservations about the wisdom of buying the Villa, Walters' offer was accepted. With John Cadwallader, then in Rome, handling the money of Walters' loan, Ambassador Henry White, who had succeeded Meyer, successfully negotiated the purchase. McKim wrote to Burnham in September 1904: "The public announcement of the passage of the bill and the purchase of a permament home are results that we may see before January 1st to congratulate ourselves upon, within ten years of the inception of the enterprise at the time of the Fair."

But as the year 1904 drew to an end the endowment campaign still lagged. To revive it McKim suggested a new plan: to raise the Fund by securing ten men willing to subscribe $100,000 each and become permanently recorded as "Founders." Late that autumn, by chance, he met Walters on a train from Boston and broached the idea to him. Without hesitation Walters replied: "I hope you will give me the privilege of being the first of ten Founders." Almost overcome by Walters' recurrent generosity, McKim could hardly eat or sleep that night. The next morning he went to see Morgan, hoping that the time had come when Morgan might make some sort of gift to the Academy. McKim launched on one of his hesitant preambles, but Morgan brusquely interrupted: "Yes, yes, Mr. McKim, and what did Walters do? Put me down for the same amount." McKim could only blurt: "But Mr. Morgan, you don't understand. Mr. Walters made a princely gift, no less than $100,000!" "All right, all right," said Mr. Morgan, "put me down for the same amount!" and turned the conversation to his new library building. When Walters heard of Morgan's pledge he urged that Morgan's name head the list of Founders, and it was done.

McKim had also been working unceasingly to organize a large dinner in Washington on January 11, 1905. It was to be held under the auspices of the American Institute of Architects with the ostensible purpose of celebrating the collaboration of the government with artists and architects on such matters as the fulfillment of L'Enfant's plan for Washington and the restoration of the White House. McKim and his inner circle had a less overt purpose: to promote the passage of the bill to incorporate the Academy as a national institution.

The passage of the bill had encountered serious snags. It had first been introduced in 1901 by Senator James McMillan. After his death Senator George Peabody Wetmore sponsored the bill, which was voted by the Senate in successive years but had always been denied a hearing in the House. This was because the powerful Speaker of the House, "Uncle Joe" Cannon, opposed it and regularly refused to recognize the Representative who was trying to introduce it. McKim was therefore especially eager that Cannon attend the dinner, at which, if plans worked out, Cannon would hear talk that might disarm him regarding the bill. Cannon was among the first to be invited, and he accepted. He even spoke some felicitous words on the merits of collaboration between artists and government. He also heard other big guns, well-loaded and primed by McKim and his associates, boom in salute to the Academy as sponsor and educator of American artists. President Theodore Roosevelt was there and spoke; Secretary of State Elihu Root spoke; so did James Cardinal Gibbons, ranking prelate of the Catholic Church in America, and so did Ambassador Jean Jules Jusserand of France. So did La Farge and Saint-Gaudens. Others benevolently present were Secretary of War William Howard Taft, presidents Nicholas Murray Butler of Columbia and Woodrow Wilson of Princeton; Henry James, Thomas Nelson Page, Senators Nelson Aldrich of Rhode Island and Henry Cabot Lodge of Massachusetts, and Charles Freer of Washington, who was about to give his art collection to the nation.

While the dinner did not bring about the immediate capitulation of the Speaker, it won him over to discuss the bill with representatives of the Academy. Cannon said he opposed any congressional appropriation of funds to support an institution in a foreign country. It was pointed out that the government would not be called upon to appropriate money for the Academy, which had always existed on private funds and intended always to do so. Cannon then fell back upon the argument that it would be improper for official representatives of the United States government, such as senators, representatives, and the ambassador to Italy, to be charter members of the Academy. In deference to that argument it was agreed to remove any such persons from the list and to accept Cannon's proviso that "no official of the United States shall be eligible to serve as Director of the Academy." After this shadow victory "Uncle Joe" laid down his arms and agreed to permit the bill to be introduced and voted upon. No time was wasted, and on March 5, 1905, seven weeks after the dinner, the House passed the bill.

The Washington dinner was followed by smaller ones given by the Academy in Boston and New York. According to Moore the Boston dinner, at which the Somerset Club brought out its famous Daniel Webster silver for the table, had as guests a carefully selected group of distinguished men and women whose support of the Academy would be invaluable. This time McKim produced a speech shorter than he had expected and more immediately successful than any had dared to hope. He launched in stumbling detail upon the aims of the Academy. "Major Henry L. Higginson stood the hesitating speech as long as his short patience would bear. Then, pulling the embarrassed speaker's coat-tails he said: 'Here, McKim, let me talk,' and with that he announced: 'I subscribe one hundred thousand dollars in the name of Harvard!'"

The New York dinner was held in April in honor of the charter members and to celebrate the passage of the bill to nationalize the Academy. McKim presided with such confidence and humor that "his speech-making deficiencies and hesitations vanished," said Moore, who was present. There was good reason for high spirits, since McKim was able to announce that half the endowment goal of a million dollars had been pledged by Morgan, Walters, Harvard College, William K. Vanderbilt, and James Stillman. Stillman was ultimately unable to fulfill his pledge, though he paid annual interest on it for some years and was made a Benefactor when that class of donors was created. In any case the halfway mark to the goal was maintained when in July 1905 Henry C. Frick became a Founder.

In 1906 the Academy added again to its assets. The trustees not only purchased the Villa Mirafiori but felt able to authorize $13,000 out of current funds to renovate it. The Academy moved in in July. It is ironic that in the same letter in which Ambassador White informed McKim that he had bought Mirafiori he added this paragraph:

Curiously enough on the very day I completed the purchase of the Mirafiori there came another proposal which would be very tempting if money were no object, namely the Villa Aurelia on the Janiculum— one of the most conspicuous houses in all Rome, standing out quite alone and bold on the top of that hill. It was Garibaldi's headquarters during the siege of 1849 and from its terrace there is the most unrivalled view of the whole city with the sea in the distance. It belongs to Mrs. Heyland, neé Jessup, who wishes to become one of the $100,000 subscribers to the fund (via selling Aurelia at $500,000 minus her gift, or $400,000, or 2 million francs). As she wants her name to be linked to the Academy she might accept less. Ownership of the Mirafiori puts us in a position of considerable independence, as would-be vendors will not feel the Academy is at their mercy.

Mrs. Heyland's asking price was considered high, and since the Academy was obligated to repay Walters' large loan and had not yet raised the million dollars it sought, the trustees spent little time in discussing the proposal. Mrs. Heyland did not press it, and the idea of acquiring the Villa Aurelia passed from the minds of the trustees—except perhaps from McKim's. But it remained in the mind of Morgan, who visited Rome that summer and privately concluded that the American Academy should top the Janiculum as the French Academy topped the Pincio. He quietly took an option on some property near the Villa Aurelia and held it for use at some later date.

Another donor came forward to help the Academy, albeit cautiously. In 1906 John D. Rockefeller, Jr., pledged $100,000 for endowment upon the condition that the balance of the million dollar fund be raised by April 1907. Had the trustees foreseen the financial crisis about to sweep across America they would have accepted his challenge with less confidence. Rockefeller at once sent $4,000, as interest on his pledge for the intervening year. Then came the panic of 1907. During the severe depression that followed, even wealthy Founders felt they could not do more than give the Academy the 4 percent annual interest on their pledges. April 1907 came and went with no new Founder's gift in sight, and Rockefeller pointed out that he was thereby relieved from his pledge. But a little later, recognizing the exceptional nature of the circumstances, he generously renewed it.

Stern economy became a necessity in all Academy operations. The trustees canceled the Rome Prizes they had hoped to offer that year. An especially serious blow came when the Knickerbocker Trust Company of New York, in which the Academy had a cash deposit of more than $18,000, declared itself bankrupt. For a year it looked as though the deposit was lost forever. The trustees immediately authorized the director to meet Academy expenses by securing emergency loans from Roman banks. Trustees dipped into their own pockets, less well-filled than usual, to help meet operating costs. By these means the Academy was kept in operation, and in May 1908 the Knickerbocker Trust announced that it would shortly repay the $18,000 deposit, and did so. Conditions in general improved, and not long afterward the Academy treasury reimbursed the trustees who had personally carried it through the crisis.

The unhappy year of 1907 brought the Academy a greater loss than temporary lack of funds. Death came to one of its oldest and greatest friends, Augustus Saint-Gaudens. The original group of men who had conceived, created, and faithfully supported the Academy for more than a decade were leaving it one by one. McKim would soon follow Saint-Gaudens.

McKim's health, never robust, had seriously failed in 1908. He became physically frail and slow and laborious in speech. In February 1909 he had made his last public appearance, to receive an honorary degree from the University of Pennsylvania. In that same month the Board at its annual meeting reelected McKim president for another year but also elected Frank Miles Day acting president "during the disability of the President." Although he was ill, McKim's interest in the Academy did not flag, and his associates kept him fully informed. In March he could rejoice when the trustees reinstated the competitions for the Rome Prizes, and again when they arranged that a distinguished artist-in-residence be invited annually to the Academy to advise and inspire its students. He did not live to see the Rockefeller and Carnegie foundations and the younger as well as the elder Morgan become Founders of the Academy, completing the million dollar fund. He died on September 14, 1909.

Charles McKim is remembered in many places, but in none more warmly and deservedly than at the American Academy in Rome. In the atrium of the Academy building that his firm was to build four years later, a tablet is set in the wall. Below it water drips gently from a lion's mask into a brimming basin in the form of a Roman sarcophagus. In classical lettering, the tablet is inscribed in Latin. Its translation reads:

CHARLES FOLLEN MCKIM

FOUNDER OF THE AMERICAN ACADEMY IN ROME

EMINENT ARCHITECT, DISTINGUISHED BY

LIFELONG AND UNSELFISH PUBLIC SERVICE

FOR THE CAUSE OF THE ARTS IN HIS NATIVE LAND

BEARING MODESTLY MANY AND VARIED HONORS AT

HOME AND ABROAD. HIS CHARMING PERSONALITY,

HIS SINCERITY AND HIS PERSISTENCE IN WHAT HE

DEEMED RIGHT WON HIM MANY VICTORIES.

THIS TABLET IS ERECTED IN HIS MEMORY

BY HIS FRIENDS AND ADMIRERS.

On the opposite wall is a similar fountain and tablet inscribed with the list of the ten Founders. McKim's name is also there, for after his death his friends and admirers subscribed $100,000 in his memory, that he might become a Founder in name, as he was in fact. The ten Founders are:

J. P. MORGAN	JOHN D. ROCKEFELLER, JR.
HENRY WALTERS	CHARLES F. MCKIM
WILLIAM K. VANDERBILT	J. P. MORGAN, JR.
HENRY C. FRICK	THE ROCKEFELLER FOUNDATION
HARVARD COLLEGE	THE CARNEGIE CORPORATION

V

The Occupants
1894-1911

THE story of the shaping of the Academy naturally unfolded in
the country of its origin. But from 1894 it was in Rome that
its staff and students were making the Academy more than a plan
and a building. Who occupied the building? Who gave the Academy character and standing? Who directed its growth? Austin
Lord had played his part in starting off a venture which may well
have seemed to him, so recently a traveling scholar, almost a continuation of his student days. When the trustees failed to find a
new director in time for the new academic year, they appointed
Will S. Aldrich, a scholar of the previous year, to be acting director. In age and experience he was not more than a year or two
ahead of the other occupants of the Villa Aurora.

Aldrich's task was to keep the frail and ill-provisioned ship
afloat. Dr. Robert Nevin, the Academy's temporary overseer in
Rome, after writing to Stanford White about the extremely bad
shape of the Academy's affairs without money and without leadership, followed that letter with one to Ware on November 4,
1896: " . . . a young man named Aldrich was in last evening in
trouble. They had no fuel for the winter and begin to need it. He
said he was asked to look after things when Mr. Lord left, but had
no funds at his disposition. I do hope you will send out soon an
Agent who can look after the business of the School in its ordinary
capacity." The appointment of Aldrich as "agent" and the provision of some money brought momentary balance to the School's
affairs, for a month later Aldrich wrote to McKim with enthusiastic
disregard for spelling that "amoung the dozzen" things to be done
he had paid all the bills. But he begged that the next rent be
made ready, as "the Italians are very suspicious when we do not
pay promptly. . . . In closing I wish to thank you for your kind
remembrance of myself."

Clearly McKim had not forgotten Aldrich or the School. How could he forget when appeals from Rome arrived so steadily and money to meet them came in so uncertainly? In March 1897 he re-received a letter from William S. Covell, Rome Prize Fellow in Architecture, who reported that he had not received the second installment due on his fellowship and that "my funds have been getting distressingly low." Lack of money forced discontinuance of the Rome Prize, and it was not renewed for nine years.

Covell's letter also provided a glimpse of the faithful and hardworking Aldrich: "While there could not be a better person than Mr. Aldrich to oversee the details connected with the management of the Villa, which both by his energy and knowledge he has looked into in a manner that could not be excelled, I feel that we have been missing much that it was intended we should have received on account of there being no Director here: a man from whom we could be getting something not so much from what he taught as by daily contact with his words and works. Such a personality, I trust it will be our good fortune to encounter next year." But there was to be no next year for Covell. He had been led to hope, by the ambitious circular of the exhibition of Academy work in New York, that the term of the Rome Prize was to be for three years. He was a victim of the Academy's almost empty treasury, and he did not return to the Villa when "Judge" Abbott took over the directorship in the fall of 1897.

Abbott's talent for practical management carried the School through the next six years. Having adopted McKim's conviction that it must "establish and cement relations with institutions of kindred purposes in Europe" and should bring its work to the "attention of travellers as well as Romans," Abbott gave much time to developing the School's public image. His warm personal letters to McKim and his more formal reports to the trustees were much taken up with accounts of entertaining important visitors and trying to find larger quarters for the expanding School. The trustees were grateful to him for bringing order and stability to the School's affairs, but one of them was critical of Abbot for the things he thought the director was failing to do. H. Siddons Mowbray, the mural painter who had gone to Rome to execute decorations for the library of the New York University Club, of which McKim was architect, wrote to McKim in December 1902:

The truth is that the original purpose of the Villa has been lost sight of completely, and at the present moment has no relation whatever to the Academy. In fact today the latter is practically on the street and the Villa is known as Mrs. Abbott's home. The *pensionnaires* creep in at night and sleep—no meals—no bath—no sitting room. They cannot ask their friends to come to see them, and in Mrs. Abbott's absence of four months in the summer, the place is in utter darkness at night. To show how utterly isolated they are, Swartz [a scholar] has been three years in the Villa and never met Mrs. Abbott. New men arriving find nothing ready for them and are either sent to a hotel for a week or two, or plainly told they are unexpected and taken under protest.

Mowbray complained further that Abbott had not seen the work of the students or been in the studios.

Abbott has no relations with the heads of Museums, and the men shift for themselves as far as permits are concerned. I find the Villa a byeword in Rome. No one can understand it. . . . Abbott lives the existence of a gentleman of no other occupation than his own social and material comfort . . . the whole thing a subject of ridicule . . . the students wished they lived elsewhere.

To find Abbott's successor the trustees looked no further than Mowbray, whose character and ability they knew. They asked McKim to persuade him to accept an offer to become director. McKim conducted the transatlantic courtship with enthusiasm. "Every reason," he wrote to Mowbray, "made us turn to you: your reputation as an artist, your presence in Rome for an extended period in the fulfilment of your great commission, your experience as a teacher, your Trusteeship of the Academy—all suggest you as the very best man we could hope to have." Mowbray hesitated and then accepted for a limited time. He and his wife took up residence in the Villa Aurora early in October 1903.

A glimpse of the life in the Villa is provided in Mrs. Mowbray's diary. She found it charming, livable, and "agreeably arranged." The "very bad" painting of Aurora in the front hall did not dampen her enthusiasm. She was hospitable to the students and their friends and spoke of one of her teas as "the first social affair the students have ever had."

She gave an account of "the opening of the Academy" on January 4, 1904. This was perhaps the first of the Academy's now familiar varnishings, when the work of its staff and fellows is shown to a few selected guests before being opened to public view. At ten o'clock in the morning, the sun was shining brightly, but it had not dispelled the Roman chill that pervaded the Sala dell' Aurora. The Mowbrays had invited royalty. As Ambassador Meyer announced "Le Roi," the waiting guests hastily doffed their overcoats and "flung them into the coatroom." Then the beautiful and surprisingly tall queen came in (in disappointingly plain dress), followed by the king, "small, and short in the leg." The royal pair was conducted through the Villa. The king was gracious and the queen especially appreciative of the exhibits. It was over in half an hour. "We had certainly dreaded it, but found it not so awful after all." That night the occasion was celebrated by a dinner in the Sala, which one hopes had somehow been heated. Twenty-five distinguished guests came: ambassadors, Italian senators, the director of the French Academy, and the "critical Waldo Story," whose approval was wholehearted: "Mowbray, it was magnificent!" For three days thereafter "the thing to go to in Rome" was the exhibition. Mrs. Mowbray added a sad little comment: "The Italians were delightfully kind and most courteous. I wish I could say as much for the Americans living in Rome."

The annual showing of the work of the Academy was being established in a traditional pattern. The next varnishing, in 1905, was reported in the *Boston Transcript:* "The honors of the day go to a single sculptor, Mr. Charles Keck." The king and queen again attended, the queen "taking occasion several times to express her satisfaction."

The difficulty in keeping as director a professional artist in the full swing of his own career had been experienced in the case of Lord. After three years Mowbray felt he must be released. He was succeeded by George Breck, who had from 1897 to 1900 been the first Lazarus Scholar at the Academy. Six years later he returned to direct it.

Breck was promptly plunged into the Villa Mirafiori discussion. Ambassador White had been commissioned to negotiate its purchase and was about the close the deal. Breck at once revealed his independence of mind. He disagreed with the trustees on the change of headquarters and said so, with understandable nostalgia for the Villa Aurora, which had housed the Academy for eleven years and himself as a fellow for three. To leave the center of Rome, with an atmosphere which American students had come so far to imbibe, seemed to him a serious "back-set."

"Going to Mirafiori," Breck wrote, "knocks [the attraction of the Academy] into a cocked hat, for it will have no . . . life class, no outside social intercourse, no nearby restaurants, long trips to town to study, measure up, get materials or models, if they will go so far at all. The food supplies are also higher and harder to get there. There are no tramways after 9:30 and poor service all day. Cabs outside the gates are, especially at night, at a ruinous rate. . . . We deal with the young and must make the Academy attractive and convenient for them while we are forming their tastes." But he was overruled. The Mirafiori was bought, and Breck, after two months in the Villa Aurora, found himself in charge of moving the Academy out beyond the Porta Pia. He did so expeditiously and cheerfully, and later was praised by trustees and others for making student life there attractive—and, somehow, convenient.

The trustees respected Breck's frankness and energy. In his first report to them he did them another valuable service by urging them to restore fellowships awarded by the Academy: "My idea of the most important work immediately before us is the setting in operation of the Academy scholarship; that in all these years we have had no scholarships directly under our control, properly belonging to the Academy." His urging was effective: competitions for the Rome Prize in architecture were held, and Harry Warren became the first holder of the prize since the days of Pope and Covell.

It was also during Breck's administration that a matter of authority which might have troubled his successors was cleared up. The trustees had suggested that priority treatment be given the graduate students from universities that made annual contributions to the support of the Academy. Breck saw at once, and with his usual directness and courage pointed out, that such a procedure might lower the qualitative standards of the Academy and that students must be admitted on their merit alone. The proposal to derive steady income by academic concessions in quality was promptly dropped by the trustees.

Breck also urged the trustees to make decisions on the optimum number of students the Academy could properly handle. He pointed out that the Villa Mirafiori could accommodate twenty-five men, but that larger studios and an adequate drafting room were needed. Other students, attracted by the Academy's growing reputation, were pressing for use of its facilities. How many student visitors should be accepted? Breck encouraged the fellows and scholars to give their opinions to trustees on these matters. They wrote to the trustees in July 1909: "The Prize holders are sure that the men who are in Rome only a few months have not sufficient time to enter upon prolonged or serious study for which the Academy stands . . . and should not represent it. On the other hand, the association of men pursuing similar courses of study would be mutually beneficial." As a result of these discussions the trustees gave the fellows the choice of staying one, two, or three years and strengthened Breck's hand by voting that student visitors might not be enrolled for less than an academic year, "that they should not necessarily be charged the same low rates as regular beneficiaries," and that they must conform to all Academy regulations.

This last rule was underscored for the benefit of an independent young man of talent who had been admitted as a scholar in mural painting. His name was Barry Faulkner. At the Academy he insisted upon planning and following his own course, and toward the end of his term in Rome Breck had to report that Faulkner "had not in any respect met the conditions of his scholarship," having pursued his education when and how he saw fit. Breck nevertheless urged that this remarkable young man be handled sympathetically. His advice was taken, and Faulkner justified his promise and even linked hands with authority when later he became a trustee of the Academy.

Under Breck's stimulus the question of the ideal age of a fellow was also discussed. It was a topic as perennial as that of general educational policy and brought out equally variant opinions. One of them came from Sherry Fry, a fellow in sculpture in 1909, who had studied previously in Europe, and who wrote:

I have seen the progress of a good number of scholarship men both here and in Paris, and their accomplishments have proven that a man should not be sent until he no longer has need of a master, and has, or is able to map out, work which he will greatly desire to do. In this case the Scholarship is a wonderful aid to him to start his career and prove whether or not he is a sculptor. On the other hand, younger men drift contentedly and very pleasantly through their three years, usually having their heads turned by the unusual social opportunities offered them. . . . Mr. Breck agrees with me that four years is not too much.

Fry spoke as a mature artist in pursuit of his profession; he had a sense of time and a fear of wasting it. But if the purpose of a scholarship abroad was to develop the maturity of a potential artist, then the answer might be different. The art critic Royal Cortissoz, in an article on the American Academy in Rome written that same year, reflected the second view: "The object of the Academy has been not so much to give the young artist training as to increase his knowledge, stimulate his imagination and purify his taste. It gives him more than instruction; it gives him atmosphere. . . . He is asked to educate himself."

These were absorbing topics for trustees to discuss, compared with the anxious grind for money. Board meetings were never long enough to thrash out such questions even if agreement could have been reached. The distance from Rome to New York was great in spirit as well as in time. It is to the credit of the trustees that they seldom over-regulated academic matters except when begged for a ruling by an uncertain director. They thought highly of Breck's good judgment in such matters. But Breck, like Mowbray, had to think of his future as a painter, and in the spring of 1908 he tendered his resignation, effective a year hence.

The trustees turned again to one of their own number, the poet and artist Frederic Crowninshield. He accepted and, with his wife, arrived in Rome in late September 1909. A visiting trustee credited him a month later with "strenuous and warm-hearted efforts" in behalf of the Academy. At the same time there arrived a new fellow in sculpture, of whom the president of the National Society of Sculptors would say three years later, "It is not impossible that this man alone may be worth to American art all the efforts the American Academy in Rome have cost." The young man was Paul Manship.

Crowninshield's path in Rome was not a smooth one. He lacked, one visiting trustee reported, "familiarity with the Roman scene." Certainly he lacked executive experience in academic surroundings. The first honeymoon years at the Villa Mirafiori had ended, and perhaps it seemed less attractive to the more independent fellows than under Breck's permissive regime. At any rate Barry Faulkner led, a few months after Crowninshield's arrival, a student protest against the division of space in the Mirafiori. Faulkner proposed that the director reduce his relatively spacious quarters and turn over the extra rooms for student use. Crowninshield did not yield on this point.

Crowninshield was almost immediately faced with two other issues, and these were of great importance. One was the problem of further adapting the Mirafiori to the needs of the growing Academy or of finding another home for it. The other was the question of a merger of the Academy with the School of Classical Studies. The two questions almost inevitably went hand in hand.

Relationships between the Academy and the Classical School had been uneasy ever since their uncomfortable partnership had come to an end in the early days at the Villa Aurora. Since 1900 the classicists had been somewhat tightly housed in the Villa Bonghi and had watched with an envious eye as the Academy moved to the ample Mirafiori with its large grounds and possibilities of expansion. It had also seen the Academy add brick after brick to its financial structure, providing it with desirable security. In his annual report Richard Norton, director of the Classical School, expressed his regret that the two institutions were not joined, but he did so in a way that hardly advanced the cause of consolidation. Though not a masterpiece of tact or graciousness, it was a revealing paragraph:

It has long seemed to many of us a pity the Academy and the School were not allied and the nucleus for a species of universality for graduate study here. A vague but nonetheless persistent fear seems to have affected certain minds that we have designs on the Academy's millions or desired to use their house; while others have suffered from the dread lest the influence of artists or would-be scholars might be undesirable. So far as money is concerned there is no more reason for us to ask the Academy for assistance than for the Law School at Harvard to expect help from the Observatory. So far as the house is concerned, no student such as comes to us, whose time cannot be spent in pleasant and perhaps art-begetting dawdling, would for one instant think of using the Academy's building [the Mirafiori]. Only persons who had much spare time could use a building so far outside the walls and distant from everything that one comes to Rome to study. So far as the influence of one set of men on any other goes, it is certain that it would be beneficial as that of any gentleman on any other always is, especially when they are working on allied subjects. No, let the Academy have its funds and let us do the same, but let them have common Libraries and rooms for lectures and study, and let them have superior officers in common. If possible let them gather around a common set of buildings and work with sympathy and understanding toward a common end of elevating the taste and maintaining superior standards of art and scholarship in America.

Financially the Classical School had done well enough. In 1903 Morgan had given it $2,500 a year for three years, and the Carnegie Corporation was sending it fellows and supporting some of its research. By 1905 its capital endowment was close to $100,000, and the number of paying students (apart from fellows) was markedly increasing. By 1907–8 it had five fellows, nine students, and seven associates in regular enrollment. It also had been pledged a gift of another $100,000, of which over three-quarters had already been paid in. It had a good library for classical study, notably enriched by an indefinite loan from Mrs. Edward D. Brandegee of Boston, comprising some two thousand volumes and five or six thousand drawings on classical subjects.

The Classical School offered lectures—"but not too numerous to interfere with still more profitable opportunities for classical education in Rome"—excursions with explanations of the monuments visited, and personal supervision of the work of its students. Each fellow was required to engage in some piece of original work during his fellowship term and to publish it "as the School may direct." Although the School could not boast that it had sufficient funds or sufficient space in the Villa Bonghi to meet its coming needs, it would not, if it should merge with the Academy, enter into that partnership empty-handed like a poor relation, nor as a junior partner, either.

Richard Norton's report had spoken of "the influence of one set of men on the other." By 1906 the influence would have included that of women. The Classical School was the first of the two institutions to admit a woman fellow when Esther Boise Van Deman was enrolled as Carnegie Fellow in Archaeology. She was followed in 1907 by Lily Ross Taylor, Bryn Mawr Fellow in Latin, and three years later by Dora Johnson, another Carnegie archaeologist. By 1909 the students and fellows of Academy and School of Classical Studies were directly influencing one another in several different ways. Members of the Academy were regularly using the library of the Classical School, though there was no comparable reason for the occupants of the Villa Bonghi to go to the Villa Mirafiori, as Norton had been at pains to point out. But the Crown-

inshields repaid past courtesies by inviting the classical students
to tea at Mirafiori. Lily Ross Taylor remembered, sixty years later,
that the wife of the School's director at that time, Jesse Benedict
Carter, insisted that the two women fellows buy new and pre-
sentable hats and gloves for the occasion. Fortunately for restricted purses, Miss Taylor added, the weather was warm and
the Roman markets were full of charming straws.

The ice between the two schools was melting and their consolidation would probably have come about in due course had not
a new event hastened it. This was the second of the large issues
that faced Crowninshield when he took office. In the summer of
1909 the Villa Aurelia fell into the lap of the Academy. Its owner,
Mrs. Heyland, had died. It will be recalled that in 1906 she had
proposed to become a Founder of the Academy by an ingenious
arrangement of sale of the Villa to the Academy, part of the funds
of the sale to be assigned as a Founder's gift. The plan having
fallen through, she perpetuated her name in Academy history by
bequeathing the Villa to the Academy, with $100,000 for its
maintenance.

Mrs. Heyland, originally a Philadelphian, was the widow of a
retired British major. She had bought the Villa Aurelia in 1881,
when it was still a partial ruin after its severe bombardment in
1849 by French artillery stationed in the adjacent grounds of the
Villa Dora Pamphili. Mrs. Heyland undertook to restore it with
the help of an English architect. The Villa's fine proportions survived her heavy Victorian hand, and the handsome structure, set
in a large garden and dominating the very top of the Janiculum,
looked straight across Rome squarely at the Villa Medici. Contemporary photographs of the interior show all the clutter of the
taste of the day: looped velvet portieres, tufted chairs, oil paintings
on easels. Perfectly fitting into this background is a surviving
word portrait of Mrs. Heyland, "languishing on a blue satin sofa
with a basket of kittens each wearing a blue bow." Eleven days
before her death she revised her will and added to her bequest to
the Academy the condition that it would "take steps to insure
against ill-treatment of Horses and Animals in Rome, it being my
hope that I may arouse in the students of the Academy of America
a deep and lasting interest in this much needed Charity and Act of
Mercy."

As soon as the terms of the will were made known they were

challenged by a younger brother of Mrs. Heyland, who claimed she had made it while of unsound mind. His threatened lawsuit, as well as all the other problems attached to moving the Academy and remodeling the Villa, gave pause to the trustees. During the following months they came and went, trying to assess the situation on the spot. Was the temptingly attractive Villa in a part of Rome suitable to the Academy? Could the building, plus its ample ground for expansion, be made to fill the Academy's needs? If so, at what cost, and at what increase in its annual expenditure?

From the beginning opinions differed strongly. Crowninshield firmly opposed the move, convinced that the Mirafiori was the better place for the Academy and could be better adapted to its requirements. His opinion should certainly not be disregarded, for he had been in the center of things and was aware of the pressure to provide for more students and more space. The Academy had been steadily growing. It was currently in operation throughout the year: there were always students whose projects kept them in residence during the summer. Competitors for the architectural prize had tripled in 1910 over those of the previous year; applicants for the fellowship in mural painting had doubled. It was important that there be more space if there were to be a reunion with the School of Classical Studies. The officers of both schools shared a sense of the mutual advantages of a consolidation, especially if it could include a fresh start in a new physical plant adapted to their joint needs.

These arguments did not move Crowninshield, and it was despite his opposition that the trustees, naturally impressed by the possibilities of the Villa Aurelia, on January 3, 1910, accepted the Heyland bequest—which compelled them to meet immediate expenses of $10,000 in settlement fees and $50,000 to buy off Mrs. Heyland's brother from contesting the will.

At the same time a joint committee appointed by the boards of the two schools was formed, and a year later both boards accepted in principle its recommendation that they consolidate. The School of Classical Studies would transfer all its property to the Academy, but its funds were to be administered separately and used only for support of the classical studies. The Academy would henceforth consist of two schools, one of fine arts and one of classics, each with its own director. Although the merger was not finally legalized* until February 11, 1913, the *rapprochement* between the two schools was complete.

By March 1911 Crowninshield had formally offered his resignation, to be effective the first of the new year. It was evident that his steady opposition to the move to Aurelia had made things awkward for him and for the trustees. That fact may explain the rather cryptic entry in the minutes of the Academy trustees: "Resignation accepted—position untenable." Whatever the causes (and Crowninshield's health had not been good), the trustees voted a resolution expressing appreciation to Crowninshield for his two years of service, with special praise for raising the standard of student work. All involved were men of generosity and good will; if there were other differences between them they have been effaced by time.

* In order to permit consolidation with the Classical School, the act of Congress incorporating the Academy had to be amended. Its educational scope was enlarged to include classical studies, and the Academy was permitted to increase its capital to $3 million. This amendment, sponsored by Senator Elihu Root, was passed on June 6, 1912. In 1924 it was again amended to increase the property limit to $10 million, and Speaker Joe Cannon's ban on government officials serving as trustees was deleted. In 1967 its capitalization was again increased by act of Congress, and raised to $25 million.

VI

The Occupants
1911-1913

FRANK MILLET was only briefly an occupant of the Academy in Rome, but he had been associated with it from its beginning, when Burnham had called him to Chicago to take charge of the decorations of the World's Fair. Millet was "one of the best fellows," said Burnham, of that talented group of artists gathered in the Shack. From then on he took his place in the small circle of Academy friends.

Millet was a painter and writer whose particular genius lay in fostering the talents of others. He was a catalytic agent in bringing men together in any undertaking. Though he never achieved a permanent place in art, there were few important commissions on the fine arts of which he was not a stimulating member. Intuitive and generous, he seemed always ready to abandon his own pursuits to help where help was needed. To win him for a friend was to acquire his loyalty for life. He brought humor, earthiness, and exuberance to his undertakings; his letters are vivid and outspoken. Those about Academy affairs speak for themselves.

He wrote to McKim from Rome in 1906:

Mirafiori? . . . the best in Rome for our purpose. I had a change of heart in Rome and am now down on old palaces for the reasons stated in my letter to the Committee. Mr. Morgan with his bric-a-brac tendencies may want the Farnesina but for our use it isn't worth a penny. As for the Strohlfern, it's rotten; you couldn't give it to me for the Academy. And the Buonaparte is really no good nor the Aldobrandini nor the Aurelia nor any of them except the Patrizi and this is of no use on account of the restrictions . . . if we could build our own buildings and show these Johnnies what architecture is! I never felt so modern in my life as I did in Rome. Nor did I ever enjoy so much the glories of the past. . . . If Mr. Morgan would buy the Strohlfern and give us 20 million to build with and you would design and plan the group of buildings, we could have the Embassy, the Academy, the Archeologs and all, in that 20 acre lot, and no one need quarrel with his neighbor.

Millet had joined the board of trustees of the Academy in 1905 and almost immediately became its secretary. In 1907 he became its treasurer. In March 1908 he wrote to Burnham:

When the Knickerbocker Trust failed [in November 1907] carrying with it our $18,000, we had no funds at all, so I assumed the position of treasurer* and opened an account at the Fifth Avenue Bank for current expenses . . . from the $4000 Mr. Morgan sent us as interest on his subscription. Then I got up a scheme to raise wind and got Cadwallader, French, Mowbray, Blashfield, Ely and myself to loan $500 each, promising payment when the Knickerbocker resumed. Now we are hard up because expenses in Rome are about $1000 a month. If Charles [McKim] were not ill I should insist on being relieved, but just now it would not be loyal to do it.

Millet did not say that when the bank failed he had at once given $1,000 to the Academy from his own limited funds.

In May 1908 the trustees asked Millet to go to Rome at their expense "to look thoroughly into the affairs of the Academy." This was not due to lack of confidence in Breck but to the expansion of Academy affairs and the increasing need of the trustees for first-hand accounts of its progress. They relied on Millet's judgment: he had been a skilled international reporter, and his reports on the Academy were the next best thing to being there oneself. Of Mirafiori he wrote: ". . . it is the most delightful place . . . neat as a pin inside and out for Breck has done his work admirably . . . airy, spacious, 70 rooms . . . students' work excellent . . . they are enthusiastic."

Eighteen months later he changed his tune. It was October 1909; he was again the trustees' emissary to Rome, "to see the Brecks out and the Crowninshields in." He concluded that the Breck administration had been too much directed toward the students, too little conscious of the image that Millet thought the Academy should present to the public. He wrote to French from Mirafiori:

"I feel as if my presence, while grateful to the Crowninshields, must be, in fact, a little irksome to the Brecks because it is inevitable we discuss changes." Millet wished to turn the Academy

---

* He took the place of Charles Barney, president of the Knickerbocker Trust Company, who had to withdraw under pressure of his bank's difficulties.

from an Americanized *"pensione* into something resembling an
institution in which the effect of production is not the human
species but works of art." He liked the students he found there "in
spite of being spoiled by too much coddling. . . . Breck has been
a very loyal and efficient *director* or rather *manager* in many ways
and for what has seemed to me an interregnum, I do not think we
could have done better. . . . My mind is easy about the future
of the Academy. It will be an institution which people here will
respect, and the director will be, as he ought to be, a personage.
Crowninshield and his wife fall into the niches and fit the pedestals
exactly."

He spoke of the changes in the Mirafiori which McKim's illness
had prevented from being accomplished. To bring them about
would

cost nothing but the labor of moving furniture and will result in a
distinct separation of the students from the official part. . . . These
changes will probably distress the minds of the old students who cannot
get over the idea that the Academy building is all for them and their
residence and wish to have reception rooms turned into a library and
living rooms for themselves. . . . We must purge at once the Academy
from the threatening element of bohemianism and vulgarity. The dignity
of the institution demands that we have spacious and stately drawing
rooms, entrance hall, dining room, etc., etc., unencumbered by peram-
bulators and bicycles and the clutter of careless youths. . . . from what
they say and from their actions I believe they think they have the
right to the entire building to use it as they desire, completely ignoring
the official character and apparently thinking it—the Villa—should be
a sort of students' club. Part of the building may well have this character. Indeed it should be so in order that they may have the intimate
association which is so useful to them.

The students had offered suggestions. ("We think you
ought. . . .") Millet considered this an impertinence and admired
Crowninshield for the way he took it. "This state of things won't
last long when he takes hold." However, he added in another letter
to the trustees of the same time that there was "an excellent class
of men working at the Academy, the best we have ever had. I have
great hopes that it is to become more and more important as an
educator. Indeed I am working as hard as I can to carry out what
I know to be McKim's ideas. . . . The Crowninshields are entering their career with enthusiasm and joy."

The Heyland bequest of the Villa Aurelia had only recently been made and was much in the minds of those who knew about it. Millet gave his opinion to French. The Villa had recently been valued at $175,000, but "while a splendid place, is unsuited to our uses. The income however would be most welcome." He concluded "the Aurelia would take nine gardeners to care for the gardens and at least $100,000 to make the Villa available for Academy use. It is exceedingly inaccessible on the very summit of the Gianicolo away up above the Spanish Academy and on the wrong side of the Tiber."

Twelve months later Millet had again changed his mind. The Aurelia had meanwhile been accepted by the board of trustees, now under the presidency of McKim's partner Rutherford Mead. Millet was excited about the possibilities of the Janiculum property. In his capacity as eyes and ears for the trustees he was once more in Rome in November 1910. He wrote to Burnham, also in Europe, urging him to come to Rome and see the Aurelia, and added: . . . "in all probability we shall have another Director before long—this is strictly between us. . . . I don't think Crowninshield will care to undergo the worry of fitting up that place and because he has always opposed our considering it as a location, I don't believe he will care to live there. . . . We know the Academy is not going along as it might, although we are turning out good men." Millet must also, in a later letter, have urged upon Burnham's consideration a candidate for director to succeed Crowninshield, for in a reply dated January 1911 Burnham expressed his mind fully to Millet on the place of women in the Academy:

The other point you urge in favor of . . . is that his wife has knowledge of Roman society and skill in playing the game. Dear Frank, that is the very thing you *don't* want. We have had mistresses in the Academy in Rome, and what has come of it? When I visited the Academy a cold chill ran down my back because I was received in a drawingroom by a woman. No man knows what this means better than you. It has not worked, and it cannot be made to. Imagine a woman presiding at the Villa Medici! Would any French artist stand it? There should be no women in Mirafiori. The students there are not boys. They do not need "the influence and refinements of a home" and they do need entire freedom to work each according to his own nature, following his own moods. Any restriction put upon him will vex and interfere, and any set formality about him frets his life. No woman can live there without making a nest for herself in the Villa, and will this nest be hidden and so used as to be negligible in summing up the spirit of the School? You know it cannot be. No woman who ever lived could so subordinate herself.

"My boys" and "what I hope for my boys." These phrases are quoted by me. The dear ladies I met in the Roman Academy used them. They brooded over the School!!

By early 1911 the pace had quickened in Academy affairs. Morgan's and Frick's checks of $100,000 each for the endowment fund had come in. The trustees were engrossed in the move to the Janiculum; Crowninshield's resignation was generally known and was to take place at the end of the year. Morgan's interest in the Academy was increasing. As soon as the trustees had, the previous year, secured title to the Villa Aurelia, he had given the Academy the piece of land near it on which he had taken an option in 1906. Then came his gift to the endowment fund in March 1911, followed by his arrival in Rome for his annual spring visit. How closely involved in Academy affairs he had become is disclosed in correspondence between Mead, who was also in Rome, and Millet in New York. Mead wrote on May 1, 1911:

> Morgan has been here. He has visited the Aurelia many times. He has openly expressed his great interest in the Academy as amalgamated, and according to everybody . . . has openly declared he will now see it through. He has also openly declared at a dinner Carter [director of the School of Classical Studies] was his candidate for Director-in-chief. He bought extensively of additional property beyond the triangle,* including the Villa [Chiaraviglio] and grounds backing on the triangle to the south, and has tried to get the Torlonia Villa extending from the triangle to the Acqua Paola. . . .
>
> All this makes us poorer than ever unless he proposes to back us up with a big endowment. He proposes, as I understand it, to put all the students on the big new piece opposite the triangle including studios, living apartments, kitchens, etc., having no students on the Aurelia site—but setting up a king there as a Director, with the library and exhibition hall, and the gardens kept up apparently for the entertainment of the American colony and visiting Americans—all rot from my point of view. He said at a dinner that Carter was his candidate for Director-in-chief, or whatever he called the head of the combined Academy.

* Mead was referring to the land between the Via Garibaldi and the Via Angelo Masina.

On May 12 and May 25 Mead sent further reports to Millet: "The situation in Rome is very mixed. Those who saw Morgan are full of hope that he is going to see the thing through, and the fact that he has bought more property would seem to point that way. He has bought $100,000 worth of land and a villa [the Chiaraviglio]. If on the other hand he proposes to turn this over to us as his additional $100,000 promised, we are worse off than before. I hope to catch Morgan in Paris and find out what he is driving at."

Mead did catch him in Paris on May 25, 1911, and described the interview to Millet:

> There is no question but that he is now intensely interested in the success of the Academy and in the new site. He believes the site is not large enough and has bought the two pieces of property I wrote you about and has his eye on the Torlonia Villa and the little Villa [Bellacci] in the corner of the big plot he has bought and which is new and was built for a Torlonia mistress and she does not want to get out and asks a big price. All this he says he will turn over to the Academy when it gets its plans ready for developing it.
>
> He says "work out your scheme; get your plans ready, and then ask for money and I will help you get it."
>
> All this is very fine but its accomplishment depends entirely on the life of Morgan. If he lives two years I believe things will go smoothly. If he should die then where are we?"

The question was partially answered in September 1911 when Mead and Morgan were both back in New York. There they had a more reassuring interview at which Breck Trowbridge, Academy trustee, was also present:

> Mr. Trowbridge and I met Mr. Morgan at his office by appointment at 1:30 o'clock Tuesday, September 19, 1911. . . . I had the sketches ready for the proposed building on the site purchased by him. . . . Mr. Morgan examined the plans carefully and showed great interest in them and expressed his approval in every particular. I also carried with me a blue print copy of the engineer's survey of the entire property, including the Villa Aurelia, which he requested me to leave with him.
> . . . He said this thing ought to be put through at once. "You ought to have weekly meetings and get your statements ready, because the whole thing must be wound up this winter. . . ."
> He is evidently eager to get to work, but must have this statement first. I came away with the firm impression that with the facts before him, Mr. Morgan will, before the winter is over, raise all the money.
> When in looking over the plans, I told him that the buildings we

suggest would cost at least $250,000 he said, "That's all right," and
when I added, "We haven't a cent of money; where are we to get the
money?" he said, "How much have you got in the bank, invested?" I
replied, we had $400,000. He said, "Use it; you are at perfect liberty
to do so. You can use mine. Use whatever is necessary for building
purposes." I suggested that there might be an objection by the donors,
on the ground that it was given as endowment. He said, "That's a
question for lawyers, but you can use mine."

On November 27, 1911, Mead again reported to Millet: "I wrote
Morgan on the 25th . . . in which I tried to commit him on the
assurance that we should be in funds to pay money on the contracts. The Committee did not feel that we could actually make
the contracts until we had an assurance from Morgan, so that if
anything happened to him, Jack Morgan might carry out his
wishes. . . . I shall daily expect some assurance from him."

On December 1 and again on December 4 Mead sent notes to
Millet, saying he was "in the dumps" because of no word from
Morgan, but on December 5 he reported to Millet that though
there was "no word from Morgan yet . . . De Forest says it will
be all right. . . . there is a perfect understanding in the whole
family and everything his father starts in on will be carried out."
On that basis the trustees went forward in the next months with the
extensive plans for property and construction having gratefully
accepted on February 13, 1912, "the property on the Janiculum
recently transferred to the Academy by Mr. Morgan." Even Mead,
who tended to worry, was completely reassured.

Meanwhile the trustees were also concerned with finding Crowninshield's successor. There was immediate need for a director who
could cope with the move to the Janiculum and all that it implied.
The Villa Aurelia must be adapted to the uses of the Academy: its
handsome rooms on the *piano nobile* should be left for the purposes
of entertainment, others on the ground floor should be made into
offices, while the upper floors should provide living quarters for
the director, his family, and Academy guests. A new Academy
building, designed by McKim, Mead, and White, was to be built
on the piece of land Morgan had bought and given. If the new
director were an architect he could oversee all this construction
and alteration.

He should also be a man who would help to adjust the Academy
to the coming merger with the School of Classical Studies. The

School would bring with it to the Janiculum its director, Jesse Benedict Carter. It would also bring a classics library, an endowment of $100,000, and annual gifts from twenty-five universities and foundations. It was clear that when the two schools and their separate administrations actually merged, a top administrative position would have to be created and someone appointed to it who would hold the balance between them. The trustees felt that during the period of creative activity the new administrator should preferably represent the fine arts.

With these considerations in mind the trustees first selected the architect. They asked Gorham Phillips Stevens, a graduate of M.I.T. and associated with McKim, Mead, and White, to go to Rome as secretary of the Academy. Stevens had been with the firm since 1902 and was warmly recommended by Kendall. It is perhaps at this point that the misunderstanding began which would trouble Academy relationships for the next five years. The trustees wanted a man who could contribute a specific talent for a certain limited period of time, but they had evidently not made that clear to Stevens. Perhaps because he sensed the temporary nature of the offer, he refused it. It was late in the year, with little time to look further even had the trustees wished to do so. They offered Stevens the directorship of the Academy for a year from January 1, 1912. He accepted. They also appointed C. Grant La Farge secretary to the board.

At the same time the trustees went ahead with their plan to find and secure the top administrator of the new Academy when it was consolidated with the School of Classical Studies. They turned to Frank Millet, confident that his tact, warmth, and experience would iron out any difficulties that might arise between the directors of the two consolidating institutions and electing him, on February 13, 1912, executive head of the American Academy in Rome with the title of secretary of the Academy. Millet accepted, unmindful of his own convenience where the Academy was concerned. Stevens arrived in Rome to take up his duties on January 1, 1912. Millet arrived as executive head a few weeks later. It is said that Millet went reluctantly "to straighten out the affairs of the Academy in Rome" which were "sadly complicated owing to the death of Mr. McKim, the ambitious building plans of J. P. Morgan," and the change of directors.

Millet spent February and March in Rome—two busy months

during which Morgan and Mead were present. Many plans for the Janiculum were discussed. In April, Millet set out for New York to report to the trustees. He crossed France and took ship on the maiden voyage of the White Star Line's magnificent new liner, *Titanic*. On the night of April 14, 1912, the ship struck an iceberg and sank. Millet died in the service of others, quietly helping women and children into boats while giving words of encouragement. The last glimpse of him was of a white-haired man standing on deck and waving his hand to younger mortals he had helped to save. The memorials to Frank Millet conveyed affection and regard beyond the usual formal terms. They spoke of his perception, his power to express ideas clearly and forcibly, his quickness to grasp and readiness to consider opposing points of view. The Academy would miss him sorely in the tangle of relationships that followed his death.

The shocked trustees soon received another blow. Within weeks of the *Titanic* disaster Daniel Burnham died. Next to McKim he had been the senior statesman of Academy affairs. Linked to it from the beginning, he had served almost continuously as a trustee. He had joined McKim in supporting it from his own pocket when its bills could not otherwise be paid. His counsel had been sought in every aspect of its growth and work; his presence was urged at all its gatherings.

But there could be no pause for mourning. Millet had to be replaced at once. Disregarding the principle of an impartial chairman to hold the balance between the two schools, the board appointed Carter to succeed Millet. For the rest of 1912, while retaining his directorship of the Classical School, Carter was to be executive head, as Millet had been. The following year, after the merger, he was to remain the top administrator and the representative of the trustees, with the title of director of the American Academy, to which the powers of executive head had been added, while also retaining the directorship of the School of Classical Studies. He was to receive immediately a fee of $1,000 to be added to his salary from the Classical School. In 1913 he would receive $6,000 for his two directorships, plus an expense account of $1,000. Stevens' salary and expense account was $3,500.

Stevens was dismayed at what had been done, and justifiably offended by the way it had been done. He did not hear of Carter's appointment until it was a *fait accompli*. He had served less than half his year's appointment as director of the American Academy in Rome. It was true that the Academy of which he was director was the Academy before the consolidation, but consolidation was not to occur until the beginning of 1913. He cabled the trustees for a clarification of his position. Mead replied by cable confirming the news of Carter's appointment and, from Stevens' point of view confounding confusion by adding: "This does not disturb your title or conduct of the Academy."

But actually things were already very different for Stevens, as they would probably never have been under the perceptive Millet. When Carter assumed Millet's powers, no further pretense of Stevens' position as director of the American Academy in Rome for the balance of the year was maintained, and Stevens felt his demotion sharply. Although the trustees cabled him to act as their "representative agent in the supervision and erection of new Academy buildings" even this turned hollow as Carter prepared the budgets, sent in all progress reports on the buildings, and made all major decisions not actually to do with the details of construction. In another effort to ease and clarify, the trustees told Stevens that his appointment was now that of director of the School of Fine Arts. But the harm had been done.

The steps by which the trustees were led to create so awkward a situation are understandable but not quite pardonable. Millet's charm and tact had made the problems of administration and administrative personnel seem less difficult than they actually were. And Carter was rather a dazzling person while Stevens' talents were less conspicuous. Carter's reputation in the world of classical scholarship was impressive. He knew Rome well and Rome knew him better than it had known his predecessors. Cultivated, able, energetic, he moved about expansively as social or speaking engagements took him frequently away from the Academy. When he offered public lectures, Roman society flocked to hear him. "The ladies swooned over him; he was a spell-binder," said one woman fellow who knew him well. Altogether he made a natural and imposing head of the Academy, which up to that time had not had a director at once so scintillating and aggravating, so charming and alarming. He captivated Morgan. He exasperated others. It was a pity, said the same woman contemporary years later, that "he was not gifted in his contacts with people. Stevens, for his part, was discreet, conscientious." The two men were temperamentally incompatible, as is clearly revealed in the diary kept by Stevens. Each was able but in different ways; they might have worked together more contentedly had they not been put in such anomalous positions.

In January 1913 Morgan returned to Rome and the Grand Hotel where he habitually stayed. He visited the Janiculum immediately. Although his health was obviously failing, his interest in the Academy seemed inexhaustible. As plans were put before him he would repeat in tones too loud to be a grunt, too genial to be a growl: "Spread it out; spread it out." Lame and ill as he was, he would not be deterred from inspecting every floor of the Villa Aurelia. Fortunately he could mount by a new elevator—the gift of the Otis Elevator Company to the Academy. There is recollection of anxious moments when he insisted on stepping out onto an upper balcony, unaided and apparently uncertain of his balance, to survey the scene below. Perhaps it was that bird's-eye view of the new building going up almost below him that brought about his offer to advance its cost. This enabled the trustees to use Academy capital to "spread it out" by the purchase of more adjoining land.

In this way the Academy acquired nearly all the property bounded by the Via Angelo Masina, the Via Giacomo Medici, the Via Pietro Riselli (since abandoned), and the Aurelian wall—the wall that had been built in the second century A.D. to keep out the barbarians, but which now sheltered American invaders. None of these properties might have been acquired by the Academy but for Morgan's loans and gifts; he did not ask for but was given as collateral a mortgage on the Villa Mirafiori. One small piece of property, the Villino Bellacci, only a few yards from the excavations for the new Academy building, resisted purchase except at an exorbitant price. Morgan would not be thwarted. He bought it and on March 29, 1913, gave it to the Academy. On March 31 this generous friend of the Academy died.

Morgan's partners immediately cabled cash for the most recent of his gifts. Altogether he had advanced $365,000 to the Academy. At first the younger Morgan declared that after he had fulfilled his father's commitments to the Academy he would feel no obligation to do more. It was, he said, "Not a Morgan Academy but an Academy representing the entire country." But his deeds belied his words: he became as generous to the Academy as his father had been. Almost at once he began by "rounding out" his father's loans by another $10,000. When in 1915 the 5 percent interest on the total Morgan loan was due at a bad time for the Academy, he waived the interest. Soon afterward he offered to cancel one dollar of the loans for every dollar the Academy added to its endowment during the year. He renewed that offer annually until in 1920 the whole loan had been canceled, thus turning the $375,000 into a magnificent gift. It was never a "Morgan Academy," but it owed a great part of its physical plant and property to the Morgans, father and son.

VII

World War I

BY 1913 the annual expense of the Academy had grown to $50,000, and Boring, as treasurer, was once more wrestling with the difficulties of finding money for the Academy's bread and butter. Carter had entered confidently on his new duties and had shown no hesitation in making large expenditures, professing to believe that the best way to secure added endowment was to spend beyond current income, thus making it imperative to raise more money. This dubious procedure is in frequent practice today; in 1913 it was regarded as worse than unorthodox by the dismayed finance committee. Carter's bland disregard of the tight financial situation and his expenditures without advance authorization gave Boring unhappy moments. On taking office Carter had, upon his own initiative, secured an option on more property near the Villa Aurelia and recommended to the trustees that they build on it a dormitory for women students. For seven years there had been women in the Classical School, and Carter was looking forward to admitting women to the School of Fine Arts. It was a pity that his disregard of the board's attitude toward unauthorized expenditures and toward resident women fellows led him to launch a commendable scheme so abruptly and at so untimely a moment. The trustees did not take up the option or greet except with silence his proposal to house women students in Academy buildings. A little later, on trustee instruction, Boring explicitly directed Carter to incur no further unauthorized expense.

Stevens also was enduring frustrations. The new Academy building had not been roofed by June 1, 1913; the contractor had fallen behind schedule and had already exceeded his estimate by 10 percent. And as if suddenly aware of the building's elevated position, the city of Rome was refusing to supply water to its upper floor. Stevens was, in short, suffering all the problems of construction.

In October 1913 Mead, Kendall, and C. Grant La Farge, secretary of the board, came to Rome to observe progress, and Carter returned from London to receive them. He then dashed off to America, where his extensive tour of brilliant lectures brought the Academy before a wider public. During Carter's absences Stevens resumed full charge, and the tension apparent in his diary eased. But by Christmas, Carter and the tensions had returned, and the year ended on a dismal note. Carter gave a Christmas dinner to the students, insisting (according to Stevens) that he alone should make an after-dinner speech. It was to the credit of both men that much of this discord was kept behind the scenes, though certainly some and probably all of the fellows were aware of it. Fortunately most of them were too absorbed in their travel plans and personal affairs to give much thought to administrative bickering.

As the year ended there was no intimation of the world-shattering events to come. New gifts to the Academy continued to be made. In February 1914 the Rockefeller Foundation made a grant of $10,000 annually for ten years toward current Academy expenses. Thomas Spencer Jerome, long resident in Capri, died in 1914, bequeathing one-third of his collection of books to the Academy as well as a sum, which later proved to be about $45,000, to establish a lectureship in his name. In April Cass Gilbert gave $5,000 to the McKim Memorial Fund. In June, Mrs. Charles Mac-Veagh offered to provide funds to plant the new Academy "campus" with large pine trees, while Mrs. Carl Schmidlapp gave the Academy handsome new furniture for its dining room. The previous spring the trustees had elected to the board, in place of Morgan, Charles D. Norton of New York, a banker. Nephew by marriage of McKim, he had caught his enthusiasm for the Academy from McKim himself, whom he greatly resembled in singleness of purpose, energy, and persuasiveness. Norton, together with Anson Phelps Stokes of the board, immediately drew up a plan for raising funds to increase the endowment. The Academy was moving rapidly and prosperously toward its opening in the fall.

To commemorate the twentieth anniversary of its founding, the Academy published a handsomely printed booklet, *History of the American Academy in Rome*, by trustee C. Grant La Farge. Also, in

the first issue of *Art and Archaeology,* Professor E. K. Rand of
Harvard wrote that the Academy's magnificent new building as-
sured centralization and efficient operation of all Academy activities. He felt confident that the School of Classical Studies had a
fine future there. As for the Villa Aurelia, it would be a truly
splendid administrative and social center. Rand did not fail to re-
mind his classical readers that "The ground is sacred with reminis-
cence of the ancient and more recent past: the Aurelian Wall runs
through the estate, and the house itself is built on the ruins of the
Villa Savorelli, where Garibaldi made a desperate stand in the
siege of 1849." Kenyon Cox, Royal Cortissoz, and Edward Robinson had also joined in the accolade, in speech and in public print.
Cortissoz had said: "You are not sent to the Academy unless you
have unmistakable gifts, and those gifts are not developed by rule
of thumb, not by lessons, not by work alone. They are to be developed by what you feel as a human being, by your excitement
and happiness under the pressure of the glorious things you see."
Cox, speaking of the logic of combining art and the classics, added:
"The artists should be able to teach the archeologists that art is a
living thing . . . the archeologists can teach the artists that art is
a continuity, that to know it one must know its past as well as its
present, and that the educated artist is something more than an
artist who is up to date." The Academy felt itself to be soundly
based both physically and educationally. Its future seemed secure.
In October 1914 it was nearly ready to be opened.

But not with ceremonies, for World War I had begun in August.
The war caught most men unprepared, scarcely able to credit its
actuality, and certainly unwilling to believe it could last very long.
Rutherford Mead telegraphed to Rome that he was bottled up in
Carlsbad; an urgent summons brought Carter back from northern
Italy. Although Italy remained neutral during August and the
Academy seemed safely remote from the invasion of Belgium and
France, by mid-September the unexpected successes of the German
armies had staggered the western world. It was as if mankind had
violently turned a corner and rushed off headlong in a new direction. The Academy, reflecting the society it served, was swept
along too. But like all institutions, it lagged behind the changed
mores of the day and for a while held to its old pattern.

Some prudent measures were taken. Norton consulted the secretary of state, William Jennings Bryan, who in turn consulted

Thomas Nelson Page, ambassador to Rome. The secretary advised that "no new man should be sent out at present" but saw no reason for closing the Academy altogether. The villas Aurelia and Chiaraviglio were not opened. The Mirafiori was closed. Its last occupants, with their lares and penates, had been brought across Rome by October 1. The new building was able to house the entire resident membership of the Academy, which consisted of fourteen students (the new holders of the Rome Prize had come anyway) and also Stevens and his wife. The lease of the Villa Bonghi had expired on October 1, and the Carters took up residence in the Bellacci. Professor of Classics Kirby Flower Smith had been appointed to assist Carter through 1914–15 as acting director of the Classical School. Thus snugged in on the Janiculum, the Academy went about its business as usual, on the smaller total budget effected by this consolidation. The plan for a grand opening had been abandoned; the Academy was lucky enough to be housed in time for the new term.

While Europe crashed around them, the occupants of the Academy appear to have been largely absorbed in their own affairs. Reflected in Stevens' diary, their days were full. Ezra Winter and Eugene Savage were taking lessons in fresco painting. The new young sculptor, Leo Friedlander, "wants to get married and is causing trouble." Everyone was working furiously to meet the deadline of the annual January exhibition of fellows' work in New York. When the boxes of exhibits finally went off after the first of the year, everyone relaxed into the more normal pastime of staging "a great rebellion" over the cost of food and the quality of the butter.

But on January 13, 1915, a fearful earthquake in Italy brought home the uncertainty of life. As destructive as German bombs, it killed or injured some fifty thousand Italians. Fortunately the Academy escaped with only a small crack in its library foundations. But Academy life soon reverted to normal. "Rodin called on us," said a cryptic entry in Stevens' diary for February 9. How much more one would like to know of this event! In March, Friedlander again jeopardized his fellowship by declaring he would marry. With admirable coolness his fiancée put Friedlander's career first and said she would wait. But when the impatient lover said he would not wait, Carter insisted that he sign a statement to the effect that he was not married and that if he did marry he would relinquish his fellowship, giving Friedlander twenty-four hours to sign or leave. Unanimously the students protested the ultimatum. Friedlander remained at the Academy, but he privately gave Stevens the signed paper Carter had asked for.

Once again Carter recommended to the trustees that women be admitted to the Fine Arts School, this time joined by President M. Carey Thomas of Bryn Mawr and by the trustees of Vassar College. The Academy board reiterated that it was not feasible to admit women whom the Academy was not able to house. Mead wrote two years later to Norton a letter that expressed the board's unshaken point of view from the outset: "It is much better to consolidate our present activities and get them working perfectly— with money to support them generously—than to branch out into . . . women's accommodations. These will come but can wait—and then let the women come forward and provide the means."

The board, however, rejoiced to announce a new fellowship in landscaping, given to the Academy in the form of $25,000 of endowment by the American Society of Landscape Architects. It also announced "the most complete competition yet" for the American Academy in Rome Fellowships. There were seventy-five entries in architecture, ten sculptors, twenty-one landscapers, and ten classicists. So sure was everyone that the war would soon end that it was also decided that travel by fellows, which had been somewhat curtailed, could be resumed by summer, and an excursion to Greece was arranged for that time. The Academy was to be closed for the summer session, however. There was the familiar shortage of ready funds and the usual borrowing from a New York bank, this time the sum of just over $4,000 to meet the estimated deficit of the year. The trustees loaned the empty Villa Mirafiori to the American Embassy, which used it for the American Ambulance Corps. The board accepted with pleasure Paul Manship's generous offer to design and execute a fountain for the *cortile* of the new building, in gratitude for his fellowship at the Academy. When it was installed a few years later it became the focal point of the courtyard, a representation of the infant Hercules strangling a serpent—Youth triumphant over Adversity. Its water falls into a basin that Norton gave to complete the sculptor's design.

In May 1915 Italy declared war on Austria. This serious news, far from uniting the forces within the Academy, was overshadowed there by another springtime skirmish between Carter and Stevens over the budget. Stevens had, in Carter's eyes, exceeded his duties when he cabled the trustees that the expenses of the Academy could be reduced below the figure Carter had submitted on the new budget. The issue was exacerbated by Carter's unauthorized purchase of coal. He had seized an opportunity to buy a large amount of this increasingly dear and scarce commodity. The trustees, influenced by Stevens' cable as well as by Carter's sudden draft, protested vigorously the unbudgeted $5,000 expenditure. The correspondence between the director and the board grew in length and acrimony. Mead wrote to Norton about Carter's habit of spending first and explaining afterward, and added: "While I have the greatest admiration for Carter, I always feel that in his exuberance he has an inclination to build up about himself a machine which will give him importance. The less machinery we have and the less show we make in Rome, the better for the Academy as a working institution."

In October, Carter went to America. At once his presence and his charm cleared the atmosphere. The budget was approved, twenty-one new stoves were acquired to burn the coal, and in December the resolution of the previous June "disapproving the Director's course of action with regard to his budget" was stricken from the minutes "with regret for the injustice inadvertently done him." The most important decision of the board that summer had been to appoint a director of the Classical School, thus restoring at last the administrative balance on paper, if not healing the breach between Stevens and Carter. Professor Charles Upson Clark of Yale, who had served as acting director in 1915, took up this post in the Academy in October 1916. Besides the annual professorships at the Classical School, the staff of the Academy now included a librarian, Albert W. Van Buren, who doubled as professor of archaeology. Carter was given the assistance of a bursar, Charles Laurie, and of a secretary. The first Rome Prize Fellow in Landscape Architecture, Edward Lawson, had come to Rome.

Winter set in, but despite the twenty-one stoves there was no heat whatever in the bedrooms of the main building. When the war began, the students, staff, and trustees (like most Americans at the time) thought of themselves as occupying spectators' seats, but in April 1916 the war came closer when Italy declared war on Germany. The Academy offered to loan the Villa Mirafiori to the Italian government as a military hospital, an offer which was grate-

fully accepted. The Villa served this purpose for the duration of
the war, under the direction of Count San Martino. The only grace
note in an otherwise grim and chilly spring was sounded by the
unquenchable Friedlander, who was found to be keeping a live
horse in his studio.

World wars end eventually; domestic wars almost never. The
internal contentions between directors began again over the 1916
budget—this time with drastic effect. Once more Stevens undertook
to present an elaborate analysis of every facet of Academy life in
order to show how expenses could be cut. His presentation makes
fascinating reading for an historian, but it was rash of him to send
it to the trustees. Carter exploded. He wrote to the finance committee that its budget plans "took it for granted that no one would
raise a hand until the end of September 1917 to increase in any
way the income of the Academy—a state of affairs which is un-
thinkable. . . . It is obvious that if we are going forward without increasing our income and replacing our expiring subscriptions,
it is only a question of arithmetic when we shall have nothing left
but our $21,000 [income from endowment]. In eight years even
Rockefeller money would run out were it not renewed. . . . I am
writing to the President of the Academy a letter on this subject."

Norton was in Rome and went over the budget with Carter and
Stevens. On March 31, 1916, he wrote to Professor Francis W.
Kelsey, a classicist at Michigan:

I like both Carter and Stevens and it is going to be a very hard case
for me to settle. I guess the budget ought to go through with only
minor cuts, but in reality Stevens is right. There is a system of life,
of servants, of wages for servants, etc. which is out of all proportion
with what Italians pay. Carter has put the thing on this basis now, and
if he started cutting down too hard, the Academy would probably lose
some of the better servants, and what is worse, all would be dissatisfied
. . . if it becomes necessary to retrench Carter has almost made his
position impossible. He does not discuss the question as practical
business, but insists on a certain standard of life and *tone*, which should
be ruined if a servant's pay were cut.

Carter sent to the board an exhaustive rebuttal of Stevens'
estimate. He described some of his possible economies: how he
could keep the Academy open without steam heat in winter, "except at intervals to dry out the dampness of the building"; how
wood was being used because coal was at a premium. The stoves

had had to be replaced by wood-burning stoves "made to our purpose by hand." The students were receiving an allowance of wood daily but had to pay for any beyond this. He described how "the gardens of the Villa Aurelia give [the students] the one thing the new building lacks." To let the grounds of the Villa Aurelia go would be shortsighted, and anyway the grass was cut free by a farmer outside the Porta San Pancrazio for his cows. Carter deplored reducing the staff of twenty-six servants, not including the four gardeners. The cleanliness of the buildings, he argued, "is one of our great moral effects on the individual students." When cheap food and lower wages for the servants had been tried in the Mirafiori "five years ago" the result had been "hospital bills that cost more than wages would have in the first place." Moreover it was thrifty to keep the servant who cleaned the studios because he also posed for the painters and sculptors. Carter pointed out that the services of the bursar and secretary "saved every one of the Directors many hours which they are free to devote to those things which make for the intellectual and artistic progress of the Academy. . . . Any proposition to remove either of these persons would seem to me unjust under present conditions when those who must of necessity pass upon the proposition can also by the same necessity have no real knowledge of the actual existing condition of affairs."

In April, Carter sailed for New York with his resignation in his pocket. Norton was now directly in the line of fire, for although Henry Walters was chairman of the finance committee, Walters was ill. Telegrams and letters went back and forth, each revealing that Carter's charm and confident forcefulness were again having their effect. In the end he returned to Rome on May 12, still director and with a budget cut by only $5,000. He had also secured a strongly urged increase in salary for one member of the faculty. In his words: "Dr. Van Buren is a married man approaching forty years of age . . . many years in service of the Academy and the old Classical School as Librarian . . . next to myself the oldest officer in point of length of residence. He has received, however, almost the smallest salary on our rolls and has absolutely no perquisites of any sort." Carter obtained an increase to Van Buren's salary of $1,000 a year.

Relieved by his success, Carter wrote fulsomely to La Farge: ". . . a command from this [finance] Committee has far more than

mere legality. It does more than require obedience; it brings
straightway to the front of our consciousness all our love for the
Academy; we leap forward to gird up our loins and accomplish
their bidding, even though the task seems impossible. Their love
quickens our love and only love can accomplish the impossible."

It was the last battle of the budget between Stevens and Carter.
But an auditor from the University of Chicago, brought in to
examine the books, reported on June 1: "It would appear that a
considerable part of the expense of the upkeep is incurred from a
desire to maintain a high standard as to appearance and the things
that go with it, all of which may be very desirable but not justi-
fiable if they involve the institution in debt." The trustees began
to consider very seriously how the Academy might retrench.

Meanwhile the big guns moved steadily nearer. In late October
1916 Italian military officers requested permission to install an
anti-aircraft searchlight on the Villa Aurelia. The Academy did not
issue a peremptory refusal; to have done so might have brought
more difficult demands. On the advice of attorneys nothing at all
was said—officially—and the searchlight did not appear. Tourists
were by that time "virtually non-existing" in Rome, but there were
thirteen fellows and fourteen other students in residence at the
Academy, almost filling it to capacity.

The new year began a different story. On January 13, 1917, the
war came home painfully to the Academy when one of its former
servants was killed at the front. On February 4 the United States
broke off diplomatic relations with Germany and on April 13 declared war. The Academy reacted sharply: its attitudes and activities changed overnight. Carter had been at work part-time for
the American Red Cross and the Ambulance Service and had already been decorated by the Italian government, but after April
the time he gave to the Academy was very limited indeed. Some of
the fellows enlisted in the Red Cross or the Ambulance Corps;
others waited for word on their status as draftees or for advice
from the State Department. After consulting the Department the
trustees voted on May 15 to close the Academy "as an active institution," though a complete closing proved unnecessary. Competitions for fellowships were to be discontinued, and those who
had already won their Rome Prizes were to postpone going to
Rome until peace came, when their scholarships would be valid.

Travel by all students was reduced to a minimum, but the trustees voted to keep the Academy "open this summer."

On July 18, 1917, Carter left "for the front" in northern Italy, to study Red Cross conditions there. Two days later, at the age of forty-six, he died, reportedly of sunstroke, at Cervignano. His last words were "I came to help Italy. It is I who needs help." Stevens recounted the bleak aftermath: "July 24. Carter's body arrived. July 25. Met Mrs. Carter. Services at St. Pauls. Coffin too big to go in tomb, buried next day. Lothrop, Train, Richardson and I present." It was a sad, small, wartime service for the man who had served the Classical School and the Academy for nine years, at that time a longer term of service than anyone else had completed. An appropriate resolution was soon voted by the trustees: "Such faults as he had were not unlike his virtues. . . . His exuberant vitality and brilliancy—the source of his strength" might easily have been misunderstood for mannerisms. A bust of Carter by Albin Polasek, FAAR '13, was put in the Academy library beside that of Frank Millet.

Stevens was asked to continue as acting director of the Academy, a post in which he had served frequently during Carter's absences. This he agreed to do.

The war had come late to the Academy but it had come with a vengeance. In October, Norton, in his uniform of brigadier general in the American Red Cross, came to Rome to investigate the possibilities of establishing a Red Cross unit there. He was soon joined by Cornelius Bliss and Joseph Lindon Smith. It was natural for the trio to cast avid eyes on the only partially used Academy buildings, which would make admirable hospitals, hostels, and staff headquarters. As a trustee of the Academy Norton felt that the Red Cross would be a better tenant than some Italian or American war agency that might conscript the buildings and later return them in bad condition. He proposed that the Red Cross pay the Academy a good rent and guarantee good maintenance of any building it might take over from the Academy. He also offered to give full or part-time appointments, in Rome or elsewhere as desired, to fellows and members of the staff. This offered a form of war service especially congenial to many of the Academy's young men, who took up the offer. The trustees rented the Villa Aurelia to the head of the American Red Cross in Italy, and Colonel

Robert Perkins occupied it with some twenty of his staff officers until after the war ended. Meanwhile, to save the main building from undesirable conscription, it was also offered to the Red Cross for a hospital of 380 beds, but the war ended before that development could take place.

In December 1917 the United States declared war on Austria, Italy's chief opponent in the trenches in the mountainous northeast. At that time the Academy was housing only ten of its fellows and former students, together with nine United States army and navy officers and its first woman resident scholar, Lily Ross Taylor, who had returned to Italy in September to pursue research and to live with Professor Clark and his wife on the mezzanine floor of the Academy building. All of the students were engaged in some kind of war work, mostly with the Red Cross, and at least one, Russell Cowles, was an "observer" under guise of continuing his painting. The Academy had rented the villas Chiaraviglio and Bellacci for the duration of the war to private persons. By March 1918 the number of resident members of the Academy had shrunk to eight.

By June 1918 some fifty thousand American troops had landed in Italy, and during the summer of 1918 all the resident members of the Academy and some of its former fellows were deeply and often dangerously immersed in war service. Two former fellows died on active duty and were later commemorated on the walls of the *cortile:* Harry B. Thrasher, sculptor, FAAR '41, and Walter L. Ward, architect, FAAR '16.

After the armistice of November 11, 1918, the Academy buildings were illuminated with every light that could be found. Thanksgiving that year was felt truly and deeply, if not solemnly. At dinner the twenty-three who were present included Charles Platt and Paul Manship, whom war services had brought to Rome. There was music, while live turkeys were paraded, gobbling excitedly, around the table: with each course a larger turkey appeared—or so the story goes. As the dessert appeared so did two doves, one with an American and the other with an Italian flag. They flew distractedly over the endangered heads of the celebrants, as turkey and wine symbolized the thankfulness of Italy and America for the war's end.

VIII

The Twenties

UNDER the shadow of war in 1914, the Academy had opened without ceremony on its hilltop. During the war years it had accommodated a dwindling student population—chiefly engaged in war work—until even its buildings were absorbed in the war effort. Now, as the year 1919 began, the last wave of wartime tenants had receded; the threat of turning the main building into a hospital had vanished, and the Academy was able for the first time fully to use its new quarters on the Janiculum.

In February 1919 Gorham Stevens was made director and in due course moved with his wife from the main building into apartments on an upper floor of the Villa Aurelia. The *piano nobile* of the Villa, with its decorated walls and ceilings, its chandeliers and parquet floors and superb views of Rome, was reserved for official Academy entertaining. The ground floor held the offices, and within a few years other rooms in the Villa were to be used as studios for fellows or as residence rooms for women students. A *villino* standing in the garden housed visiting fellows and scholars. When the iron gates beside the gatekeeper's lodge at the foot of the villa drive were closed, the Villa Aurelia became a small world of its own.

Under the south windows of the Villa the land drops steeply down a bank to the Via Garibaldi, which cuts across a corner of the original Aurelia property. This detached segment of garden, together with the Via Chiaraviglio and its grounds, form a wedge-shaped piece of land bounded on its farther side by the Via Angelo Masina. Across Angelo Masina stands the new "main" building with its neighbor, the little Villa Bellacci. Stevens dreamed of a bridge from the Villa Aurelia over the Via Garibaldi and down to the severed garden plot beside the Villa Chiaraviglio, from which one would need only to cross the Via Masina to reach the main building, thus partially knitting together a campus so awkwardly intersected by streets. The bridge never materialized, but in time Stevens managed to close another small street behind the main building, so that today the Academy land runs unbroken to the Aurelian Wall. He also kept a sharp eye out for property on the other side of the Via Giacomo Medici to the east of the main building. In all his negotiations he was very careful to assure that the new acquisitions would be tax free, which required firm handling and steady pressure on the authorities. Or, as Grant La Farge reported with delicacy to his fellow trustees: "The Italian Government has again in a notable way shown its friendly feeling toward the Academy by exempting its property from taxation."

The trustees appreciated Stevens' management. In a letter to Charles Norton, Ambassador Page wrote: "Our friend Stevens seems to be doing extremely well, going along methodically and earnestly." Lily Ross Taylor, the first woman fellow to live in the Academy (in 1916 in the main building and later in the Villa Aurelia) and a distinguished classicist, remembered Stevens as "obsessed with protecting the property of the Academy."

The Academy was also fortunate in the devotion of its librarian. In 1914 Albert Van Buren was arranging and cataloguing the volumes on the classics that had come from the Villa Bonghi after the merger of the two schools. His assistant, Stanley Lothrop, arranged the books in the mediaeval and modern fields. The library was augmented in 1917 by Mrs. Carter's gift of her husband's classics library, and in 1918 William Herriman, painter, an incorporator of the Academy and its first Roman trustee, left it three thousand books of considerable value. But the total number of volumes looked like a mere handful in the large empty rooms where the stacks were not quite finished, the furniture was barely adequate, and the lighting system was at best temperamental. Moreover both the librarian and his assistant worked only part-time, serving also as lecturers in their respective fields. For all that, Van Buren was optimistic. He and Lothrop prepared a pamphlet to celebrate the library's establishment on the Janiculum. It boldly described the small collection as "devoted to everything that has to do with the history of human life in Italy from the earliest times, and also the history of human life in other countries in so far as that may be expected to throw light on Italian civilization or as being influenced by it." A definition so eclectic enabled Van Buren to fish for books with a wide-mouthed net. But wide as it was, it caught no fish in America for some time. Large giving to a new institution in a foreign country immersed in war did not attract donors. As for the Academy, its own finances, after providing for its bread and butter, left no margin for the expansion of its library. Even today this important part of the Academy has not wholly recovered from the penury of those earlier years.

In 1919 the sculptors' studios could again be heated, and domestic service in the living quarters of the eight fellows in residence (two architects, two painters, two sculptors, a classicist, and a landscape architect) was resumed on its former scale. The Academy was beginning to move forward again; it could even boast a presidential visit when Woodrow Wilson came for ten minutes on January 3, 1919, en route to the peace conference in Paris.

The trustees, reacting in part to the overblown image of the Academy they thought Carter had created, adopted conservative policies. Inflation and wildly fluctuating currencies added to their caution. On January 2, 1919 they sent Boring to Rome to consult Stevens and Del Frate, the Academy's solicitor, regarding the disposition of the various Academy properties.

In past budget discussions it had been strongly hinted that the Villa Aurelia was expensive and ill-adapted to the uses of the Academy, and should be got rid of. Boring and Stevens talked over the problem with the current ambassador, Thomas Nelson Page. The American Embassy was disposed to buy the Villa and cabled an offer to the trustees. Had it been sold the future of the Academy might have been very different. Buildings can determine policies as surely as policies determine buildings. But the offer was declined as inadequate, and a further plan to rent the Villa to the embassy was in turn abandoned, since to derive income from it would jeopardize the Academy's tax-free status. The villa remained to gild the Academy image.

While he was still in Rome, Boring turned his attention to the Villa Chiaraviglio, which had been rented to a gentleman of Rome after the Red Cross had vacated it. Three weeks after the lease had been signed it was discovered that the new tenant proposed to use the Villa for his mistress. This, the trustees felt, was unsuitable. Though their point of view probably surprised its victim, the lease was broken and the threat of moral defilement by association was escaped. The Chiaraviglio was taken off the market, reconditioned, and thereafter used for Academy purposes. The Villa Bellacci housed the director of the School of Classical Studies as it had from the outset.

In New York the board of trustees continued to consist of notable representatives of the arts and classics and other public-spirited men. Though there was no bylaw that forbade it, no woman had ever been put on the board. The New York office, reorganized in 1919 by Roscoe Guernsey, transacted Academy business, administered the committees for the selection of fellows, kept the records, and became an invaluable center for the trustees, former fellows, and friends of the Academy.

In broad strokes, this was the physical outline of the Academy after World War I, and it remained much the same for the next fifty years.

But the history of the Academy's affairs presents no such tidy or enduring an outline. Change was in the air, a profound change in the arts which was to carry the Academy along in its course, supplanting McKim's era of devotion to tradition, continuity, and good taste. "Good taste" had been a respectable phrase. If hard to define, at least everyone was sure he knew when it was lacking. Gradually it was to be dissipated by more popular criteria, and finally replaced by untrammeled self-expression. Anything that checked this trend was to become irrelevant to artistic concerns. In the early twenties the fellows were acutely aware of the new stirrings. But they had been trained in the past. Some of them now look back ruefully on the time when, like Janus on the Academy seal, they faced both ways at once and could not move wholeheartedly in either direction.

The classicists, in their role as scholars and chroniclers, were relatively unaffected by the change. Painters also rode the wave more easily. After all, their profession had staged a successful revolution almost within living memory. If the Academy's collaborative projects seemed somewhat sterile to them and to their sculptor colleagues, it was a price they were willing to pay for their three years abroad. But the architects were engulfed by the rising tide. The postwar world was a different architectural world. Permanence —building for all time, of which Rome was the great exemplar— had been proven by the war's devastation to be illusory. Fluidity and mobility were taking its place. The soaring cost of construction in any case wiped out classic materials and embellishments. A young architect must keep abreast of the new and cheaper materials being devised to fill the need. In an advertising-conscious society the eye-catching design was the thing, while for the urban planner the quick and profitable turnover in land use was a prime factor to be given precedence over the ideal layout. Solutions for housing mankind and building for twentieth-century life were more likely to require ecological studies than spatial concepts.

During the twenties and more rapidly in the thirties this change took place. At first there were few to purchase the more extreme expressions of the new art. But as the older patrons who could still afford to order and pay for a product suited to their tastes were replaced by corporate patrons, and then by mass demand, the standards of the marketplace superseded those of academia. The study of ancient monuments began to seem no more relevant than looking into a glass-topped case at an object of delicate craftsmanship, beautiful in its way but now serving no purpose except as a relic of a discarded culture. Color, proportion, and setting still stimulated the appreciative eye, but the relics themselves could not be studied as specific answers to the problems of the day—or so at least many fellows began to think. The grandiose *projets* required by the Academy made them increasingly rebellious, and their solutions correspondingly lifeless.

"*Chefs d'oeuvre* and immortality are to be found by following the road of precedent," said Stevens. He was of the old school; he would gladly have stemmed the rising tide of unorthodoxy. In an effort to counteract the loss of stability he sensed in the Academy's *esprit* (a word that appears again and again in his diary), he wrote in his annual report for 1919: "The object of the American Academy in Rome is not to afford opportunities for a few individuals to perfect themselves for the practice of their chosen professions. The ideal is to create an atmosphere in which a limited number of carefully selected artists and scholars may develop that synthesis of intellectual culture which will make them worthy to preserve and continue the great traditions of the past, in order that the standard of art and literature may be handed on from year to year, constantly strengthened and improved."

The trustees, themselves tossed on the seas of change, were inclined to be reassured by Stevens' championship of familiar values, as well as by reports like that from their fellow trustee, Breck Trowbridge, who visited the Academy in 1919. "The Director has

succeeded in laying the foundation of a tradition . . . he has
created an atmosphere which inspires high ideals, which is con-
ducive of creative effort . . . complete freedom of thought and
action but in which there is no taint of that sordid Bohemianism
which so often invades artistic communities."

But Stevens, who was to continue as director for another thirteen years, could not arrest world change or return the Academy to
its former paths. In the end he was a victim of a revolution to
which he could not adjust himself. In 1919 he was principally concerned with the effects of inflation on the lives of the fellows as
well as on the Academy budget. During the war years when the
fellows had received payment for their war work from other sources
than the Academy, a Suspended Fellowship Account had been set
up from the unused income. Stevens was now able to draw on this
limited nest egg to augment funds of students and fellows in serious
need. As for the senior members of the staff, most of them had no
choice but to grin and bear their financial difficulties. There were
some generous gestures. Stevens had accepted his promotion to the
directorship without increase in salary; Lily Ross Taylor offered
to forego the stipend of her classics fellowship, as did Allyn Cox,
the painter, his prize money for 1919. The trustees were also
struggling with inflation in America and were acutely conscious of
the shortages at the Academy. Norton, Blashfield, and West secured
the approval of the board to form a national council for the Academy as the basis for a nationwide campaign to increase its endowment. Alumni of the Academy, who had formed themselves into
an association in 1912, reactivated their council and began to do
good work in helping returning fellows to find jobs and to exhibit
their work annually at the Grand Central Art Gallery in New York.
Gradually the upswing started. It reached a crescendo in the later
twenties, only to fall steeply again when the bubble of inflation
burst in 1929.

The Academy's financial upturn was sparked by the sale of the
Villa Mirafiori. Henry Walters had originally loaned $128,000 to
the Academy for its purchase. Later he waived the loan, both
interest and capital. The Mirafiori had been appraised in 1918 at
1,200,000 lire or approximately $190,000 net. In February 1919,
while Boring was still in Rome, Baron Alberto Fassini offered to
purchase the Villa at this price and made a down payment of one
quarter. He agreed to pay the balance when the hospital that had

been established at the Mirafiori was finally closed. However, before this occurred he sold his option to the religious order of the Sacred Heart, and it was this society that made the final payment to the Academy in October 1919. "Thus," wrote Stevens in his annual report to the trustees that year, "the Villa Mirafiori, with its extensive gardens, fine ilexes and firs, after having been used by the Academy for eight years, and loaned to the Italian 'Mutilati' for three years and a half, has been sold." Even after the cost of its improvements had been taken into consideration, it represented a considerable profit to the Academy.

Early in 1920 the younger J. P. Morgan extended for another year his offer in 1915 to cancel one dollar of the Academy's large debt to him for every dollar it added to its endowment. That offer had, since he first made it, brought almost $100,000 to the Academy endowment. Before August 1920 the amount was raised in full by another stretch of effort, and the Academy was free to use the income from the $375,000 of the Morgan gift. In 1917 the Carnegie Corporation had granted the Academy $25,000, George F. Baker had given it $50,000, and Arthur Curtis James had given $10,000. Margaret S. Burnham gave $25,000 to the Daniel Burnham Fund for Fellows in Architecture.

Also by 1920 the Jesse Benedict Carter Fund for a fellowship in classics had reached nearly $25,000, and other gifts in cash, though smaller than in the last good years before the war, were coming in. In 1922, however, John D. Rockefeller, Jr., gave $200,000, and in 1923 Mortimer L. Schiff gave $10,000 after a visit to the Academy. Contributions from Benefactors (those who gave $1,000 or more) had come from forty-two persons or corporations. Ninety-two members of the Association of Academy Alumni had, by their subscriptions, become life members. The School of Classical Studies was receiving annual gifts from thirty-two contributing universities and colleges. At the end of 1922 the Academy endowment had risen to almost $2,000,000.

Though inflation and the fluctuating lira created great difficulties, the Academy budget was increased to $80,000 for 1924–25, and in November 1925 the executive committee reported for the first time in its history that "the finances of the Academy are in satisfactory condition . . . with a substantial balance in the income account for last year."

Other gifts were coming in. In 1925 William S. Richardson,

whom ill health had compelled to retire from an active architectural career with McKim, Mead, and White, settled in Rome and bought a villa at 6 Via Giacomo Medici, across the street from the Academy. His interest in the Academy and his knowledge of the fine arts made him a valuable neighbor. When he was appointed annual professor in the fine arts for 1925–26 he refused a salary and thus made a gift of it to the Academy. A little later he raised, on his own initiative, more than $8,000 to purchase an adjacent lot for the Academy and himself contributed $1,000 to the fund. In January 1927 he spoke of making a will bequeathing his villa to the Academy, subject to its lifetime use by his sister.

Thanks in great part to a grant from the Carnegie Corporation of $5,000 a year for three years beginning in 1925 (a gift that the Academy trustees hoped might upon its expiration be renewed), the annual stipends of most fellowships were increased by $250. In 1926 Samuel L. Parrish (for whom McKim had designed a house in Southampton, Long Island, in 1889) provided endowment for three years of a fellowship to be called the Parrish Museum Fellowship. In 1927 Mrs. George Gordon endowed a fellowship in landscape architecture, and in 1928 another landscape fellowship was partly endowed and partly pledged by trustee Walter Brewster in his wife's name. The largest gift of the period was made by the Rockefeller International Education Board, which in February 1927 offered a grant of $1,000,000 for the improvement of grounds and such other needs as the trustees might designate. At once the trustees increased the stipends of the fellows to $1,500 and the budget for 1927–28 leaped to $100,000. The Academy acquired another piece of property when a neighboring *trattoria* called "The White House" was purchased to provide living quarters for Academy employees. Back of it (to add a touch of economy greatly valued as good times vanished) the Academy maintained a poultry farm consisting of 172 hens, 3 ducks, and 11 pigeons. Roosters and drakes are not mentioned, reversing Academy policy toward housing the sexes.

Having voted in 1928 a retirement age of sixty-six for all members of the academic staff, the trustees tackled the question of retirement allowances. This was especially difficult because there were no men on permanent appointment in the academic sense. Except for Van Buren, the members of the teaching staff had served for only a few years and then returned to their former, or to other,

McKim *center*, Mead *left*, and White

An unnerving visitor. Mussolini with Mrs. Garrett, wife of the American ambassador, flanked by Gorham Stevens and Mrs. Stevens

The Academy *center*. The Villa Aurelia *far right*. In the triangle *left corner*, the Villa Chiaraviglio with the Villa Bellacci opposite. The Villa Richardson, with tower, *far left*

The Villa Aurelia, front entrance

The Villa Bellacci

The Academy courtyard with the Manship fountain and the Kendall cypresses

The Villa Chiaraviglio

The Villa Richardson

The library

The lounge

Chester Aldrich "trying to explain 'a collaborative' (without much success!)" to the King of Italy and Ambassador Phillips

The dining room

Colleagues: Director Frank Brown and King Gustavus of Sweden

Cosa. Arx and Capitolium *far distant and aerial views*

academic positions. Under these unusually fluid conditions, the Academy had not been able to afford to establish adequate retirement funds, even if the beneficiary paid half the cost. Most professors at the Academy had been holders of annuities with the Carnegie Foundation. The Academy asked the Foundation whether it would continue those annuities during the terms served by their holders in Rome. The Foundation replied that it could not, but it agreed to renew them when the men returned to their academic institutions in the States.

The last eighteen months before the stock market break of late 1929 saw the trustees optimistically embarking on further expenditures. The budget was increased to $138,000. The Villa Aurelia, which had been variously called "an academic frill" and "a Roman white elephant," was given some repairs. It had been twice on the point of being offered for sale, and the trustees, uncertain whether or not to keep it, had spent little on improving it. Now it was given new piping and a water pump. Fifty thousand dollars was also appropriated for bookcases, a card catalogue, and other improvements of the library in the main building, though part of that sum was diverted for the maintenance of other buildings and the grounds. By the end of 1928 the Academy's financial holdings totalled nearly two and a half million dollars, apart from the value of its plant in Rome.

The stock market collapse of 1929 was a shock, but it did not at once impair the operations of the Academy or, indeed, prevent a few last fruits of prosperity from dropping into its lap. In November 1929 the trustees learned that Rutherford Mead had bequeathed more than $100,000 in trust for the Academy (it proved on settlement to be about $250,000). And in 1931 the Carnegie Corporation, which had so steadily supported the Academy, pledged $5,000 a year for three years to the library.

One turns with relief from the first shadows of the depression to the story of the development of a music department during the decade—a development that had rapidly brought public distinction to the Academy. The idea of a music department had been raised before the war. Edward Macdowell, the pianist and composer, was an incorporating trustee of the Academy in 1905 but did not continue on the board after February 1906 due to illness. He had already urged his fellow trustees to establish music fellowships at the Academy. Mrs. Macdowell sent to Charles McKim on May 11,

1905, direct quotations from Macdowell's memorandum: "For years it has been my dream that the Arts of Architecture, Painting, Sculpture and Music should come into such close contact that each and all should gain from this mutual companionship. That students in all these arts should come together under the same roof, and amid such marvelous surroundings, seems almost too good to be true."

Macdowell then outlined at length to McKim his carefully worked out plan for music fellowships in a "Musical Department of the Academy in Rome." It was almost certainly the lack of any funds for music or of any promising prospect for their acquisition that kept the Academy trustees from attempting to establish music fellowships at that time.

Felix Lamond, an English organist married to an American and settled in New York, had frequently been in Rome and knew the Academy well. In 1913 he suggested to his friend, the Academy trustee Daniel Chester French, that a fellowship in musical composition be established. Sixteen trustees of the Academy met in New York to discuss it, but although sympathetic to the idea they decided they must reduce their debt to Morgan before undertaking a new project. Lamond, however, quietly persevered and during the war collected some $2,000 for music at the Academy.

In 1920 Charles Norton turned his interest and energies to the support of Lamond's suggestion. He approached the Carnegie Corporation, which reacted promisingly by asking formal assurance from Academy trustees that they would give a music program top priority in their plans for expansion. To this the trustees replied that "a division of Musical Composition" was "the most urgent development" that they had "in view at the moment." Meanwhile Harry Harkness Flagler offered to secure $25,000 toward a "Fellowship in Music in the name of Walter Damrosch," providing the Academy would raise a like sum within the year. Trustees also agreed to this commitment.

On July 14, 1920, Norton presented to the trustees a plan, already approved by their executive and finance committees, for the creation of a department of musical composition. Though Norton was neither musician nor educator, he had clearly taken good advice in both fields, for the plan he proposed showed expert knowledge of the requirements of both professions. It provided for a professor, as well as three fellows in musical composition ("these to be unmarried men") who were to live at the Academy for not less than six months in each academic year of their three-year fellowship. They were required to visit other music centers in Europe, with a generous travel allowance. At the end of each year the fellow must submit to the director an original orchestral or choral work. The fellows were to spend their time in creative music rather than in attendance at courses and lectures. "No instruction in music shall be provided for or allowed at the Academy." They were to be given liberal stipends, studios, and complete freedom other than the stipulations already noted. The trustees were to elect to their membership at least one recognized authority in music, to organize open competitions for the music fellowships, and to appoint juries to award them. Norton's proposed budget for the new department included the costs of pianos and other non-recurrent expenditures totaling $35,000 and an annual operating budget of $15,000, which he had reason to think the Carnegie Corporation would assist in providing.

The trustees approved this plan, and at the October meeting the budget was raised by borrowing $36,000 from the Academy's general endowment. After final and satisfactory consultation with the Carnegie Corporation, public announcement of the Academy's establishment of a department of musical composition was made.

The project moved briskly. In July 1921 Lamond, in company with Boring, arrived in Rome. There they worked with Stevens to fit the new department into the Academy's buildings and operations and to arrange for the necessary furnishings and equipment. Lamond became the first professor in charge of musical composition, and he and his wife soon afterward took up residence in the Villa Chiaraviglio.

In New York musical matters also moved with unprecedented speed. Augustus Juilliard and Harry Flagler, among others, contributed very generously to the fund for music fellowships. Mrs. H. Fairfield Osborn headed a group of women who raised over $10,000 at an impressively sponsored benefit concert at Carnegie Hall, and later, in 1924, Mrs. Osborn sent to the Academy treasurer $8,000 from another benefit performance. A competition was held, and fellowships bearing the names of Walter Damrosch, Frederick Juilliard, and Horatio Parker were awarded to three remarkable young men: Howard Hanson, Leo Sowerby, and Randall Thompson. Sowerby was in Rome before the end of the year; Hanson, although actually the first winner of the Rome Prize in Music, had commitments in America that held him there until January 1922. Randall Thompson followed within a few months.

The new department flourished. Besides regular concerts held at the Academy to present compositions of the fellows, their works were also heard at the Circolo Romano and the Augusteo in Rome, at the Salle Pleyal in Paris, and at the International Festival in Geneva. Walter Damrosch and Deems Taylor were made trustees. In 1925 George Eastman gave $15,000 to finance the copying or printing of the manuscript compositions of the fellows. In 1929 Myron Taylor gave $25,000. In 1931 Elizabeth Sprague Coolidge sponsored and financed a series of concerts at the Villa Aurelia which drew capacity audiences. The remarkable record of the first fellows was sustained by their successors through the twenties. Leo Sowerby became professor of composition at the American Conservatory in Chicago; Howard Hanson, director of the Eastman School of Music of the University of Rochester; Randall Thompson, professor of music at Wellesley College and later at Harvard; George Herbert Elwell, 1924–27, professor of composition at the Cleveland Institute of Music; Walter Helfer, 1925–28, professor of music at Hunter College in New York; and Robert Sanders, 1925–29, professor of composition at the Bush Conservatory in Chicago. All these men were well known to their contemporaries for their compositions, as was also Roger Sessions, 1928–31. It was a brilliant beginning. The music fellows not only found their years at the Academy creative but also found Rome a place where they could hear the works of the great composers of the day being conducted by the men who wrote them. Possibly even more exhilarating, they themselves were invited to conduct their own works at such places as the Augusteo.

In 1960, a friendly critic of the Academy looking back over the years said: "In the 1930s it was the Academy's archeologists . . . who stole the limelight from the composers." Actually the composers were not robbed of the limelight. They merely moved over to let the classics fellows share it. What Dean West of Princeton had written of the Academy's School of Classical Studies in 1921 was even more true in 1932: "We have furnished our universities with nearly 150 professors trained in the humanistic as opposed to the pedantic spirit. We have also trained a group of curators for museums and a fair number of gifted writers and critics." No one questioned the excellence of the work being done by the School or its contribution to American scholarship.

By 1929 the classical staff had given advice or help to more than one hundred American and European scholars and students beyond those enrolled at the Academy. As far back as 1921 the trustees had cautiously approved a summer session in classical studies, "not under the name of the Academy" but sponsored by "an interested group of Trustees." It had become so successful that in 1923 it made a full-fledged debut with the imprimatur of the Academy and with five students. Under Professor Grant Showerman, who had been annual professor of classics the previous winter, American teachers and students of the classics enrolled for lectures on Roman history and literature, instruction in modern Italian, and tours to ancient sites nearby. Enrollment grew from five to thirty-nine, and then to fifty-four in successive years, and increased until there was talk of limiting it—but the depression settled that matter.

For some time funds had been set aside to publish the work of the classics fellows. Volumes entitled *Memoirs* and *Papers and Monographs* brought impressive examples of research to the learned public. Lily Ross Taylor wrote on Roman architecture and religion. Marion E. Blake studied and wrote on the Roman ruins on the Janiculum, some of which were on Academy property. Louise Adams Holland catalogued the bridges of Rome, and Esther Van Deman plotted the courses of the Roman aqueducts with such effectiveness that she became known, with affectionate pride, as "Aqueduct Annie." Her work was said by one authority to be "the Academy's greatest single contribution to archaeology" up to that time.

Indeed research, chiefly in archaeology, expanded notably at the Academy. It was spurred on by the assurance in 1929 of Conte Constantc, representing the Italian authorities, that the Academy archaeologists—heretofore excavating under Italian direction—could soon look forward to an excavation of their own in Italy. In addition to work on Horace's Sabine Farm near Tivoli and the baths of Hadrian's Villa in Tivoli, the archaeologists, using special scaffolding some fifty feet high, studied and photographed sculptured reliefs on the arch of Septimus Severus. Howard Hanson, fellow in music, recollects finding himself holding a tape measure on top of St. Peter's dome for his friend Victor Hafner, fellow in architecture. As Hanson was subject to acute vertigo, the ideal of collaboration between artists could go no higher. Though the purpose of the measurement was not archaeological, a discovery was made. They found a crack in the dome of St. Peter's. As word of this spread, visitors at the church were seen to crane their necks nervously, and the Roman hierarchy, at first merely irriated, hastened to build a scaffolding and make repairs.*

During those postwar years there were notable events at the Academy. It had celebrated the twenty-fifth anniversary of its founding in 1894 with a fanfare that circumstances had not permitted in 1914. A special exhibition of creative work by the staff, fellows, and students was held at the Villa Aurelia, which officially "opened" the Academy. The king of Italy was one of 350 guests who, in spite of a strike of Roman cabmen (which probably inconvenienced the king less than other guests), made their way up the Janiculum to the varnishing. Later the annual exhibitions were regularly attended by the king and queen, and the guest list swelled to 700. In 1921 Ambassador Richard Washburn Child had unveiled in the *cortile* the fountain designed for it by Paul Manship and surrounded by four superb cypresses given by William Kendall. In 1927 the music department, from its beginning devoted to performance as well as composition, had produced before 800 guests, including Rome's musical elite, a ballata entitled *The Happy Hypocrit,* written and conducted by George Elwell. In 1929 the first Jerome Lecture was given by Professor John G. Winter, and the first Academy student ball set for later balls a pattern of uninhibited gaiety. In 1931 Benito Mussolini, escorted by Ambassador John Garrett, visited the Academy. Although his tour of the main building was somewhat unnerving to his hosts, it was not perfunctory on *il Duce*'s part. He insisted on entering nearly all of its studios and talking with the artists at work in them. In fact the entertainment of numerous important visitors became an alarmingly time-consuming duty of the director and his small staff.

The roster of professors and fellows at the Academy included a high percentage of names of current or future distinction. Francis

---

* According to an Academy classmate Hafner was not awarded a diploma because of the embarrassment to the Academy created by his over-alarming statements. Other reasons are given in the records, and Hafner's drawings of the dome of St. Peter's were later used by the engineers who strengthened the dome, and who paid tribute to their quality.

Henry Taylor, later to be director of the Metropolitan Museum of Art in New York, was a visiting student, as was Thornton Wilder, who wrote *The Cabala* while at the Academy. An outstanding sequence of sculptors included C. Paul Jennewein '20, Tom Jones '22, Gaetano Cecere '23, Edmond R. Amateis '24, Walker Hancock '28, and Sidney Waugh '32. In classics and the fine arts the Academy staff included among others such names as G. L. Hendrickson, Francis Kelsey, George H. Edgell, Rhys Carpenter, and Charles R. Morey.

The number of academies in Rome was increasing. The British School came in 1912, followed by Czechoslovakia, Bulgaria, Egypt, and Switzerland, whose scholars and artists perched themselves on the minor Alpine slope above the Via Ludovisi on the premises of the Villa Aurora. There was some communication and an occasional social gathering between the fellows of other countries and those of the American Academy, usually initiated by the Americans. All foreign students in Rome found themselves profiting by the action of the Italian government in declaring some 418 of the finest private villas in Italy to be national monuments and therefore open to the public on occasion. For a special rate of about five dollars students could gain admission to them all. They also enjoyed other fringe benefits such as reductions in fare on Greek and Italian rail and steamship lines. The American Academy was also allowing each of its fellows in painting and sculpture $50 a year for the hire of models. Each of its fellows in music had an annual grant of $1,000 for travel, and the Academy defrayed the expenses of all fellows on their initial trip from New York to Rome. When these advantages were added to those of free residence, free studios, and inexpensive Academy meals, the actual value of an American Academy fellowship approximated at least $2,000 a year. Satisfaction with life at the Academy seemed general, and pride in their fellowships was indicated by a request from the fellows that they be allowed to append the letters FAAR to their names—a request gladly granted by the trustees.

If Stevens' administration seemed largely a period of material consolidation, those who knew him saw a side of him that is scarcely revealed by the bare notes in his diary or by the minutes of trustee meetings. He had a scholar's love for history, particularly as expressed in architecture, and when he took students on field trips they found themselves spellbound by his re-creation of the places they visited, which he peopled and brought to life for his audience. In his own words, he made the students "drink of the marvellous well of accumulated experience which is only to be found in Rome." His later researches—especially on the Athenian Acropolis when he became director of the American School in Athens—are still used as a basis for the work there. His care for the beauty of the past and his championship of the artist in man won him the affection of the fellows even when they clashed with him over details of Academy management and make it less surprising to find him urging the trustees to establish an atelier in the center of Rome. Characteristically, he put his reasons for it on practical grounds: "to provide a place more convenient to *pensiones* and sightseeing, and [to provide] equipment for drafting and to a limited extent painting and modelling for American practicioners of the Fine Arts who choose to stay in Rome for a limited time." The Academy was to be open to these artists, who could get criticism from its staff, use the library, and obtain student permits and privileges to visit the sights of Rome. In 1927 such a place as Stevens had in mind was found at 73 Via San Niccolo da Tolentino, immediately above the studio Saint-Gaudens had occupied from 1871 to 1874. The arrangement was almost at once successful. The studios filled. The imponderable results of the venture were found in the stimulation fellows and students received from these confreres. When in 1930 ten artists were working there (including Bartlett Hayes, later director of the Academy, who recalls paying fifteen cents a day for his studio), the Academy renewed the lease for another ten years.

The enrollment at the Academy swelled with prosperity and sank with the depression, which, like the wake of a passing ship, did not wreak its worst on the Academy craft until some time after the event. In 1922 the number of fellows and students in residence reached a new high of forty-eight; by 1929 the enrollment was sixty-six, including those not housed at the Academy. In the early 1930s the number of competitors for the fellowships fell off, partly due to necessary economies taken by the trustees in lowering fellowship stipends and shortening the term of fellowship to two years. Another factor affected enrollment: under the New Deal the government offered jobs to unemployed young artists, and this drew off some who might have applied to the Academy.

More significant in the long run was the unsettled climate of the fine arts, which made difficult the election of fellows suitable to the taste of conservative juries, and which produced stalemates within the Academy itself. In 1930 the jury in Rome for the collaborative competition prize declined to award it for the best creative work of fellows in residence, because it found the quality of the work disappointing. In 1931 it again made no award, reporting that "the attitude of the Fellows in general . . . has been perfunctory." Boring, visiting professor of fine arts in 1930–31, concurred and so reported to the trustees. It began to seem inevitable that the requirements established by the Academy would have to be made more flexible or possibly abolished altogether.

No one was more troubled by all this than Stevens. He had every reason to be tired and some reasons to be disappointed. He had ridden out the years of war, of postwar adjustment, of economies, and of brief prosperity only to see hard times returning and a decline of the *esprit* he had tried to maintain. In 1929 he told the trustees that they might have his resignation whenever they wished. They did not ask for it until 1931, and though Stevens acquiesced almost with relief, he was emotionally depressed and recorded in his diary that he was being slow in despatching his "hemlock letter." When he did do so the trustees accepted it, but they could find no successor and asked Stevens to continue until they did. Stevens, the Academy's faithful friend, stood by until James Monroe Hewlett took his place in the late summer of 1932. Then he departed.

Stevens had been with the Academy altogether twenty years. He had been a director of the School of Fine Arts, an acting director of the Academy and then its full director for thirteen years. Indeed for fourteen years if one counted 1912, that first year when he had come to Italy with the title of director of the American Academy in Rome. Within five months of his arrival he had found himself outranked and his honor an empty one. To his diary he had confided his feelings in a stiff, brief entry on August 8, 1913: "In last year's annual report . . . I am not given among the former Directors of the Academy." Perhaps this account may help to give him his due.

IX

World War II

IN THE twenties and early thirties the Academy lost many of its oldest friends. Charles Norton died in 1923, a trustee upon whose vision and contagious convictions the board had come to depend. William Rutherford Mead, for nearly a score of years the president of the board, died in 1928 and was buried in the Protestant Cemetery in Rome. He used to say that his name, in the famous partnership, was between McKim and White "to keep the two damned fools out of trouble." A brusque man, often rough-tongued, he was forthright, clear-headed, and wholly devoted to fulfilling McKim's dream of an Academy in Rome. Daniel Chester French, of the original circle of the Shack, had been one of the first to become a trustee, a position which he held "with undiminished ardor" up to a short time before his death in 1931. Henry Walters, who died in the same year, was another serious loss to the Academy and to the nation as well. Seldom has there been a man of such modesty and power combined. It was his initial generosity that had turned the Academy into reality.

Remarkable men filled these empty places. In 1924 Chester Aldrich of the New York architectural firm of Delano and Aldrich came on the board. Dean Clarence W. Mendell of Yale became a trustee in 1926. A classics scholar of robust temperament, he stimulated the School of Classical Studies and gave especially strong support to the library. Everett Meeks, director of Yale's School of Fine Arts, was elected trustee in 1927. Charles Platt, a distinguished New York architect who had been vice-president of the board, moved into Mead's place as president in 1929. He died in 1933, after a short term of four years. (Less than ten years later his son, William Platt, also an able architect, was to carry on his father's interest in the Academy, where he has served as a trustee ever since.) Charles Platt was succeeded by John Russell

Pope, architect and mural painter and the first winner of the Rome Prize when the Academy was the American School of Architecture. In 1934 Herbert Winlock, Egyptologist and director of the Metropolitan Museum, joined the board.

The Academy was fortunate that it could call on men of such caliber. In the early thirties it had come to a dead center. The depression was at its deepest. Pledges to the endowment fund were being defaulted; there were fewer contributing institutions—themselves affected by the depression—to the Academy; the value of its capital was dwindling and its income decreasing. Fellowships in architecture and landscaping were reduced to two years in 1931, to be followed by the same reduction in painting and sculpture. The course of the newly appointed J. M. Hewlett as director had not run smoothly and had been brought to a mandatory end. Exactly what comprised the difficulty is discreetly veiled in the records. In any case Hewlett served only from October 1932 until July 1934, when he was given leave of absence with salary ("less such sums as he owes the Academy") until the end of his three-year appointment in 1935. The Villa Aurelia was closed, and the Academy as well for the summer of 1934. The atelier on the Via San Niccolo da Tolentino was given up. The Academy ran on its momentum during the following winter. Trips for the fellows, usually conducted by the director, were arranged by the American Express Company. The alumni in America rallied to help: New York's Grand Central Galleries made a particular effort to get good publicity for its 1935 show of the fellows' work, awarding prizes and broadcasting the results on an NBC program that included music by Samuel Barber, FAAR '37. In the spring Howard Hanson gave a concert dedicated to the Academy in the Eastman Theater of the University of Rochester. That summer the Academy was again closed.

Meanwhile the special committee to find Hewlett's successor had told the board that it would "search for an artist of maturity and distinction, a man of great breadth and in sympathy with classical studies." The last phrase reveals the duality of the Academy, composed of two schools and requiring a director who could hold the balance fairly between them. The trend away from tradition is also implied in the "search for an artist" sympathetic with the classical point of view. The man they were looking for must understand the working needs, temperaments, and habits of the scholars and artists who shared this single community. Outwardly its members might all appear to be fellows together of the American Academy, but at a deeper level their divergent purposes must be recognized. To the scholar the classical world was a gold mine for research. To the artist it was a giant display of western man's development in art. If, like his contemporaries, he were to react against its influence, at least his reasons for doing so should be more valid because of his experience at the Academy. A director who could open the mind of the artist to the excitement of the intellectual world or the eyes of the scholar to the delights of beauty might unite these disparate disciplines.

The search soon ended triumphantly in the board itself. Chester Holmes Aldrich, after a long and successful career as an architect, accepted the post. The trustees could not have made a happier choice; once more wind filled the Academy sails. It brought with Aldrich his sister Amey to act as official hostess and unofficial aide to the director. Her wide mind, humor, directness, and kindness made her friend of staff and fellows alike. Both brother and sister were much traveled, familiar with Italy, fluent in its language, and already known to many of its scholars and artists. Chester Aldrich was deeply musical; Amey Aldrich could write enchantingly. She never put her talent to use professionally, but she did leave to the Academy the legacy of a little booklet on the history of the Villa Aurelia which, in scholarly fashion, digs into its remote past when its site had been used by the Romans, whose traces on the Janiculum are still discernible. The Aldriches assumed that members of the Academy would be, like themselves, spacious in outlook, generous in spirit, and cultivated in manners—an assumption that had a deep effect. Their portraits are sketched with a few more strokes than usual because the quality of their personalities so strongly influenced the Academy during their all too brief regime.

Aldrich was fortunate in the time of his arrival in October 1935. The depression had begun to wane, and at his request the trustees added to the staff an administrative assistant in the fine arts. This was another piece of good fortune for the Academy. Aldrich was acquainted with Bernard Berenson and had come to know John Walker, Berenson's protégé at I Tatti. Walker was persuaded to come to the Academy, where he soon showed the qualities that later made him director of the National Gallery in Washington.

The brightened financial future began to be reflected in a renewal of gifts. The Carnegie Corporation extended its grant to the library. In 1936 Boring, the Academy treasurer, came to Rome and reported to trustees that everything was "in excellent condition, everybody happy, and everything going well." It was to be Boring's last view of the Academy into which he had poured more than forty years of unstinting service, having been at McKim's right hand from the outset. He died in 1937, bequeathing a remainder interest in his estate to the Academy. Blashfield had died in 1936. Like French, he had been one of the first artists to join the board. John Russell Pope, perhaps the Academy's most distinguished fellow in architecture, died in 1937. Pope was succeeded as president of the board by James Kellum Smith, FAAR 1923 and since 1929 a member of the firm of McKim, Mead, and White. The transition of authority took place without disturbing the excellent relationship between director and board.

In spite of these changes and losses, signs of high morale continued through 1937. Fourteen fellows and members of the staff went with Chester and Amey Aldrich and Ambassador and Mrs. Phillips on a cruise through the Greek islands. Henry Rowell, who taught classics at Yale, was persuaded to stay as director of the summer session. A new young professor of classical studies was appointed—Mason Hammond of Harvard and Oxford, who was henceforth closely associated with the Academy in several capacities. In the fall of 1937 Christopher Grant La Farge, secretary of the board, came to Rome and picked up the refrain of Boring's report the year before. He could speak only "in terms of the highest commendation of the admirable work being done by the director and Miss Aldrich. In this very favorable and stimulating atmosphere the Fellows are responding well." La Farge's prose was stiffly corseted for the board minutes, but he must have smiled as he wrote so solemnly in praise of the old friends now under his trusteeship.

The possibility of another world war began to loom in 1938. In the first war scare of Munich, Aldrich consulted his friend Ambassador Phillips, and on his advice told the Academy fellows that those who wished might leave immediately for home. None left. But during the following year, with war an imminent threat, the Academy began to take stock of its situation. On the side of gain its budget showed a surplus for 1937–38 and an impending credit balance for 1939. Mrs. John Russell Pope had made a gift of

$10,000 and Mrs. Arnold Brunner a bequest of $20,000. The stipends of fellows were increased to $2,000, and for the first time since Gorham Stevens' directorship the treasurer reported that "on the whole the finances are in fairly good condition."

On the negative side, a change was taking place in the fine arts that would strongly affect the Academy's position. In 1938 work in the creative arts at the Academy was so exuberant that the classicists felt outmatched and uneasy. The advisory council of the School of Classical Studies gravely recommended that the professor in charge of classical studies should be a scholar of outstanding distinction. Had the council been more prescient it need not have been troubled by the temporary ascendancy of the creative arts. In April 1938 a matter had arisen that hinted at the Academy's future dilemma. Recipients of the National Academy of Design awards in mural painting had regularly utilized their fellowships at the Academy in Rome, but shrinkage of funds during the depression had forced reconsideration of the arrangement. Judge McCarthy, the referee in the case, ruled that the fellows of the National Academy of Design need not be required to study primarily in Italy. This was a blow to the finances of the American Academy, but a greater blow to the study of fine arts in Rome, for the judge's decision had centered about the opinion that the development of modern art made it possible for a young painter to secure training and inspiration without exposure to the classical world.

By 1939 Aldrich was reporting that "the political disturbances throw dark and flickering shadows over us all." The Academy was carrying on nevertheless with "its steady and fruitful work." That spring the director and Miss Aldrich and the classical fellows visited Tripoli, their way paved by Berenson. A summer session under Rowell was scheduled, a new budget of nearly $108,000 was approved, and Rhys Carpenter was appointed professor in charge of classical studies—an accession which should have allayed any doubts regarding the quality of leadership of the School of Classical Studies.

In June 1939 the king of Italy once again opened the annual exhibition, of which the critics said "the standard was much higher than in previous years." The summer session was held under Rowell, but because war seemed imminent only seven students enrolled. And yet "it is so peaceful here," wrote Miss Aldrich. Venice in June (for the Veronese show) proved "just as gay and splashing as ever and Roman cares are not very carking (whatever that is)." Nevertheless members of the Academy, especially those with families, were discussing whether they should leave Rome before war engulfed them. Chester and Amey Aldrich went home to America to get "a solid rest," leaving John Walker and Mason Hammond absorbed in organizing the photographs in the library—a "monumental piece of work," as Aldrich afterwards called it.

In one sense the Academy also went home that summer, and in triumph. The New York World's Fair and the San Francisco Golden Gate Exposition—two defiant gestures of a peaceful world in the face of war—were opened in 1939. Thirty-three fellows of the Academy were represented: thirteen sculptors, nine architects, eight painters, and three landscapers. The quality and power of their work brought highly favorable comments from critics.

On September 2, 1939, while the Aldriches were at sea on their return to Rome, Hitler invaded Poland and the war began. The decks of their ship had been brilliantly painted with stars and stripes on which searchlights were trained at night. "I thought they ought to be painted on our bottom to be logical," Miss Aldrich wrote to a friend.

However it was a relief to find ourselves actually in Naples harbor, and no land ever looked so peaceful and lovely to us as those vineyards and hemp fields we motored through to Rome. It seemed almost too good to be true to find everyone here at the Villa to welcome us except the kitchen boy, who came the next night to salute us in his *bersaglière* plumes. They are all so glad to have us back. Everything is uncertain here; just our coming gave them a feeling of confidence. We don't know yet whether the Academy will open. Cables are flying back and forth. We shall stay anyway and hope they will let us keep going in a small way. By "they" I mean the N.Y. Trustees of course. . . . A few students are here, some have fled for home, some are trying to get cabins and some are lost somewhere in Europe and we hope will turn up. It takes ten days to get mail from England. . . . It seems a very strange world and a strange war and a strange winter ahead of us. And yet the land is so lovely, the weather so beautiful, and everyone so calm that there is often the illusion of its being as usual.

Chester Aldrich went at once to the American Embassy. Italy had not yet entered the war but it seemed certain to do so very soon. The Italian authorities saw no present need for the Academy to close, and the American ambassador advised that it continue until further notice but that no new students be brought to Rome. The State Department took a more cautious view. It urged all Americans in Italy to come home and declined to issue passports to Italy for new students. The trustees went into hurried session and ended by giving the fellows abroad the option of returning to America at once "and completing their fellowships here [New York] or elsewhere, or of continuing their work abroad until otherwise directed."

When the Academy opened on October 1, 1939, seven fellows and seven other students were on hand, comprising all those who had remained in Europe except one who had been given permission by the trustees to remain in Oslo for his studies. By the end of the year Aldrich reported that "of all the Classical School only Professor Van Buren remains in Rome." Rhys Carpenter, unable to get to his new post at the Academy that year, said of Van Buren that "no Professor in Charge of Classical Studies could find a more devoted nomenclator, a more exhaustively informed exegete, a more generous comrade, or a more helpful friend." Even those trustees who could not readily translate this learned praise but knew Van Buren could subscribe to the last two tributes. Dr. G. K. Boyce, a former fellow in classics, had been appointed librarian for three years from October 1, 1939. He too was for some time unable to get a passport to Italy but finally managed to be at work there before April 1940, and immediately won favorable reports to the trustees. Later in 1940, when the Academy seemed certain to close, he offered to return to his former post in America and relieve the Academy of his salary. The trustees then accepted his offer with regret and appreciation.

Aldrich offered to forego his salary and to bear personally part of the expense of maintaining the Villa Aurelia. His offer was gratefully declined. He and his sister remained in Rome. Miss Aldrich's letters give the flavor of 1939–40 as no formal records can:

October 29, 1939. All is quiet here—too quiet—but we are keeping on with our little family of seven and everyone here is so glad we do so as it is thought very valuable to have neutrals keep up the normal tone of life. The French Academy is open though their ten Fellows are at the front, and the one woman they expected to have, decided to go to do war work. They just keep it open, *quand même*.

January 5, 1940. There will be seven of our students and one Fellow (on a trip up the Nile) and as that leaves only four behind, one fat girl having just set off alone for Timgad and not speaking a word of French, it seems a good chance to take. We all feel the uncertainty of the spring, a sense of horrible possibilities around the corner and of looking our last on all things lovely every hour. We had a wonderful Christmas, even with our small Academy. The Fellows gave a fancy-dress ball which was unusually successful, the same nice girls you remember with some pretty French girls added; then we had a party here Christmas eve and a Christmas dinner at the Doria's [at the Doria-Pamphili Villa next to the Academy]. And on top of Christmas we had such a snow storm as Rome has never seen, drifts in our garden, people skiing on the Janiculum, and all the population out to see the sight. As half Rome wears bare legs and lives in unheated houses, the storm had its disadvantages. Even here we were . . . cold.

April 17, 1940. We have the most lovely picnics now that the weather is better, long tough three hour walks. Last Sunday there were fourteen of us with three dogs, and all the walk was across meadows, on hills, and in woods. I noticed when we sat down for lunch that English, French, Italian, Roumanian and Polish were being spoken.

May 29, 1940. Most of our students and many of our friends are sailing this week on the *Manhattan* so I will let one of them take this to N.Y. I hope when you see the postmark you will not think I have gone home, for I am sitting right here trying to look the war in the face. It is the most gloomy and unbelievable time I have ever lived through and yet we are so fortunate compared to most people. . . . All is still uncertain here but we now expect that in a few days or weeks Italy will be in the war. The clouds are gathering around us and there are ominous signs. It is not likely to make *much* personal difference in our situation. . . . Our present plan is to stay on here keeping the three students who don't want to go home, and keeping the buildings open as we can, then close down if we must, but we two live on here at the Villa to watch the property. The Ambassador is seeing Ciano tomorrow, for us, to see if he thinks our property will be all right. If we can, we will go off now and then for a few days in the country. It is still possible we may be allowed to use our American car; all others go out of commission June 1. Santa's husband [Santa was an employee] has been called, though 60 years old and is buying mules. None of our men have been called yet and we are sure to be able to keep Joseph [the major-domo] as he is over age. Up to now our daily life goes on undisturbed.

On June 10, 1940, Italy entered the war on the side of Germany and on July 6 Miss Aldrich wrote:

Next week we shut up the Academy. The last two Fellows leave by air.
. . . We still have our cellar refuge with its pickaxe and brandy and
bandages but the last alarm was a false one, and I don't even get out
of bed though most of the servants go down.

July 21, 1940. We are staying in Rome until we get rid of the last
two students whose departure keeps being delayed for lack of Portu-
guese visas. . . .

September 10, 1940. Chester has the disagreeable job this week of
discharging, into a workless world, almost 25 employees, many of
whom have been twenty years at the Academy and regard it as home.
They get large indemnities, but it is none the less painful. But we must
close; we have no choice though we hope to keep our Library open for
miscellaneous students this winter, especially as the Vatican Library is
closed, and those of most of the other Academies. Our hill is very
peaceful except for the guns and the ten young soldiers manning them
on the top of our Gate [the Porta San Pancrazio]. We have had no
air warning for some time though my coat and shoes are always ready
by my bedside.

The letters stopped when, in October 1940, Chester Aldrich fell
seriously ill. In December he and his sister were both in a hospital
in Rome, she after a minor operation and he after a very serious
one. He died there the day after Christmas. He had been, the trustees recorded in a fine memorial tribute, "ever on the side of the
angels." With quiet New England resolution Miss Aldrich gathered
up the Academy reins. She immediately volunteered to the trustees
to stay on in Rome and fill her brother's place in the now almost
empty Academy. The board at once cabled its acceptance and
offered Aldrich's salary to her. This she declined.

The following months were filled with decisions and counter-
decisions on closing the Academy. It was finally decided to do so.
Miss Aldrich sailed for the United States in June 1941 with the
wife of the ambassador, but not before she had seen that all Academy affairs in Rome were in the best possible order. Responsibility
for its plant was vested in Hale Benton, assistant to the director,
Ricardo Davico, secretary, and Colonel Peter DeDaehn, acting librarian. All Academy buildings were closed except the main building with the library, and the Academy was placed under the protection of the Swiss embassy. By good luck trustee Myron Taylor
was in Rome at the Vatican as "personal representative" of President Roosevelt and remained there throughout the war.

In November 1941 officers of the Italian war ministry inspected the Villa Aurelia as a site for air defense—a repetition of what happened in World War I. Again the delaying tactics of prolonged discussion resulted in the hilltop of the Janiculum escaping this military use.

On December 7, 1941, Italy declared war on the United States, and the occupants of the Academy, having automatically become enemy aliens, found it impossible in early 1942 to draw funds from the Credito Italiano. The Swiss embassy came to their rescue and offered to advance 20,000 lire each month to the Academy. All seemed well for the moment, but someone in New York blundered, for the Swiss received a curt cable asking why they had interfered. At once the offer to the Academy was withdrawn, and on May 11, 1942, Benton set out on a difficult and devious journey to New York to discuss what could be done. He returned with no solution. Those left in Rome had perforce to use their own personal credit.

In May 1942 the Italian government was about to place seals of sequestration on the doors of Academy buildings. The Swiss again intervened successfully and also renewed their offer to advance money to the Academy provided the United States would assure them of ultimate repayment. But as the Academy was a private institution no such assurance could be given by the U.S. government. It was only through the skillful intervention of Myron Taylor that the knot was cut and arrangement made (in which "the Vatican was very helpful") to pay outstanding bills—which had risen to some 90,000 lire—and to give the Academy a monthly advance. At last Colonel DeDaehn could cease his efforts to keep the Academy in credit "by acting in Italian films and playing the balalaika in Roman cafés." By that time at least thirty-nine fellows and former fellows of the Academy were serving in the armed forces and at least an equal number in other government war agencies and the Red Cross.

Though unable to send funds to Italy, the Academy put to good use its funds available in New York. Having felt compelled to abandon for the time its competitions in the fine arts, the board found another way to support its program. In 1942 it appropriated $5,000 for use in cooperation with the American Artists for Victory, which sponsored young artists in making posters and art decorations for navy ships and army war camps. This plan was so successful that in 1943 the Academy made added appropriations to a total of nearly $20,000 to the Citizen's Committee for the Army and Navy. In the Academy's part of that program 115 triptychs as well as murals, medals, and sculpture were commissioned. The program of awards in classical studies at American universities was also continued.

In October 1943 a new proposal for the use and preservation of the Academy's properties in Rome came before its trustees. The President's Commission for the Protection of Historic and Artistic Monuments in Europe voted resolving "that if the Trustees of the American Academy in Rome were to offer the facilities of the Academy . . . for work connected with the protection and salvage of artistic monuments, the Commission would welcome such an offer." While the matter was under discussion, Leon Fraser, international financial expert, influential officer of the Red Cross, and trustee and treasurer of the Academy, suggested that there might be alternatives to the commission's use of Academy buildings. The State Department might like to use them as annexes or residences for its greatly increased postwar embassy staff, or the Red Cross might make advantageous use of them as in World War I. The war in Italy ended before any of these wartime uses of Academy buildings went into effect.

The generous and ever-helpful Swiss had meanwhile blocked another sequestration attempt by moving some of their embassy staff into the villas Chiaraviglio and Bellacci and the main building. And when in January 1944 German officers forced their way into the Academy buildings, the Swiss took prompt diplomatic action and prevented the Germans from establishing themselves on the Janiculum.

In late 1944 the war in Italy was drawing rapidly to an end, and by the beginning of 1945 the trustees began to turn their minds to the Academy's peacetime future. The Academy finances were not in bad shape. Although wartime awards had been made of fellowships in American universities—a highly successful venture—and although some expenses in Rome had continued, the Academy's unspent income was accumulating: in 1947 it reached $350,000.

In July 1944 the trustees appointed their colleague and secretary, Professor William Bell Dinsmoor of Columbia, as acting director, but the State Department refused him permission to travel to Italy at that time. Later, when Dinsmoor might have gone, Myron Taylor sent word that he opposed any move toward reopening the Academy "under present conditions," pointing out that Rome was still in "the zone of operations" and that in some respects the situation had "deteriorated greatly." Taylor urged that the trustees postpone any thought of opening for another year— certainly until peace was declared. He felt that the trustees should consider "a complete reorganization, and not a hasty but a deliberate selection of staff." He added his emphatic opinion that the Villa Aurelia should be put up for sale. It was, he wrote, "a burden for everyone who had undertaken to live in it, and it bore no substantially desirable relation to the activities of the Academy."

The trustees accepted Taylor's advice on keeping the Academy closed for the time being. During 1945 they met frequently to deliberate on the Academy's future, finally resolving not to sell, at least for the moment, the Villa Aurelia. Some months later their minutes recorded that "all agreed that the present accommodations, without the Aurelia property, would be inadequate for the Academy activities in the postwar period." The war in Europe ended in May, but Italian economy remained in chaos. It was clear that nothing productive could yet be done with the Academy in Rome.

Professor Van Buren's retirement was due at the end of 1945, and the trustees very properly voted him financial support. He had been a 1906 fellow of the School of Classical Studies before its merger with the Academy. In 1908 he became librarian of the School, and then of the Academy after the merger. He was also a lecturer and later a professor. He had given up his post as librarian but retained his curatorship of the small Academy museum of which he had been virtually the creator. The museum consisted mostly of ancient fragments unearthed during the Academy's many years of construction and alteration, the finest examples of which had been mounted on the walls of the *cortile*. It is lucky that all discoveries were not so permanently affixed. One handful of objects had been brought to Van Buren by an excited gardener. They were pronounced to be early Roman glass, scrupulously labeled as such, and shown in the museum. But even Homer nods. It may be hoped that Van Buren never learned of their later removal from the collection by the Academy's most celebrated archaeologist. They turned out to be pieces of vermouth bottles doubtless flung from a window by a student in a moment of happy insouciance.

Van Buren's thirty-eight years of service and unfailing presence

at the Academy, even throughout the wars, had made him the very
embodiment of the Academy. A vignette appeared in *The New
Yorker* on June 24, 1944, in Daniel Lang's "Letters from Rome":

Professor Van Buren, who has remained uninterned because several
Italian scholars stood as guarantors for him with the Germans, was
found in Rome by a former student, Lieutenant Colonel Henry Rowell,
now the A.M.G. Education Officer for Rome. As soon as Rowell entered
the capital, he made straight for his old professor's office in the
Academy. . . . Outside, the Italians were cheering and Allied tanks
were rolling by. Inside the office, the atmosphere was still. Van Buren
was there all right, bent over a book. Rowell walked up to him and
tried to make his presence known with as much restraint as possible.
"The Professor said hello to me and he was very nice," Rowell told
me afterward, "but he was reading Dessau's 'Inscriptiones Latinae
Selectae.' I think I made him lose his place."

A second vignette is brief and moving. Late in April 1945 Captain
Gordon C. Atkins (in civilian life a teacher of the humanities in
San Bernardino Valley, California) took Van Buren to mess in his
quarters. Van Buren cried at the sight of mashed potatoes. He had
not seen them in years and had been dreaming of food.

In 1945 the Academy made provision for "leave courses" for
members of the United States military personnel, consisting largely
of lectures by distinguished scholars stranded or resident in Rome.
But among the men in service there were four fellows who would
never return to the Academy. First Lieutenant Henri Emil Chabanne, FAAR '34, landscape architect; Private First Class Theodore Harrison Gibbs, FAAR '38, sculptor; Sergeant Erling Charles
Olsen, FAAR '39, classicist; and Captain Harry Poole Camden, Jr.,
FAAR '27, sculptor, had been killed in action. The trustees paused
in their deliberations to record appropriate memorials.

In April 1945 Professor Dinsmoor resigned *pro forma* the acting
directorship of the Academy, and his place was taken by Professor
Charles Rufus Morey, former head of the Department of Art and
Archaeology at Princeton, at that time in Rome as cultural coun-
selor at the embassy and head of the Office of War Information in
Italy. In October 1945 the Academy offered further help to the
United States government and its armed forces by making its
housing and food available, within practical limits, to the personnel
of the embassy and the military establishment. At once the villas
Chiaraviglio and Bellacci were occupied by a secretary and an at-

taché of the embassy, with their families. Officers taking the leave courses lived in the main building.

Early in 1946 Morey reported that the Academy could continue its Service activities through the coming summer. A little later, to the satisfaction of trustees, the State Department sent word that the Academy might reopen its normal program in the autumn and that it would issue passports for this purpose. At a meeting of the board in May, Henry Allen Moe reported that his special committee recommended the appointment as the new director of Laurance P. Roberts, then a captain in the army. Roberts was a graduate of Princeton in 1929, was married, and before the war had been the highly successful director of the Brooklyn Museum. Since he was not likely to gain his discharge from the army before October 1946, it was understood that he would begin his duties at the Academy by January 1947. A nominal staff was appointed to supervise the plant pending his arrival.

For six years after the death of Chester Aldrich in 1940 the Academy had lived without consistent leadership, its policy shifting to meet the exigencies of the day. Its survival was largely due to old loyalties and to extraordinary friends-in-need. Of these the Swiss government ranked perhaps the first. Much was also owed to Myron Taylor and to the Americans in wartime command who, when the question of the use of the Academy for war purposes arose, kept in mind what would be appropriate to "its future, long-term usefulness as a national American asset." That it was never taken over for purely military purposes but served only in non-military activities is an indication of the respect in which it was held and the place it had won for itself. Of the remnants of its staff who held on through the war, though often unpaid and poorly nourished, enough cannot be said in praise. The fabric of the Academy had proved tough and enduring.

X

Change and Growth

THE Academy fabric had proved tough, but by the end of 1946 it was also shabby and worn. Renovation was needed and needed soon. The war had not only damaged tangible property; it had uprooted society from its old ways, made it more flexible, and given it fresh concepts. Nearly everyone connected with the Academy was ready for a new start.

The leadership of Roberts was eagerly awaited. He became available two months earlier than the trustees had expected. Demobilized in late September, he was able to be at the meeting in New York of the executive committee on October 2, when important changes that had been under discussion during the war years were approved. The most startling of the trustees' decisions was to admit women fellows in the fine arts and to abandon the rule against married fellows. The age limitation of thirty for all fellows was also removed. The duration of fellowships was reduced to one year, with the possibility of renewal for a second or even a third year, and it was hoped that the economies thus effected would allow the support of more fellowships. The creation of one new fellowship in the history of art—first suggested by Chester Aldrich—was authorized for 1947. Of the five other fellowships offered in classics, two were in future to be awarded to candidates of high professional level. It was also proposed that a program of artists and scholars in residence be made a regular feature of the Academy year. The Academy was to be fully reopened a year hence, and competitions promptly organized so that the prizewinners could be in Rome by October 1947. Meanwhile, although the Academy might not be in perfect running order by that time, it was thought safe to offer a 1947 summer session.

When Laurance and Isabel Roberts arrived in Rome early in December 1946 they found the Villa Aurelia empty and desolate.

The Villino was being used by Rufus Morey, acting director, until his successor could take over. The villas Chiaraviglio and Bellacci housed personnel from the American embassy, while the main building was fully occupied, mostly by servicemen on leave study. No rooms were ready for the new director and his wife, but their friend John Wesley Jones, first secretary of the embassy, who was living in the Chiaraviglio, put them up until other space was available.

An immediate task of Laurance Roberts was to clear the main building of its occupants, which included the Davicos and the Bentons. Both men had been mainstays of the little Academy garrison during the war. Both had been with the Academy for many years; Davico since 1920, when he had come to organize the photographic section of the library and had stayed as the Academy's secretary, and Benton, who had been assistant to the director since 1927. To terminate their service was hard, but it was done with mutual good feeling. They were made aware by Roberts of the Academy's appreciation of their work. Benton's place as assistant to the director was temporarily filled by Lamont Moore of the National Gallery in Washington, who, although he could stay for only a year, was of the greatest help to Roberts in getting things underway. The GIs soon vanished from the main building as their turns came to be demobilized.

It was a scramble to put the Academy plant in order. The Villa Aurelia, closed since 1941, had been plundered during the war of everything movable to furnish other Academy buildings. The rest of its battered furniture had suffered from being stored in the cellars of the main building; only two marble consoles and a large red lacquer cabinet, too cumbersome to move, remained in its empty rooms. The trustees authorized $50,000 to put the Aurelia in shape, and under the skilled direction of Laurance and Isabel Roberts, the northeast wing was transformed into apartments with studios for fellows. The old kitchen became the present living room, while the dining room, new kitchen, and servants' quarters were installed in the southeast corner. The Roberts furnished the Villa largely with their own possessions, many of which they left to the Academy. It is to their generosity and taste that the Villa Aurelia owes a good portion of its equipment today.

The summer session took place as planned, under Henry Rowell's guidance. Every morning nineteen students set off with him to visit ancient sites. In the afternoon the students listened to a lecture on the historical and literary background of the material they were studying. Once a week they made a trip to some more distant place of classical interest. In Roberts' first report to the trustees he wrote that Rowell had "made each day a more exciting one of discovery than the last, and gave his pupils a picture of Roman civilization sound in fact, full in detail, and exciting in conception, which rekindled their interest in the classics." Before the year ended the board formally voted approving the summer sessions as an integral part of the regular Academy program. The "summer school" had come a long way since its tentative and cautious debut twenty-six years earlier.

That summer the trustees made an appointment of importance in Academy history. Owing to war conditions Rhys Carpenter had been unable to fill except nominally his long-postponed professorship in charge of classical studies. He was succeeded by Professor Frank E. Brown of Yale, FAAR '33, who had led Yale's team of excavators at Dura Europus, and who now began a search for Etruscan sites near Viterbo. (The success of his later findings is described in Chapter XII.)

In October 1947 the Academy sprang to full life again. There were eighteen fellows, with George Howe, architect, Samuel Barber, composer, and Henry McIlhenny, art historian, as artists and scholars in residence. Eight of the fellows were married. They were housed with their children—known as the Little Fellows—in the main building. But dormitory life for families proved too tumultuous, and the experiment was not repeated. Thereafter married fellows were given additional funds for quarters nearby, and later still the garden next to the Villa Chiaraviglio was made into a playground.

In persuading the trustees to increase the special allowance for married fellows, the director pointed out that the amount involved could be made up in part by the nominal rent of their rooms to artists-in-residence. Roberts hoped to make of the Academy a forum of artists and scholars where the students could share their Academy experience with men and women who had already made a mark in their professions. The success of the venture, and the variety of interests represented, may be seen in a random list of those who came: Edgar Wind and Agnes Mongan, art historians; Gisela Richter and Mason Hammond, classicists; Jean Labatut, architect; George Biddle, painter; Elizabeth Bowen, Archibald MacLeish,

John Ciardi, and Van Wyck Brooks, writers; Nicholas Nabokov and Aaron Copland, musicians; Ivan Mestrovic and Carl Milles, sculptors; and Donald Oenslager, stage designer. At first the trustees questioned the use of Academy funds to support those who were not American citizens. A committee was appointed to go into the matter, with Randall Thompson and Francis Taylor among its members, both sympathetic with Roberts' objective. In the end the issue was resolved by the generosity of trustee Wallace Harrison and of his partner Max Abramovitz. Recognizing the significance of the program, they established a fund to relieve the Academy of expense for the foreign artists-in-residence.

Life at the Academy was also much enriched by the men and women whom the Roberts brought as their personal guests to the Villa Aurelia. They entertained largely and skillfully; it was no wonder that the Villa was cheerfully nicknamed the second American embassy. The wide range of the Roberts' interests, and their perception of quality in people, reached far beyond the adornment of their own dinner table and greatly influenced the Academy. Staff and fellows alike began to reflect their discernment.

Isabel Roberts had a talent for administration, which she had demonstrated when acting director of the Brooklyn Museum while Roberts was in the army. It appeared also in her selection of personnel. The excellence with which she put together a staff—many of whom still continue to serve the Academy—has been testified to by her successors. She regularly inspected every aspect of the Academy's housekeeping and exemplified her own principle that success lay largely in finding the right person to train for the job.

Though it is invidious to name some and not all of those brought to the Academy by the Roberts, two must be mentioned. When in 1945 Roscoe Guernsey retired as executive secretary of the New York office, his place had been temporarily filled for a year by Meriwether Stuart of Hunter College. Roberts proposed as Stuart's successor Miss Mary Williams, who had held several other offices with distinction. She accepted the post in November 1946 and has since filled it with outstanding skill, tact, and loyalty. Her annual visit to Rome links her closely to the Academy itself. She probably knows more of its history and workings since 1946 than anyone else. It is hard to imagine how the administration in New York could function without her. A second valuable addition to the staff was also a woman. In 1951 Roberts persuaded Princess Margherita

Rospigliosi to become the Academy's secretary in Rome, a position she held until her retirement in 1969. She was a friend as well as a devoted employee of the Academy, putting herself at the disposal of its members for the smallest service or for the opening of Roman doors that might otherwise have been closed to them. When she left, tributes and gifts came from many parts of the United States from grateful men and women to whom she represented the day-to-day humanity of the Academy.

Roberts believed that quality of character was important in choosing new fellows. He was the first director to meet with the juries in America, and sometimes with the competitors. On occasion he even asked the juries to reconsider their choices. How well-equipped was the candidate with judgment, balance, and self-discipline to meet a Roman experience which might prove too heady for the young artist of average American background? It was this question of which Roberts constantly reminded the juries when they were dazzled by a show of talent.

The creation by Congress of the Fulbright fellowships in 1949 brought the Academy the opportunity to welcome many of the recipients. By mid-May 1950 it was accommodating Fulbright fellows in all the fine arts and the classics. Some of them, older men and women already distinguished in their fields, came as artists-in-residence, among them, over the next years, Allen Tate in literature, Franklin Watkins in painting, and Frederick Woodbridge in architecture.

Applications for Academy fellowships continued to mount; the summer sessions expanded, especially because the new Fulbright scholars in classics came in numbers. A pleasant summer tradition had begun when the trustees urged that President James Kellum Smith make regular visits to Rome "at a time convenient to him" and at Academy expense. The result was an annual hegira to Italy by Smith and his family, where for several weeks he took part in the life of the Academy and made himself conversant with its problems and its personnel. The ties between board and director were strengthened in two more ways. The travel allowance of the director was extended to cover two trips to New York annually. And so illuminating had been his first report that Roberts was asked to write the board a monthly letter on the Academy. This was the forerunner of today's printed *Newsletter*, for which there was no budget in Roberts' time.

Academy morale was high. The enrollment of twenty-eight fellows in October 1950 was one of the largest on record. The initial excavations at Cosa under Frank Brown had shown great promise. Spring concerts were begun at the Villa Aurelia, playing the works of American composers before capacity audiences. Financed by the Koussevitsky Music Foundation and with the personal interest of Mrs. Olga Koussevitsky, they constituted a landmark in European recognition of American musical talent. Roberts and his wife, as knowledgeable in travel as in art, conducted trips for the fellows to northern and southern Italy.

There had been another development of considerable importance to the Academy after the war. This was the International Union of the Institutes of History, Archaeology, and Art. Promoted by Professor Morey during his war years in Rome, it was organized to support the mutual interests of the various non-Italian national academies and institutes in Rome. It also incorporated what had been before the war the German Archaeological Institute, with its important possessions in Italy. Both Rowell, who was a moving spirit in the enterprise, and Roberts served at one time or another as its president. In the summer of 1948, and largely under the prompting of Roberts, the Union had sponsored a joint exhibition of the work of the students in the member academies. Held at first in the Palazzo Cafarelli, it was such a success that it was later shown in Rome's foremost gallery, the Palazzo Venezia.

Under the sponsorship of the Union and with the close cooperation of Mason Hammond, professor of classical studies in 1956, Roberts offered Academy space to Ernest Nash, a German scholar. Nash was attempting a complete collection of photographs of Roman remains (wherever to be found). The Academy library already had a small number of these; room in it was provided for Nash, and the Fototeca—a deposit of photographs as its name indicates—came into being. The Fototeca is a joint enterprise of the Union and the American Academy, the latter's share being to house it and to help find funds to finance it, which it has received from the Bollingen and Mellon Foundations. It is not, strictly speaking, a function of the Academy, and its funds are handled by the Union, whose support comes from memberships and foundations. But its value to the Academy is inestimable, as it is to all scholars who use it, and **it** continues to grow steadily under Nash.

The fifties brought to the Academy holders of other new fellow-

ships besides the Fulbrights. The American Academy of Arts and
Letters proposed to support a fellowship in literature at the Academy; it made an initial grant of $3,000 for the first year and ap-
pointed a selection jury of Malcolm Cowley, Allen Tate, Mark
Van Doren, Glenway Westcott, and Barry Faulkner—a jury that
must have impressed the public as well as the candidates. The first
fellow elected was Anthony Hecht; the second, William Styron. In
1953 the National Academy of Design, undeterred by the ruling of
fifteen years earlier, sent its Abbey Fellow in Mural Painting to the
Academy. In November 1956 the Academy learned that the Dum-
barton Oaks Foundation of Harvard had appointed a senior fellow
in landscape architecture, and promptly offered "every facility and
privilege of the Academy" to the appointee. And when the National
Gallery in Washington created the David A. Finley Fellowship in
Curatorial Training—long since envisaged by Chester Aldrich and
John Walker—the Academy at once offered its hospitality. During
1958–59 Nathaniel A. Owings, a man of vigor, imagination, and
talent and a member of the architectural firm of Skidmore, Owings,
and Merrill, had been architect-in-residence. On his return to America he offered the Academy, through a family foundation, the sum
of $3,000 a year for three consecutive years to establish a fellow-
ship for "an instructor or professor in an architectural school or
university, to spend a year or more at the Academy." If the out-
come were successful Owings proposed to continue the gift indefinitely. For such an offer to come from one who had recently had a
close personal experience of the Academy was in itself a compli-
ment, and it was quickly and gratefully accepted by the trustees.

It is interesting that in line with all these fellowships the board
at one time considered that the Academy might grant degrees. That
nothing came of the proposal was a matter of the board's judgment,
but that it had come up at all was a measure of the Academy's
standing.

To the skill of its finance officers is due much of the vigor and
confidence with which the Academy moved forward in those postwar years. No more constant or nagging problem had faced its reopening in 1946 than the inflation in Italy. The lira had been fixed
officially at 225 to the dollar, but on the black market the dollar
brought 500 lire or more. As prices rose the Academy paid dearly
for its necessities by its determination to observe Italian government rules. The concerned trustees finally found an adequate solu-

tion by purchasing blocked accounts at a rate more favorable than the official exchange—a procedure within Italian government regulations. During those years the fellows' stipends seemed barely enough, even though their rooms were free and the cost of their meals had been held down to $1.50 a day. In spite of the financial pinch, Academy fellowships were much sought after (in 1948 the number of applicants had reached 137) but the trustees were anxious about the situation and were frequently reminded of the need to raise the fellows' allowances. They were not able to do so until 1957. Not only had Italy's inflation dogged Academy budgets, but inflation in America, an accompaniment of the Korean war, was taking its toll of capital values. As a prudent measure in 1954 the finance committee increased Academy holdings in common stocks to 50 percent of its total investments. The Academy's real property in Rome at that time was given a paper value of $8 million and its securities in America of $4.5 million.

The years that followed were marked by continuing inflation, outward prosperity, and optimistic expansion. Rising costs led to rising annual budgets. A system was adopted to bring the proposed Academy budget to the trustees earlier in the year and in greater detail for finance committee consideration, but it continued its inevitable rise. In 1948 it had been about $127,500. In 1956 it was nearly $250,000, against an estimated income of $218,000. By good management the Academy weathered this period and in 1957 added $5,000 a year to the total allowance divided among the married fellows, made large outlays for repairs, and even offered a prize of $1,000 to the winning team in the flagging collaborative artist competitions.

Various factors eased the effects of inflation. A trustees' committee had been set up to raise endowment, and there had been many gifts since the war. In 1947 Jules Guérin, an illustrator of McKim's day and a mural painter whose works decorated many public buildings in America and Europe, left a legacy of over $200,000 to the Academy. A bequest from Janet B. Grover brought $25,000 to the fellowship fund and another from the Sarah Jones Trust about $47,500. The Kate Lancaster Brewster Fellowship in Landscape Architecture received added funds after her death that brought the fellowship's endowment to some $50,000. The Bollingen Foundation made grants for the archaeological work at Cosa, and the Avalon and Old Dominion Foundations, established by Paul Mellon, helped to support various undertakings. The Carnegie Corporation continued to grant funds to the library, which Dean Mendell reported was at long last excellently equipped for its immediate purposes. Its current librarian, Peter DeDaehn, had come to the Academy as a White Russian émigré colonel. He had made himself useful in a score of ways but particularly in the library. He became assistant librarian in 1924 and librarian in 1948.

Since the war four villas had been offered to the Academy. One was the Richardson villa on the Via Giacomo Medici across the street from Academy property. Richardson left it to his sister Miss Ethel Richardson. Aware of the shortage of housing at the Academy and unwilling to maintain so large a house for herself alone, she suggested selling it, with the first option to the Academy. After protracted negotiations it was formally agreed that Miss Richardson should bequeath it to the Academy in consideration for its maintenance during her lifetime and permission to retain a small apartment for herself. Hospitable to all members of the Academy and its guests, she lived there until her death in 1963.

In 1947 Mrs. Henry Clews offered to give her Château de la Napoule on the French Riviera to the Academy as a memorial to her husband, but the trustees, on their guard against expansion, no matter how tempting, which might dissipate the energies as well as the funds for maintenance of the Academy, reluctantly declined the gift. In 1949 General Helbig offered to give to the Academy his historic Villa Lante, magnificently overlooking Rome on the edge of the Garibaldi Park near the Villa Aurelia. This was even harder to refuse, but the trustees found that it would involve them in complicated legal and tax problems, and sadly declined. And when Walter A. Weiss of the Arts Fund in New York offered to rent a villa in Taormina for the use of Academy fellows, the trustees again concluded with regret that they must not deviate from their determination to keep the Academy's commitments within strict bounds. Had the financial world been more stable the trustees might have accepted one or more of these offers. But there were immediate obligations to be met: the budget was extended to the limit and so were the energies of the Academy's small staff.

Losses in capital values during the fifties were matched by inevitable losses in personnel. Francis Henry Taylor died in 1957. His refreshing and unpretentious approach to the arts and his electric shafts of wit were missed at meetings of the board. His place was taken by Rensselaer Lee, art historian and professor at Princeton, who would later become president of the board. It was a blow when President James Kellum Smith resigned in 1958 on grounds of ill health. He had presided over one of the most progressive periods the Academy had ever known. Michael Rapuano, former fellow in landscape architecture and a trustee since 1946, was elected to succeed him, and Henry Rowell was made vice-president. In March 1959 Mario Settini was appointed business administrator of the Academy at a salary that, though modest for the times, exceeded the total budget of the Academy's beginnings in 1894.

As the decade ended, so did Laurance Roberts' successful leadership of the Academy. In January 1959 he asked the president to tell the board that for personal reasons he wished to resign. He had served as director for thirteen years and believed the Academy would profit from fresh energy and new ideas. Rapuano, Harrison, and Henry Allen Moe did their best to dissuade him, but in the end they yielded to his wish and agreed to release him by January 1960.

The committee appointed to find a new director solved the problem to everyone's immediate and future satisfaction when it recommended Richard Arthur Kimball, a graduate of Yale and of the Yale School of Architecture. The trustees knew that in securing Kimball they would add the counsels and service to the Academy of his wife, Josephine Dodge Kimball, whose demonstrated executive ability was balanced by rare charm and warmth. The committee's recommendation was unanimous, and the trustees approved it unanimously.

During his years at the Academy, Roberts had been paid many tributes for his outstanding leadership. One of these was a letter to President Smith from the Committee on Fine Arts, which read in part: "We believe that you, Sir, and the Director, have brought the Academy to a position of eminence, both here and abroad, unsurpassed since its founding. We believe that this has been accomplished by following, not a restrictive course but—far more difficult —a course of enlightened artistic liberalism." More direct praise came to Roberts when he retired. He was awarded the first newly designed Medal for Outstanding Service to the Academy. But perhaps he was pleased most of all when word came from the men and women with whom he had worked, who also acknowledged their debt to his wife. A group of former fellows and associates of the

Academy wrote of his "distinguished regime" and recorded their "great admiration, deep affection and lasting gratitude to Laurance and Isabel Roberts. . . . He had the grace and wisdom to treat us as adults." The musicians added a significant comment: "If a list were composed of all the compositions played for the first time by American symphony orchestras in the last ten years, it is a modest guess that 75 percent of the composers would be found to have been guests of the Academy." It was a good record.

XI

The Latest Decade
1959-1969

THE Kimballs—for they immediately made themselves thought of as joint partners in Academy affairs—brought a characteristically friendly touch to their undertaking. From the moment of their arrival in December 1959, their doors stood open to any Academy member from staff to fellow, and the personal relationship that resulted gave to the phrase "the Academy family" a very warm meaning.

The phrase had a literal meaning as well. During Kimball's years at the Academy never less than 50 percent of the fellows were married; many had children. In 1961 the proportion of married fellows rose as high as 80 percent. Their well-being was of concern to the director, who was acutely conscious of their financial anxiety during the very period when they were supposed to be free from it. At once Kimball put his architectural talent to work on a master plan for Academy development, which included housing. But maintenance, repair, and the alteration of existing space for more economical use had to come first. The Academy plant required a bigger water supply. The main building had extensive heating and plumbing problems. The retaining walls of the Villa Aurelia garden were bulging out ominously over the heads of pedestrians in Garibaldi Park below. The trustees authorized $100,000 to remedy these problems and to make other practical changes during the next six years. Nothing could be done about the housing for married fellows that Kimball had visualized in the garden behind the Academy, even though the Italian authorities had, astonishingly, overlooked the regulation against any more buildings on the Janiculum and had given permission for the new apartments. In the end, in view of the plight of married fellows, Kimball obtained a revolving loan fund from which they might borrow at 1 percent interest a year. The trustees set this up with an initial sum of $5,000.

By 1964 Kimball had also to find space for ten thousand more volumes in the library, which, always steadily growing, had received new impetus when Josephine Kimball turned her attention to it. Shortly after she came to Rome, she put behind it all the weight of her experience in running a highly successful bookshop in New York. When she started the Friends of the Library she drew on her own wide acquaintance in the book world, which helped to bring substantial funds for the purchase of books. It has continued to do so ever since. The library began to add at least fifteen hundred volumes a year from this source, as well as gifts in kind. Gisela Richter, the classics scholar, had retired from the Metropolitan Museum to live near the Academy. In 1963 she offered to bequeath her own books and a fund to purchase more—an offer most gratefully received by the trustees.

In 1965 Lewis Einstein, a retired American diplomat living in Europe, gave to the library eighty-four rare volumes, and he later bequeathed $15,000 to house his gift securely and appropriately. Sometime during the first months of the Kimballs' sojourn in Rome, Einstein had come to visit the Academy and to call on its new director. He was a remarkable friend of the Academy and a remarkable benefactor as well. In the mid-fifties he had met Isabel Roberts in Florence, where he had a villa, and thereafter he formed the habit of coming to the Academy or of seeing the Roberts in New York or Washington on their trips to the United States. It was quite natural for him to call on the Kimballs when he came to Rome early in 1961. He took an instant liking to the new director and his wife.

For a long time Einstein had been thinking of giving some of his possessions to the Academy. He proposed to the Kimballs that en route to the United States that spring they break their trip in Paris, where he was then living, and that they look over his collection with a view to a gift or two in the near future. Thus the Kimballs found themselves in March in Einstein's apartment just off the Avenue d'Iena, where he showed them his books, his beautiful seventeenth and eighteenth century French and Italian furniture, and his storerooms in the same building, overflowing with the fruits of his discriminating taste.

The Kimballs learned more of their charming host. As a very young man studying for the foreign service—he was eighty-three when he met the Kimballs—he had become the friend of Justice

Oliver Wendell Holmes, thirty-five years his senior. For nearly that many more years the two men corresponded, as the *Holmes-Einstein Letters*, published in 1963, revealed. Einstein had meanwhile had a distinguished foreign service career. He also wrote of politics and history, but his greatest interest was in art, and he loved best the art of Italy—a fact known to another friend, John Walker, who asked him to write the guide to Italian painting for the National Gallery in Washington.

During the years of Kimball's directorship the relationship grew. After every visit of the Kimballs to the Paris apartment a fresh flow of books or furniture would come to the Academy. The Villa Aurelia benefited from these gifts: the tapestries in the front hall, the mirrors in the dining room, the rug in the living room (woven for Einstein when he was posted in Peking)—these and other furniture and china were his gifts. He wanted a paneled room built in the library for his books; he wanted to bequeath to the Academy his Paris apartment as a meeting place for scholars; he tentatively discussed giving new fellowships to the Academy. When he died in 1967 the Academy found itself the beneficiary of the bulk of his fortune. Unfortunately his family, for whom he thought he had made ample provision, contested the will. In the end a settlement was arranged. The Paris apartment went to the family, and the Academy received approximately a million and a half dollars from its generous friend. Closely allied to his interest in art had been Einstein's pride in the position America held in the cultural world of Europe. He found in the Academy and in its directors, Roberts and Kimball, a worthy outpost of American culture. His wish had been to fortify it, and he did so magnificently.

Kimball was hard put to find space for incoming books, but he did so ingeniously and to the satisfaction of DeDaehn's successor as librarian. For DeDaehn's retirement had come in 1961, a matter of regret to everyone after forty years of his active and stimulating presence. The blow was tempered by the promotion of the assistant librarian to his place. Signora Inez Longobardi was also well known to the Academy. She had come as cataloguer in 1926 and had been responsible, with DeDaehn, for the library's reputation as "the most accommodating in Rome." Signora Longobardi is still the librarian, and the constant use of the library by scholars of many nationalities and by students from other academies testifies to her skill and care.

Other gifts came to the Academy during Kimball's regime. In 1961 the Crown Zellerbach Company of California gave a fellowship of $4,000 in honor of the recently ended service as ambassador to Rome of its president, David Zellerbach. Halstead Vander-Poel, an American friend of the Academy living in Rome, gave 200,000 lire annually for archaeology. Richardson Pratt, a recent loss to the Academy board, of which he had been secretary from 1945 until 1959, left it $25,000. By 1961 the committee to raise endowment had secured $500,000 toward its goal of $2,750,000, and ten contributing universities had agreed to give $500 annually instead of $250. A very personal and much appreciated gift was made to the Academy when Walter Damrosch's daughters gave a bas-relief of their father, whose initial sponsorship of music at the Academy started the fund that had finally established its music fellowships.

Gifts like these were especially welcome, for in 1963 Michael Rapuano had presented to the trustees the serious need for a substantial increase in endowment. The inflated dollars of Academy income no longer covered Academy expenses, and from now on it might have to make dangerous inroads upon its capital. Persuaded by Kimball, some trustees joined him in redoubtable efforts to get foundation help. The Avalon Foundation pledged in 1965 a grant of $90,000 to permit an increase of fellows' stipends to $2,400, with an allowance for the children of married fellows up to $600 a year. The Old Dominion Foundation, also through the agency of Kimball, granted $75,000 for fellowships. The Academy was at last able to ask a cost price for the meals it served, as well as to adjust fees to cover the cost of some of its other services.

Other gifts continued to come in. Clarence Percival Dietsch, fellow in sculpture in 1909, bequeathed $5,000 to the Academy; Mrs. Harold T. Clark gave $5,000 and Mrs. Richardson Pratt $5,000. A touching bequest of $100,000 was left by Gorham Stevens, who died in 1963. All these were deeply appreciated, showing as they did that the Academy was not forgotten by its friends. But the financial future was still uncertain, and the Academy needed far more substantial help.

By the early 1960s it had become apparent that there was a serious lacuna in the Academy's fellowship program. Aside from the history of art there were no fellowships for humanistic studies in the long period extending from the end of the Roman Empire to the baroque seventeenth century. To fill this gap the Bollingen Foundation in 1963 through the agency of Rensselaer Lee generously gave $50,000 to provide two fellowships each year for a period of five years and a subsequent grant of $30,000 in 1968 to continue them for another three years. These Post-Classical Humanistic Fellowships made possible studies in medieval and Renaissance history, literature, philosophy, and musicology based on Rome and thus considerably broadened the Academy's scholarly range.

In 1963 there were several alterations in fellowships. It was ruled that no candidate for a fellowship in the fine arts could be appointed until after a satisfactory personal interview with a member of the jury or a trustee. The trustees discussed the right of fellows to earn money from outside sources while on fellowship, but with a nod to hard times, they left the matter in abeyance. They did, however, formally vote that no person receiving funds from any other fellowship or institution might be granted an Academy fellowship. The Academy regretfully terminated, as impracticable, the fellowship in creative writing sponsored by the American Academy of Arts and Letters. To counterbalance this loss, it was announced that a new fellowship in musicology would be offered shortly.

In 1965 another fellowship was given by the Foundation for Environmental Design through the Academy's staunch supporter Nathaniel Owings. Kimball encouraged Owings in this project and had a hand in working out the terms with him, and the proposal was accepted by the board. The fellowship was to be effective experimentally for three years, from 1966 through 1969.

Medals for outstanding service were awarded to a remarkable pair of women who had achieved great distinction in classical studies: Lily Ross Taylor, a former fellow, and Gisela M. A. Richter. Both had been Jerome lecturers. Both had spent much time at the Academy to the special benefit of classicists and to the great pleasure of all. Gisela Richter had been generous in books and funds and had also bequeathed to the Academy her charming apartment nearby.

For lack of funds there was a lull in the excavations at Cosa (described in Chapter XII) and Professor Brown returned to Yale. But he continued his efforts, assisted by Academy officers and trustees, to find money for the undertaking, and in 1961 the Bollingen Foundation promised to give the Academy $10,000 for three years.

It was decided to renew the excavations. Brown accepted indefinite appointment as professor in charge of classical studies, effective October 1963, but he came to Rome as early as May, and work at Cosa resumed that spring.

Brown had succeeded Henry Rowell as professor of classical studies. Rowell continued to run successful summer sessions, increasingly attended by Fulbright scholars, who formed at least two-thirds of every group ranging from thirty-five to forty students. Under Rowell's aegis a proposal from the American School in Athens for a joint fellowship providing a year of study at each of the two institutions was accepted. Rowell was one of the few trustees who also served the Academy as both professor and administrator. In 1963 he relinquished direction of the summer school to Professor S. Palmer Bovie but continued as vice-president of the board.

During those years the Academy and especially the classicists had a stroke of good fortune in the almost constant cordial association of one of the world's most distinguished archaeologists. Professor Axel Boethius, advisor to Gustavus III of Sweden in that king's own archaeological interests, had spent some years in Rome as the first director of the Swedish Institute there. Upon his retirement he and his wife bought an apartment near the American Academy. He used its library daily in connection with his scholarly writing, and the inspiration that the quality of his mind and the generosity of his spirit gave to students at the Academy was beyond measurement. He conducted groups of fellows to ancient sites, advised them in their work, served on the library committee, and upon occasion brought the Swedish king to the Academy. He was admired, respected, and indeed loved by the Academy community.

The lively stream of Academy events flowed along established channels. Annual exhibitions of the fellows' work were opened by Ambassador Frederick Reinhardt. Spring concerts drew their enthusiastic audiences. Artists and scholars in residence, among them Otto Luening, composer, and Eric Sjöqvist, archaeologist, came and went. The era also brought the reluctant rejection of another gift of a villa, this time on Anacapri. Attractive as the villa might have been, the trustees declined because of "previous commitments in Italy."

The board underwent its inevitable changes. Myron Taylor died in 1959, the last of the old guard whose association with the Academy stretched back to the days of McKim. Barklie McKee Henry, Gilbert Highet, and Gordon Wasson came on the board. Wasson, a banker in the House of Morgan, served as secretary of the board from 1960 to 1963, when his place as secretary was taken by Sherman Baldwin and his place as trustee by James Kellum Smith, Jr., secretary of the Rockefeller Foundation, whose father had given such notable leadership to the Academy. The Academy owed Baldwin a great debt for his legal services over the years, untangling the complexities of foreign legalities and steering the Academy into safe waters. When Walter Baker, long a devoted and generous trustee, retired as treasurer in 1965, Smith filled in for a year until a new treasurer was found in William Johnstone, a recently retired vice-president of Bethlehem Steel who has since ably presided over the Academy's finances. Gardner Cox became a trustee in 1963; so did Elliott Cook Carter, Jr., FAAR '54. They had been respectively painter-in-residence and musician-in-residence during Kimball's directorship.

In 1965 Kimball was approaching retirement age. During the previous autumn, when he was in poor health, he had told Rapuano that "while he did not know precisely when he would retire" he thought the trustees should start thinking about his successor. The trustees very reluctantly accepted the inevitable. To lose the Kimballs was a serious business; to replace them extremely difficult. The board knew how much the Academy would miss the director and his wife in ways both large and small. There would be no more Kimball Christmas parties with puppet shows for the Little Fellows and presents for all, no more Kimball Christmas dinners with flaming plum puddings for the Academy family (ninety-eight of them, one year). The Kimballs' special kind of personal interest in the welfare of the fellows would also be missed by many who had come to rely on their sympathetic understanding, their encouragement, and their outspoken admiration of talent, which had drawn out the best in the men and women with whom they had worked. Kimball was awarded the Academy medal with this citation:

To you the Trustees of the American Academy in Rome owe an affection which they cannot adequately express and a debt of gratitude which they can never repay. Your warm humanity, wisdom and buoyant spirit made the Academy a happy home of high endeavor, which has raised the Academy to a pinnacle of good repute never before attained. We part from you with affection and regret.

They could not let him go entirely. A special committee was formed to arrange with Kimball his "further services to be rendered to the Academy for the next several years." Kimball continued to serve as a consultant, on fee, and kept in close touch with Academy affairs.

The trustees had appointed a committee to find Kimball's successor, but in September 1965 it reported that it proposed not to put any name in nomination until it had ascertained whether Frank Brown would be available for the directorship. When asked, Brown replied that he felt an obligation to utilize his long training as scholar and teacher; he did not see how he could do so if he must also meet "the administrative, social and promotional responsibilities that dissipate the real effectiveness and diminish the real dignity of the office." The reply pleased the trustees, whose confidence in Brown increased with his frank estimate of the job. They decided to tempt him by the offer of a competent assistant, as well as by the continuation of his professorship in charge of classical studies, and they asked him to come to New York to discuss these terms. Brown came and was persuaded, and by November 1 he and his wife were installed in the Villa Aurelia and he had taken up his new duties.

To relieve Brown of many of the daily details of administration, the board appointed Joseph Day Deiss vice-director in January 1966. Deiss had taken bachelor's and master's degrees at the University of Texas and then worked in industrial public relations in New York before setting off to Europe to write. He was author of several books, and his monograph on Herculaneum must have been a special link between himself and the archaeological director. It is regrettable that the appointment was not wholly successful. This was in part due to the number of decisions only a director could make and the number of functions at which no substitute for the director was acceptable. It was also due in part to Deiss's illness, which took him from active service in the fall of 1968. In any case, at the end of his short tenure the experiment of a vice-director was not repeated.

In the spring of 1966 the Academy held its first conference on urban problems under the optimistic title of The City as a Work of Art, to which experts came from Denmark, Switzerland, America, and many areas of Italy. The conference had been the result of Kimball's planning, and it aroused wide interest. It had a refreshing sidelight when Rome and its environs were used for observational field trips.

The new fellowship in environmental design began that fall and helped to offset the disappointment in the loss of another potential series of fellowships that the Academy had been very eager to receive. In 1963 John Walker had informed the Academy trustees that Chester Dale, the National Gallery's great benefactor, had left a bequest for fellowships of $5,000 each in painting, sculpture, and the history of art. Walker had proposed that these fellowships be used at the Academy. The Academy had accepted the suggestion and had been awaiting the outcome. In March 1968 Walker seemed to have secured agreement on the plan, but questions regarding the selection and management of the potential fellows were unresolved when in November he was forced to inform the trustees that the new legal counsel of the National Gallery had rejected as "contrary to the Testator's intention" the sharing of the Dale Fellowships with any other institution.

However, the Academy continued to attract other scholars who contributed the wealth of their learning. Ernest Nash reported over 12,500 classified and catalogued negatives in the Fototeca, which was a further attraction to classical study in Rome. It had changed its descriptive title from "the deposit of photographs of ancient Italian architecture" to "the Union collection of photographs at the American Academy." The geographic scope of the collection had gone beyond Italy.

A remarkable art historian had also come to work at the Academy. Richard Krautheimer was born in Bavaria and went to America in 1935. He remained no professor of the history of art, first at Vassar and then at the Institute of Fine Arts at New York University, which during his time there became outstanding. He came often to Rome, lived near the Academy and later in an Academy apartment. He worked there on his great *Corpus of Early Christian Basilicas*. He also brought with him the mutual advantage of a close connection with the New York Institute. Some of his students became fellows at the Academy—notably trustee James S. Ackerman, FAAR '52, now professor of fine arts at Harvard. In November 1968 Krautheimer was presented with the Medal for Outstanding Service to the Academy as a scholar who had "contributed incalculably to the distinction of the Academy as a center of research in art and archaeology."

The 1967 annual show of the fellows' work was an unusual success, with 350 guests at its opening by Ambassador Reinhardt and its 800 catalogues exhausted within a week. "Browsers" continued to invade it until the closing date. It had been held in the courtyard of the main building. The old museum was being moved from its space next to the entrance, and the whole northwest corner of the main building was being made over into an excellent series of exhibition rooms, which would open in time for the 1969 exhibition. The museum came to rest on the ground floor of the Villa Chiaraviglio, where the office of the professor of classical studies is also located. Most reports on Academy buildings and grounds are dreary reading, but one catches the eye. A plague of mosquitoes drove the archaeologist-director (or a henchman, very knowing in such matters) to dig for the source of a damp breeding ground beside the main building. It turned out to be a portion of the emperor Hadrian's aqueduct (built in A.D. 109) which was found to run twenty-eight feet below the *cortile*. It was drained. The mosquitoes vanished.

Demands on Brown's archaeological expertise increased when the Italian government asked him to direct the organizing, sorting, and classifying of excavated material in the Regia of the Roman Forum. Brown was already deeply involved in the excavation of Cosa, itself nearly a full-time operation, and yet he managed to continue to take his students on "Walks in Rome" to see the remains of Republican Rome and hear his comments on them. He instituted "Shop Talks," at which members of the Academy heard one of their group discuss his, or her, special project. These talks were a great success. Brown also continued to supervise the publication of the Academy's scholarly papers, *Memoirs* and *Papers and Monographs,* which now totaled over fifty volumes, and to which he himself was adding volumes on Cosa. It is difficult to imagine how he could have spread himself so widely over all that was done.

But no one could relieve the director of the burden of Academy finances, which he shared with the trustees. The year Brown had assumed office—that is, by December 1966—the market value of Academy holdings had fallen from approximately $8,300,000 to $6,900,000. At his first meeting with the trustees Brown confronted them with the usual assessment of the stringent financial situation, which, if the proposed changes and repairs to plant were to be made and the Academy's current program were to be carried out, would lead to deficit financing. The trustees were familiar with the refrain, but President Rapuano urged that the board consider at once how to add $2,000,000 to endowment. The Bollingen Foundation had to withdraw its support; the Ford Foundation, when approached, felt unable to help; to raise money was becoming increasingly difficult when even foundations felt the pinch. In 1967 Rapuano was authorized to consult a public relations firm.

In Brown's time the Academy's annual expenses and income ran roughly as follows: it spent $106,000 on fellowships, $125,000 on wages of Rome employees, $50,000 on staff, $61,000 on the New York office, and $62,000 on all the rest. Income from investments was approximately $315,000, from contributing universities and colleges about $63,000, and from philanthropic institutions some $26,000. The Academy was nearing its seventy-fifth anniversary. By curious, if not significant, coincidence, its budget was nearly seventy-five times greater than in 1894.

Gifts continued to come from many friends, and the Academy made a gift also. In 1967 the trustees did not hesitate to appropriate $5,000 to help restore the works of art damaged in Florence's fearful flood; members of the Academy in Rome raised over $1,000 for the same cause by a benefit concert. The library received some superb gifts. Its friends continued to send in steady amounts. In 1966 the Kress Foundation began an annual grant to the library of $2,500. Mrs. Frederick Hilles gave $50,000 in 1968 to be used as a fund for the purchase of books in memory of her cousin Marjorie Morse Dawson. That same year the American Musicological Society began to raise $5,000 a year to establish a music library at the Academy, while the library was also the beneficiary of one of its most loyal members when Professor Van Buren, who died at the age of eighty-nine, bequeathed his own collection of books and $172,000 as well.

Other friends gave generously, notably Mrs. Winthrop Rice, Whitney Shepardson, Richard Webel (FAAR '29), Stephen Currier, and Nicholas Roosevelt. The Association of Fellows of the American Academy sent $2,000 for Cosa, which was continuing to receive foundation support. Two other items were the equivalent of gifts: the official ruling of the United States Treasury that the Academy was entitled to full exemption from federal taxes, and the renewal of the Rinehart Fellowships in Sculpture, which the

Peabody Institute in Baltimore had abrogated in 1963. But, as almost always, the balance of credit to debit remained very precarious.

There were irreplaceable losses. Deaths of former fellows included Leo Sowerby, Paul Manship, and Barry Faulkner, and of members of the board, Whitney Shepardson and Barklie McKee Henry. It was especially hard to face the loss of Michael Rapuano when in November 1967 he asked the board to relieve him of its presidency as soon as possible. The magnitude of the work and responsibility of the post had so increased that, he said, a man could no longer carry it and his professional work at the same time. It took a full year to find his successor in trustee Rensselaer Lee, who bravely shouldered the load. Coming from the Department of Art and Archaeology at Princeton, Lee could not have devoted the time required had he not just become professor emeritus.

His first task was to find a new director. Frank Brown had carried on as long as he could, but his doubts in accepting the post had been confirmed. Fifty-five years earlier the trustees had appointed the head of one of its schools as director of the Academy, while continuing him in charge of his school. Although many of the circumstances of 1913 were different from those of 1968, an administrative principle had been twice violated. The results were equally hard on everyone—director, fellows, and staff. Brown had had four years of double-headed responsibility, most heavily felt when the vice-director had been unable to continue. It seemed to friends of the Academy that there was a waste of the talents of a great archaeologist and teacher when Brown was distracted from his leadership of the School of Classical Studies. In October 1969 he returned to his former position, to the delight of the classicists and congratulations from his well-wishers.

In August 1969 the president of the board announced "major administrative changes designed to give greater strength and effectiveness to its operations in Rome." A new office of executive vice-president, to serve in the New York office, had been created to take much of the load of Academy business from the shoulders of the president and to raise funds for the Academy. The trustees appointed to that post Reginald Allen, who had been an executive with the Philadelphia Orchestra, the Metropolitan Opera, and the Lincoln Center. He is married to Helen Howe, monologuist and novelist. They went to Rome to direct the Academy from October

1969 to March 1970, so that he could thoroughly acquaint himself with every facet of the institution he was thereafter to manage from New York. In March 1970 the new director would take over, having by then become director emeritus of the Addison Gallery of American Art at Phillips Academy in Andover. He was Bartlett Hayes, Jr., old friend of the Academy as an art historian in residence. The success of the new arrangement will be recorded in the next history of the American Academy. Its seventy-fifth birthday, which this account celebrates, took place in October 1969.

XII

Cosa

ONE more chapter must be added to the account of the Academy's first seventy-five years. Archaeological excavations were not, until 1948, a regular activity of the Academy. Students in classics had assisted, somewhat sporadically, in excavations at Hadrian's Villa and at the Roman Forum, working under the direction of Italian archaeologists in accordance with regulations of the Italian government. But after World War II a change in policy had made it possible for the Academy to secure permission to conduct its own excavations provided it could acquire a promising site and adequate funds. It was then that its trustees appointed Frank Brown professor in charge of the School of Classical Studies and director of excavations.

Brown arrived in Rome in July 1947. Before the year was out, it was reported at a trustee meeting that "Dr. Brown had been looking into the possibility of a site for excavation . . . and is interested in Ansedonia, an Etruscan site about eighty miles north of Rome on the Tuscan coast." The trustees were much inclined to go ahead with the work but could not then commit the Academy to finance a new undertaking. When, however, in the spring of 1948 the Italian government sanctioned preliminary soundings with excavations to follow should the soundings give promise, and when the owners of the site, the Marchese and the Marchesa San Felice di Monteforte, generously gave permission for the use of their land, the trustees voted funds for a modest beginning.

The modern town of Ansedonia lies on and below the shoulders of a high promontory just southeast of the landlocked lagoon and town of Orbetello. The outward face of the promontory drops steeply to sea, and on the inland side it is separated from the fat lowlands of the Maremma by the old Via Aurelia, which, sometime during the second century B.C., the Romans had pushed out from the Forum Aurelia to connect the promontory with Rome. On its craggy summit lie the remains of Cosa, a fortress-town whose ruins, except for the solid city walls, were covered with thorn and rosemary bushes growing from the pitted limestone outcrops until the excavations of 1948 began to clear them away.

Rome's choice of the promontory had been a strategic one. Rome had been at war with the Etruscans of the neighborhood for a century but had finally defeated them and cut them off from access to the sea by treaty. It now sought to consolidate its position by establishing a fortified colony at the most favorable spot on the Tuscan coast. The promontory offered natural advantages. Its high escarpment on the seaward side made its summit difficult to attack, while the town walls were defensible on the less steep slopes of the landward side. The configuration of beach and lagoon at the foot of the promontory made possible a port ingeniously contrived by the Romans, as later researches revealed.

Whether or not Cosa had been the site of an earlier Etruscan or a still earlier Pelasgian town had long been debated. There had been Etruscan settlements nearby. Archaeologists of the nineteenth century, reaching their conclusions without benefit of excavations, and basing them first on references by Virgil, Horace, Strabo, Livy, Valleius, and Pliny and secondly on what were believed to be Etruscan methods of wall-building, thought Cosa to have been built on the site of an Etruscan town named Cusi. But the findings of the Academy archaeologists led to a different conclusion. It is now known that the Cosa which they uncovered was built in 273 B.C. by Rome's military engineers.

The history of Cosa is brief. The town was founded as a military outpost north of Rome, for much the same reason and in the same year that Paestum was founded to the south. Cosa's port was a naval stronghold which also flourished commercially as a material link in the chain of supplies to Spain. Its strength is revealed in an historical footnote: when in 77 B.C. Lepidus led to Cosa the survivors of his defeat at the hands of Catullus, he was able to secure there enough ships to embark them all for Sardinia. It was fitting that the dolphin should have been the symbol of Cosa.

Its importance dwindled a few centuries after its founding. The surrounding countryside had become thoroughly Roman; local warfare was but a memory; the western Mediterranean was pacified. Military and naval grounds for Cosa's existence vanished.

The harbor silted up, malaria struck from nearby stagnant marshes, and the youth of Cosa drifted away to seek better opportunities elsewhere. Tradition records that by the first century A.D. a fugitive slave found the place so solitary that he was able to hide there in safety. During the dark centuries that followed even the name of Cosa was forgotten, or recalled only as "empty and demon-haunted." The false renaissance of the thirteenth century brought Cosa back to life for a few years, but after taking part in local rivalries and embroilments, medieval Cosa was almost totally destroyed in 1329 by a punitive Sienese army. From that time the hill lay untenanted, untilled, and almost unknown for more than six hundred years.

The Academy's first campaign of excavation at Cosa began on May 1 and lasted until June 23, 1948, the normal span of the annual excavation season. The satisfaction in discoveries that followed was tempered by constant awareness that funds were limited and continuance uncertain. Excavations were conducted with the greatest possible economy. Brown wrote:

In this as in following campaigns the cordial generosity of the owners of the site, the Marchese and Marchesa di Monteforte, relieved us of the necessity of spending a part of our limited budget for the lease and purchase of land. Similarly the heavy expenses of building living and working quarters and of buying excavating equipment which would have exhausted the funds at our disposal, were avoided by an arrangement with the contractor engaged in developing the locality as a summer resort. He placed a newly-built villa at our disposal, and we in turn hired fifteen or twenty workmen and the equipment, from him. This arrangement was continued through the second campaign May 1 to June 30, 1949.

After giving a warmly felt tribute to the Italian government for permission to excavate Cosa and for the interest and help of the personnel of the national and local offices of antiquities and fine arts, Brown continued: "Our first three weeks in Cosa were naturally spent on careful mapping of the site, and survey of the visible remains on its surface. The results of this survey . . . furnished us with the outlines, amazingly complete, of the town plan of a Roman colony of the third century B.C."

The work began to reveal the nature and significance of the well-known but little understood site and to throw light on a most crucial but obscure period of early Roman history. Cosa had been drawn up as a single conception and laid down as a single act, and that a Roman one. The excavations largely centered on the highest point of the saddle-shaped summit, clearly the *area sacra* of the town. At the outset the Romans had built a small platform there. Standing on it, augurs could observe the flight of birds and other signs and portents to do with the auspicious laying out of the city. Near the platform Academy archaeologists found a small natural crevasse which held the remains of burnt offerings traditionally made before actual building might begin. Subsequently the altar of this sacrificial pit became the focal point about which Cosa's temples in the *area sacra* were oriented.

Before the first four campaigns of excavation, 1948 through 1951, had ended, two temples were uncovered. The *via sacra* that led to the temples was also revealed and below, in the forum, a large basilica-odeum of the second and first centuries B.C. These structures and their arrangement followed the usual pattern for new colonial towns, as did the town plan itself. From the Capitolium, the largest temple on the summit, the *via sacra* ran down the swale of the saddleback and up to the other crest (as yet unexcavated). With the exception of these two areas on the crests and the oblong forum lying below and between them, the rest of Cosa was a grid of streets running so closely up to the walls themselves that little or no unused ground was found within the thirty-four acres enclosed by the walls.

The walls, which contained three fortified, arched gates and one postern, were a notable feature of Cosa, and a great part of them still stands, firm, dramatic, and beautifully constructed. Varying in height from twelve to thirty feet, and five or six feet thick; strengthened by twenty towers of up to forty feet in height, whose remains are still visible, they circled for a kilometer and a half the boundaries of the fortified city. The large polygonal stones are, on their outer surface, so smooth and closely fitted without mortar that they seem like an intricate picture puzzle standing on edge. Many of Cosa's citizens probably lived outside the walls but came within them in time of war for refuge and in time of peace to market, to govern, and to be governed. Refuting the guesses of earlier speculators, the Academy archaeologists firmly concluded that "nothing was observed or found which might be attributed without question to the hands of Etruscan builders," and that "Cosa was a compact example of late Roman colonization, the

fruit of long practice and tradition." "Two events give absolute
dates: the founding of the colony in 273 B.C. and its reinforcement
by a thousand new colonist families in 193 B.C. Coins found in
significant contexts date other events between these fixed points."

In January 1952, Brown reported to the trustees that the four
years of excavation had justified his most optimistic expectations.
The site, he told them, was rich in new evidence about one of the
least illumined periods of early Roman history, and further excavations should throw even more light on it. But if it were to be
continued the Academy should have a qualified archaeologist to
supervise the diggings. With the expectation that Brown would
shortly be called back to Yale, the trustees within six weeks acted
upon his advice by appointing Lawrence Richardson, Jr. as deputy
director of excavations. He and his wife, Emeline Hill Richardson,
added a distinguished chapter to the research at Cosa.

Success bred success, but inevitably it bred expense. From the
beginning the trustees had found it difficult to maintain this ad-
mittedly important undertaking without imperiling other, regular
activities of the Academy. Brown and his associates had achieved
remarkable results with extremely small funds, but each year
continuance became increasingly uncertain. The archaeologist who
directs work of this scope should have assurance of steady financing for a period of at least ten years. Brown had worked quietly
and continuously to secure outside help but had not so far been
successful. Regretfully the trustees saw him return to Yale in 1952
as Thacher Professor of Latin. In 1954 the excavations at Cosa
faltered; in 1955 they were indefinitely discontinued. Richardson
and the Academy men did some digging at Paestum, but Cosa was
not forgotten.

At the October 1955 meeting of the trustees another plea was
made for Cosa. Walter C. Baker, chairman of the committee on
classical studies, urged that the work was too important to abandon
and that a special effort should be made to secure funds to continue it. Partly as a result of this, and at their request, Brown
addressed the trustees on February 21, 1956, on "reactivating"
the excavations. But though they greatly desired to do so the
trustees were obliged to record that renewal of the work "cannot
and should not be a charge on the overall budget of the Academy
to the detriment of its principal functions."

The situation was discouraging. Then at last help came to the

Academy. The Bollingen, the Old Dominion, and the Thorne foundations provided funds that directly or indirectly brought the Cosa project back to life. Late in 1956 the trustees approved a budget that included an appropriation of $6,000 to renew excavations. In January 1962 Brown accepted an appointment to be effective the following October as professor in charge of classical studies at the Academy. In November 1963, Director Richard Kimball reported to the trustees on plans to start digging again.

The Academy at this point hoped to secure permission to erect a building at Cosa at an estimated cost of fifteen thousand dollars, to provide storage for the valuable findings, as well as to house the workers' tools, with the thought that this building might ultimately become a museum of artifacts and works of art found there. A few months later the San Felices not only gave the Academy permission to build the much needed building but offered to give the land for it and for a road leading to it. Meanwhile Columbia University had asked to join the excavations and to share the costs, while leaving the direction in the hands of the Academy. All these were offers that the Academy could not fail to accept gratefully.

So it was that on May 3, 1963, after an interval of ten years, Brown again started work at Cosa. In addition to four scholars in art and architecture from Columbia, his team included three fellows of the Academy and two former fellows. The new building went up. The nucleus of the long-planned museum had been begun. The next summer the excavators not only cleared around a third temple, finding many terra-cotta and mural decorations that had belonged to it, but they made a rare find, which brought them to the front page of the world press. Toiling under an unusually hot Italian sun, a worker uncovered a pottery jar buried beneath the floor of a closet, which proved to contain 2,004 Roman denarii dating from the early second century B.C. to about 72 B.C. They were in excellent condition, some fresh from the mint. It was the largest find of coins uncovered by a professional team of archaeologists in Italy.

Free at last from financial worry, successful years followed at Cosa. Further gifts from the Old Dominion Foundation and further contributions by Columbia made it possible to have two teams of excavators at work on separate assignments. In 1965 the Thorne Foundation gave a grant toward the cost of the museum-workshop.

Harpur College of the State University of New York at Bing-
hampton joined the enterprise in 1968 under Academy direction
and shared the cost. Also in that year the National Endowment
for the Humanities gave funds to support an amphibious survey of
Cosa's port.

The survey was excitingly successful. Divers studied the plan
and structure of the artificial outer harbor as well as stretches of
the ship channel leading from it to a lagoon below the promontory.
They found elements of an ancient mole, including sections of the
wooden construction frame that had endured for over two thousand
years. They found what appeared to be the base of a large statue.
It began to be possible to reconstruct the original lay of land
and water, and the steps the Romans had taken to adapt the site
to their purpose. Where the promontory jutted into the sea it was
flanked on either side by beach and long petrified dunes that paral-
leled the shore and formed barriers behind which lay lagoons.
Where dune abutted cliff at the southeast face of the promontory,
it had been dredged away to open a channel into the lagoon. To
keep its entrance from silting up, a curving mole was built out
from the cliff. Incoming boats came out of the sea swell within
the protecting arm of the mole before turning under the steep face
of the cliff, which had been scarped vertically for about one
hundred and forty meters, to run up the channel into the tranquil
lagoon.

A further piece of ingenuity helped to keep the channel mouth
free from silt and attests to the engineering skill of those who conceived it. A deep, natural fissure ran at an angle from the mouth
of the newly made channel to the outer sea-face of the promontory.
It was cleared and deepened so that water from the sea rushing
through the fissure into the channel could scour it and keep it free.
When later the fissure itself became blocked, yet another was contrived for the same purpose. Cosa's lagoon-harbor was, in this way,
admirably secured for ancient shipping, enclosed, sheltered from
prevailing winds, and protected by the fortified town not five
hundred meters above it. A similar barrier of dunes landlocked a
lagoon to the north of the promontory, making a second placid
sheet of water dominated by the hill. All these waters, then as now,
teemed with tunny and sardines, eels, anchovies, and other fish.

The story in sequence and detail of the archaeological excavations and findings at Cosa is admirably told in two volumes written

by Professor Brown and published in the Academy *Memoirs* of
1951 and 1963. A third volume is in preparation. Emeline Hill
Richardson's authoritative book, *The Etruscans* (Chicago, 1964),
supports the findings with its study of the quantity of terra-cotta
objects unearthed at Cosa. No summary could do justice to the
scholarly content of these writings, nor to the meticulous, method-
ical, inspired reconstruction of Cosa's past from the rough remains
of the ancient town. But an attempt must be ventured here to evalu-
ate the significance of the work.

Archaeologists have a particular interest in Cosa because of the
unity and completeness both of its purpose and of its physical construction. It was a creation out of whole cloth, by a group of col-
onists of known origin and at a known date. Within a relatively
short time of its founding it was completed, and it underwent few
structural changes before its "early" or Roman period came to
an end, again at a known date. It was a remarkable example of a
certain period of Roman colonial building marking the severance
from the influence of Cosa's Etruscan neighbors and revealing the
classic "Italic" style of Rome that prevailed from the middle of the
second century B.C. for another century, before Greek influence
became dominant. That the founding of Cosa was a repetition on a
smaller scale of the traditional founding of Rome was of special
interest to the archaeologist, since most vestiges of earliest Rome
have long since vanished under later building. In addition "the
excavations uncovered such enormous quantities of architectural
terracotta decorations that it was possible to recreate the complete
decorations of all the temples excavated there, with all their patch-
ings and refurbishings, from the date of their construction to that
of their abandonment." They not only helped to determine the
chronology of the temples; they also gave a full picture of one set
of decorations of a known period, heretofore obscure and difficult,
from which future terra-cotta finds may now be more accurately
dated.

When the publications on Cosa appeared scholars expressed
their opinion of the work done there. Professor Erik Sjöqvist
wrote of the Capitolium, its largest temple, "What it means to our
knowledge to get the remains of such a temple painstakingly in-
vestigated and intelligently interpreted cannot be overestimated. It
is a great contribution to the history of Roman architecture." "No
whole Italian site has been dug with such care," another leading

scholar, M. W. Frederickson, wrote of Cosa. "The united talents
of F. E. Brown upon the structure of the two temples and the Capitolium; of L. Richardson upon the architectural terracottas, and of
Mrs. E. H. Richardson on the sculptures, have produced a re-
markably congruent account of an intricate site, which not only
illuminated the history of the town, but also . . . the darker mists
of Republican archaeology" (*Journal of Roman Studies*, 1963).
Frederickson added that Cosa was the most imposing monument of
its kind in Italy. "Few places anywhere more powerfully stir the
imagination."

The Academy as an institution for education and research
gained in standing and prestige. As the first excavation undertaken
by the Academy under the new and more flexible policies of the
Italian government, it was watched by the archaeological world,
and its success redounded to the Academy's credit.

To the fellows and other students who had been privileged to see
a closely controlled and clearly planned piece of archaeological
work unfold, it was a rare opportunity. No comparable teaching
of field archaeology for students could be found elsewhere in
Italy. Moreover they shared in every aspect of the labor of this
illuminating research.

Probably the most exciting discoveries have already been made
at Cosa, but there remains much to be done. Meanwhile the visitor
may wander among the uncovered foundations of the ancient city.
Some of its cisterns are still filled with rain water, their arches
half hidden under roots of olive trees that grow abundantly over
the promontory. Most of the magnificent outer wall still stands, and
under the afternoon's slanting sunlight it assumes an austere and
moving beauty. The *via sacra* with its wide, well-fitted paving
stones leads to the summit where the great temple walls, partly
shattered, but in part erect, dominate the scene. The museum-
workshop is near the entrance to the excavated area. It is characteristic of the whole Cosa enterprise, reflecting both its professional
quality and its sense of being a family affair. Director Kimball
lent his architectural talent to its design; Professor Brown and the
resourceful mason-caretaker, Ivo Picciolini, adapted its details to
the demands of function and site. Where money was not available,
devotion and ingenuity filled the need. The court has many levels,
some paved as they were found, by Roman hands. Under the
shadow of olive trees that have been left where they twist up out

of the paving, there is an open shed. Here students may spread their current finds, and here the amphorae and the vines somehow bring together the Italy of ancient Rome and the Italy of today.

Those of the Academy who uncovered Cosa, who struggled to finance it, who endured a pinch in their own budgets to carry it on, cannot but feel a lasting satisfaction in the distinction the excavation brings to the Academy.

XIII

The Future

THE Academy's first seventy-five years justify pride in its past but do not provide grounds for unqualified satisfaction with its present. Its foundations have been so shaken that one cannot escape the questions: where does the Academy stand today and where will it stand tomorrow?

Before evaluating its position a sharp distinction must be drawn between its two schools. The appropriateness of the Academy's School of Classical Studies in Rome is not in question. Italy is an excellent place for it: facilities for the study of classics in Rome, and in the Academy itself, are among the best to be found. The School has attracted scholars of first-rate quality and has steadily made important contributions to the history of civilization, to archaeology, and to the study of classical philology. The standing of the Academy in these fields is deservedly high. It is probable that if its trustees were to decide to devote the Academy to classical studies alone, the need for reassessment would vanish. What follows is therefore principally concerned with the Academy's School of Fine Arts.

Seventy-five years ago Charles McKim was quite clear in his mind as to the purpose of this School. Since its educational aim was to maintain the classic tradition, the School should be placed in Rome and devote itself to studies of all that Rome had to offer. At the outset Professor Ware was the only founder who openly disagreed with the strict regimen that McKim's ideal required. Ware felt that the maturing artist should have greater freedom to work out his own cultural destiny. McKim had his way, and the School of Fine Arts was established on the principle that the artist, especially the architect, could not go far in his profession without a thorough grounding in the techniques of the classical past, a steeping in its history and in examples of its culture. Since this was a rational, clear-cut ideal; since it was supported by staff and fellows who accepted it; since it was in accord with current opinion, the Academy had public approval during those first decades.

The causes of the shift in public opinion regarding the education of the artist must be left to the art historian, but shift it did, with notable acceleration after each world war. Like most institutions, the Academy reacted slowly. It adapted its original program to the new concepts sporadically and incompletely, without wholeheartedly accepting or rejecting them. The voice of the critic grew louder and more adverse, characterizing the work of the fellows as "academic," "imitative," "lifeless," and full of "ingenious stylizations and archaic tricks." The prestige of the Academy fell as the caliber of many who applied for its fellowships declined. In 1957 Francis Taylor, looking back to 1920 when he was at the Academy, told his fellow trustees:

In my student days the Academy was, in a sense, a protracted finishing school for persons of little better than average talent who had received the Prix de Rome. The conspicuous absence of our graduate Fellows now in their late forties or fifties from the great national exhibitions of American art is not a circumstance which one can lightly dismiss by making "Modern Art" the whipping boy. It is a phenomenon which strikes deeply at the root of the matter. . . . The emphasis upon the cosy and the *comme il faut* had reached such a point that at the end of the War there were many thoughtful persons who questioned whether or not the Academy should be revived except as a research institute for archeology and the history of art.

To paraphrase another critic, the limp hand of yesterday's taste lay heavily on the Academy during the twenties.

Gradually the Academy eased its formal requirements. Collaborative projects were abandoned. The fellows were given their heads: Francis Taylor went on to say in 1957 that they were "no longer treated as seminarians; they are recognized as mature individuals to whom the administration is readily available on demand, but not disposed to hold their hands or breathe down their necks."

By that time the Academy had swung almost a full circle, but in doing so it had blurred its public image. Where there had been a regimen there was now none, and the Academy that had once stood clearly for a traditional education in the arts was now hard to distinguish from other schools of art, except that it was in Rome. Its intellectual structure, its purpose, and its methods were continually defined and redefined, depending upon those who administered it, those who attended it, and those who wrote about it.

One of the latter was Herbert Kubly, a professional writer and professor, who in 1962 wrote a privately circulated essay describing the Academy after spending a year there as a "guest-in-residence." He reacted favorably to its permissiveness. He indicated his sympathy with the fellows' desire to escape from the "irrelevance" of classical and medieval culture and from the limitations of past Academy educational traditions. He wrote with approval that the Academy offered "no school, no plan of instruction; it has no teachers," but was "a workshop of predominantly youthful scholars and artists . . . engaged in an astonishing variety of projects."

This was, he concluded, a far better program than the initial aim of the Academy "to spread the gospel of classic revival in the arts" and its attempt to emulate the French Academy, that regrettable "bastion of traditionalism" and deplorable exponent of an outworn "pattern of conformism." He applauded the move of the Academy "to meet the needs of changing times" by admitting wives and children of the fellows to Academy living quarters and turning one of its gardens into a playground where "as many as fifteen toddlers could be seen romping there at a time."

But Kubly recognized that the new dispensations caused new difficulties. "Wives bring their own set of problems . . . idle wives may create mischief." Moreover, with no guidance from the Academy's staff, the less mature fellows often wasted time at the beginning of their year. They failed to choose firmly and permanently between the variety of opportunities in study, in creative art, and in the varied attractions that Rome offers in such profusion. They were drawn away from hard, steady work by the enticements of travel and by social life far beyond their previous experience. Kubly consoled himself that the "inspired indifference" now practiced by the Academy staff would in time induce in its fellows that "disciplined regularity" which would assure greater success in the arts and justify their wasted months.

In 1969 Russell Lynes described the Academy in an article in *Harper's.* He too had been its guest for some months, but he saw no "disciplined regularity" ahead for the Academy. After reporting that even its administrators were privately regretful that not enough of its fellows were "first class ones," he wrote that "the Academy is an anachronism in many respects, but it buzzes with a vitality that an anachronism has no business to. . . . It ought to be hopelessly out of date, but it isn't." Lynes discovered, however, that many of the fellows did not agree with him. What more, he asked them, could artists want than this freedom to work, and the place to do so under nearly ideal conditions? "The answer is, 'Plenty.' "

"Rome is a dead city," a composer said to me. "Musically, Berlin is more interesting."

"It's like there's no reason anymore for a painter to come here. . . . It's like being lost for two years when you ought to be making it at home."

"There's nothing new in architecture here. There's Nervi, but he's old and he's really an engineer. Rome is beautiful, but I don't learn anything from it that's going to teach me how to house people in the ghettos back in the States."

And a sculptor who thoroughly enjoys being in Rome said, "From my point of view it's great here. I get my stuff cast [in bronze] at half or less what it costs me at home. But that doesn't mean anything to the kids. Bronze to them is archaic; they work in plastics and junk . . . you name it!"

Lynes found that most of the fellows he talked with, except in the School of Classical Studies, "contended that they would just as soon be anywhere that they could work, as be in Rome. It's a free ride to Europe, though, and 'What the hell!' "

Indeed, if contact with man's artistic inheritance is no longer "relevant" to the artist's education, why should he go to Rome? In 1969 there are many full-fledged schools of art in America; in 1894 there were almost none. Numerous scholarships and fellowships are now granted to young artists either to those schools or to study abroad at any spot of their choosing. Talented young Americans have opportunities today unimaginable in McKim's time. These are facts difficult to ignore. Should the Academy wish the Rome Prize to be the hallmark of unusual talent, it would again have to carve out a special place for itself in the world of art.

One of its trustees put his finger on this lack of crisp definition, of unique characterization of the Academy today. Barklie McKee Henry told the trustees in 1963 that the Academy had "no sharp intellectual focus. It seems more like a collection of established customs and habits than an exciting intellectual adventure." The sudden death of this valuable trustee brought to an end what might have been a discerning exploration of the Academy's purpose. A few of the administrative changes Henry proposed have gone into effect, relieving its top officers of some burdens and giving them more time to reflect. But perhaps the most logical, although to some it seemed iconoclastic, of Henry's proposals—that women be elected trustees—received the least recorded consideration by the Academy board. He did not amplify the suggestion, since by that time the trustees must have understood its significance. He undoubtedly recognized the special contribution women could make as members of the board, in their understanding of the needs and points of view of women fellows, as well as in their capacity for hard, practical work.

Henry also sensed the loss of tone the Academy had suffered, and made some suggestions how to recover it. Had he lived he might have come to the realization that even these proposed reforms did not go deep enough. If the Academy wishes to project a compelling image of a unique school of fine arts, it must think its program through more clearly and state it in more clear-cut terms. If what it has to offer is primarily quality, then it will presumably attract quality, and its public image will take care of itself.

What has the Academy to offer? It offers time: a year or more, gratis, in which the artist is freed from the stridency and pressures of competition in America; time to develop his particular skill; time in which to absorb, to reflect, to ripen. It offers him a work-place of his own, food, shelter, income, travel money, entreés, the stimulation of gifted companions, the prestige of the Academy. It offers him Rome.

It should perhaps offer him something more: a personal challenge within the Academy itself. At present the Academy demands little from its artist-denizens. Many of them accept the role of takers rather than givers, transients who move through the Academy's halls with apparent indifference to any self-imposed obligation to their benefactor. This is not just a reflection of today's casual mores. For fifty-five years the Academy on the Janiculum has turned out creators of beauty with almost as little effect upon its own physical aspect as if they had never set foot there. There is little evidence of concern for its appearance from those who have inhabited it, few traces of the landscape architect's hand or the painter's sense of color, or legacies of those nostalgic accretions that come from years of use. To an outsider the Academy's atmosphere is as impersonal as a post office.

Perhaps the Academy should be no more than a lodging. Perhaps it can have no other identity than its buildings. But what of the staff and the guests-in-residence? Are they (any administrative duties aside) simply onlookers, fellow lodgers? Or are they living symbols of the Academy itself, chosen for their quality, and guardians of its tone? Who else can sustain warmth and humor, dignity and standards, and possibly even encourage a few traditional ceremonies—if they are meaningful ones—that can give continuity to an institution? Who else can provide that "intellectual focus" of which Henry spoke; can be the abrasives that sharpen wits, so that living up to the Academy is a challenge? The expectation that its fellows would want to meet excellence with excellence in all aspects of Academy life should give added value to the Rome Prize.

There are other questions that might be asked in a reassessment, of which the most important might be how wisely the Academy has selected its fellows. To measure the qualitative potential of a creative artist is the most difficult of all selective tasks. It requires the subjective judgments of men of demonstrated perceptivity. How rare such men seem to be! The wise perception of talent and character is, as Chaucer suggested, the most delicate and difficult of the arts. Genius of a special kind is needed to recognize potential genius of a special kind. Like thieves, it takes a man of quality to catch a man of quality. The choice of men to serve on selection juries of the Academy becomes one of its most crucial functions.

Administrative officers of the Rhodes Scholarships and the Guggenheim Fellowships, and of some university graduate schools, have long recognized this fact and have made the selection of selectors a constant subject of analysis. They must not only select men of rare perception; they must also study the records of the beneficiaries they have chosen and judge the selectors accordingly. One wonders how closely and persistently the trustees and officers of the Academy have studied the perceptions, the possible biases, and the batting averages of each juryman of award. One wonders how thoroughly each juryman has tested his own judgment by analyses of the performances of prizewinners for whom he voted.

But the finest imaginable selection committee cannot choose worthy candidates if worthy candidates do not apply. It has been proposed that Academy fellowships be awarded only to those candidates who are not only of high quality but have a real desire to study in Rome—possibly filling only a few of the available places and allowing fellowship funds to accumulate. Supporters of this plan feel that it would greatly enhance Academy morale as well as raise the standards of the Academy, its public reputation, and its attractiveness to talented aspirants.

Another suggestion envisages the gradual development of an academy for the arts and classics along the lines of All Souls' College in Oxford, which has long served as a stimulus to its fellows, to Oxford, and to England's intellectual elite. The Academy would seem well adapted to become a quiet residential center for distinguished fellows of all ages, on varying terms of stipend and residence depending upon the circumstances of each case. Many might hold residence fellowships on a long-term or indefinite basis and maintain a consistent tone for the institution. To such a residential group would frequently be added the stimulus of distinguished guests from many countries and many areas of culture, briefly resident or with regular dining and common-room privileges. Such a development, it has been argued, would place less emphasis than the present Academy upon preparing young men of graduate student age for professional careers. It would attract men with already established reputations who do not feel they ought to be "making it at home," and who would strike intellectual sparks from one another at the highest level of the creative and scholarly arts. Such an institution should in addition become a notable center of individual guidance and encouragement for Americans who come to Rome on their own initiative and perhaps at their own expense, partly for the associations the Academy might give them. Such a plan, like the previous one, should improve the quality and morale of the Academy by limiting its residence to those who valued it highly. Both plans might prove less expensive than the present one.

Other friends of the Academy have offered suggestions that, in various forms, propose that the Academy affiliate with one or more American universities, foundations, or associations of high distinction, which might share its costs, select its fellows, determine its program, and direct its operations—or do none of these. The proposal brings to mind the Harvard association with Berenson's I Tatti, and the considerable number of study centers in Europe sponsored by one or more American universities. Most of these proposals favor the retention by the Academy of its financial and administrative independence.

Of other suggestions, one that at first seems the most drastic might prove the simplest and most practical. The Academy would announce that until further notice its existing fellowships would be available for use at whatever place in the world the newly elected fellow might propose and the Academy approve. Supervision of such fellows might seldom be necessary but where needed could be arranged without difficulty or appreciable expense. In fact, it might develop that existing overhead expenses of the Academy would decrease and a larger percent of its operating funds become available to support its fellowship program. Such a plan does not lack precedents, including the Fulbright and Guggenheim fellowships. Given a free choice, it might be that a considerable number of the fellows might elect to go to Rome, where the Academy would certainly be in operation for the use of fellows in the classical studies.

There is no need or intention to end this account of a distinguished American institution on a falling note. Although its trustees are faced with issues more difficult than were their predecessors, the Academy's present problems are by no means insuperable. Earlier trustees were chiefly concerned with material problems: money, buildings, expansion, and the all-too-tangible crises of world wars. Such problems, like most enemies of Hercules, could be wrestled with and thrown to the ground—where they remained. But the current issues derive from imponderables, and though thrown down may, like Antaeus, rise to fight again. Those who determine the Academy's future must have patience, balance, courage, and, above all, imagination. Early principles, ancient loyalties, fixed values, established systems—as well as new idols, vague emotions, easy rationalizations, and the uncertainties of the uninformed—all these must be seen for neither more nor less than they are. Each can become an obstruction to ultimate wisdom. The solutions, like the challenges, must be initially in terms of abstractions, and this is the hardest of all cooperative tasks. But the Academy's record for three-quarters of a century is not lightly to be dismissed. It provides reason to believe that it will continue to renew itself, to win distinction in its service to the arts and letters. After all, it bears the seal of Janus, ancient Roman deity, who guards the gates to heaven and ever presides over the beginning of things.

Appendices

Dramatis Personae

A need for brevity has compelled deletion from this account of many references to other builders and friends of the Academy. The following list includes their names as an essential part of the record.

ABBEY, EDWARD AUSTIN, 1852–1911. A mural painter, he exhibited regularly at the Royal Academy from 1890; worked with McKim on the Boston Public Library decorations; and in 1905 was one of the incorporators of the American Academy.

ABBEY, MRS. EDWARD AUSTIN (Mary Gertrude Mead), d. 1925. She married Abbey in 1890 and in 1925 bequeathed in her husband's name the Abbey Scholarships in Mural Painting to be jointly administered by the National Academy of Arts and the American Academy.

ABBOTT, FRANK FROST, 1860–1924. Professor of Latin at Chicago 1894–1908 and at Princeton 1908–24, he was annual professor at the American School of Classical Studies in Rome 1901–2 and a trustee of the Academy from February 1911. He was president of the American Philological Association and published ten volumes on classical subjects.

ABBOTT, SAMUEL APPLETON BROWN, 1846–1930. Originally a lawyer and called "Judge" by McKim and others, he was police commissioner in Boston 1887–89 and a trustee and sometime president of the Boston Public Library 1895–04. In 1892 he traveled with McKim in Europe, and also on later trips. He was a trustee of the original American School of Architecture in Rome and its director 1897–1900. In 1905 he was one of the incorporators of the Academy.

ABRAMOWITZ, MAX, 1908– . He received an M.S. from Columbia in 1931 and after two years at the Paris Beaux Arts settled down to the practice of architecture in New York, later becoming a partner of Wallace Harrison. He was also associate professor of fine arts at Yale 1939–42. He was awarded the Legion of Merit for his services in World War II and is a Benefactor of the Academy.

ACKERMAN, JAMES SLOSS, 1919– . B.A. Yale 1941 and Ph.D. New York University 1952, he was a research fellow of the Academy 1949–52, and in 1964 he became a trustee of the Academy. Since 1960 he has been professor of fine arts at Harvard, and was chairman of that department 1963–68. He is a distinguished historian of Renaissance architecture.

ADAMS, EDWARD DEAN, 1846–1931. An international banker and director of railroads, he was a trustee of the National Research Council, the Kahn Foundation, the Metropolitan Museum, and the American Commission for Devastated Europe after World War I. McKim, Mead, and White designed residences for him on Madison Avenue in 1885 and at Rumson, N.J., 1888–91. He was a trustee of the Academy and in 1913 succeeded J. P. Morgan as a member of its finance committee. His gift to the Academy made him a life member in 1910.

ADAMS, FREDERICK B., JR., 1910– . He went from college into a business career in New York and was soon a director of several companies and foundations and president of the New York Historical Society and the Bibliographical Society of America. Those interests led him from business into the directorship of the Morgan Library in 1948, in which post he was notably successful; he retired from it in 1968. He was a trustee of the American Academy in Rome 1966–71.

ADAMS, HERBERT, 1858–1945. He studied architecture in Paris and won many awards for his work. He was sometime president of the National Academy of Design. He was a trustee of the American Academy in Rome 1909–45 and vice-president 1941–44. His gifts to the Academy made him one of its life members.

ALDRICH, CHESTER HOLMES, 1871–1940. He studied architecture at the Paris Beaux Arts 1898–1900 and from 1903 was practicing in New York as a partner in Delano and Aldrich. He served with the Red Cross in Italy 1917–19 and received three Italian decorations. He was a trustee of the American Academy in Rome from 1925 and its director in Rome 1935–40.

ALDRICH, NELSON WILMARTH, 1841–1915. A member of the House of Representatives 1879–83, he was senator from Rhode Island 1881–1911 and very influential among Republican senators.

ALDRICH, WILL S. He was a Rotch Scholar 1894–97 at the American School of Architecture in Rome during its first three years and in interim charge of the school 1896–97. He was an architect in the offices of McKim, Mead, and White 1903–10.

ALLEN, REGINALD, 1905– . He served on the board of directors and then as manager of the Philadelphia Orchestra Company until 1949 when he went to New York as business manager of the Metropolitan Opera Company. From 1958 to 1962 he served as executive director for performing arts at Lincoln Center. In September 1969 he became executive vice-president of the American Academy in Rome and presided over its affairs there until succeeded by the new director in March 1970, when he took over the direction of its New York office, where he served until December 31, 1971.

AMATEIS, EDMOND ROMULUS, 1897– . He was born in Rome and studied at the Beaux Arts Institute of Design in New York 1916–17. He served with the U.S. Army in France 1917–19 and then returned to the New York Beaux Arts Institute 1920–21, after having attended briefly the Academy Julian in Paris. He was fellow in sculpture at the American Academy in Rome 1921–24 and has since received various awards for his sculptural work. He has been president of the National Sculpture Society and currently lives in Florida.

APPLETON, FRANCIS RANDALL, 1854–1929. He was an attorney in New York and an overseer of Harvard 1903–29. Son-in-law of Charles Lanier, he served as intermediary between Lanier, Charles McKim, and the elder J. P. Morgan in McKim's effort to secure Morgan's aid to the project of an American Academy in Rome.

APPLETON, JULIA AMORY, d. 1887. She was the daughter of Charles H. Appleton of Boston and Lichfield, Mass., from whom she inherited a modest fortune. In 1885 she married, as his second wife, Charles McKim, but she died suddenly on January 3, 1887. By her bequests and McKim's more specific arrangements, about two-thirds of her estate went to establish traveling fellowships in architecture at Harvard and Columbia, which became attached to the American School and Academy in Rome.

ASH, PERCY, 1865–1933. He was University of Pennsylvania Travelling Scholar at the American School of Architecture in Rome in 1895. He became professor of architecture and dean at George Washington University 1903–10, professor of architecture at the University of Michigan 1910–12 and at the University of Illinois 1913–18. He was engaged in private practice of architecture in Philadelphia from 1918.

BABCOCK, CHARLES, 1829–1913. He practiced architecture in New York 1853–58, and then studied and took orders as a priest. He was rector of a church 1864–92, but also served as professor of architecture at Cornell 1871–97.

BAKER, GEORGE FISHER, 1840–1931. He was a leader in the financial world of New York and chairman of the board of the First National Bank of New York 1909–1931, meanwhile serving as a director of various large companies. In 1917 he gave $50,000 to the American Academy in Rome.

BAKER, WALTER CUMMINGS, 1893–1971. He was an active and valued member of the board and the finance committee of the American

Academy in Rome 1950–65, its treasurer 1958–65, and long a member of its committee on classical studies. He was made a Benefactor of the Academy for his gift of $5,000. On his death he bequeathed the Academy $50,000. He was posthumously awarded the Academy Medal for Outstanding Service.

BALDWIN, SHERMAN, 1897–1969. He graduated from Yale in 1919, then studied law, and from 1929 was a member of the firm of Lord, Day, and Lord in New York. He became a trustee of the American Academy in Rome and succeeded Gordon Wasson as secretary of its board in 1963. He was a trustee of Vassar, the Metropolitan Museum of Art, the New York Botanical Gardens, the Brearley School, and Pomfret Academy. He was posthumously awarded the Academy Medal for Outstanding Service.

BARBER, SAMUEL, 1910–   . While a student of music at the Curtis Institute he produced several compositions highly regarded by critics and musicians. He was a fellow in music at the American Academy in Rome 1935–37 and artist-in-residence there 1947–48 and briefly 1949–50. He was also recipient of a Guggenheim award in 1945 and of the Pulitzer Prize for musical composition in 1958. His home is in Mt. Kisco, New York.

BARNEY, CHARLES TRACY, 1851–1907. He was president of the Knickerbocker Trust Company, a member of the New York Stock Exchange, and a director of financial and insurance companies. As chairman of the University Club's building committee he worked closely with McKim, 1896–97, whose firm was architect for residences he built in 1885, 1895, and 1902. He was an incorporator of the American Academy in 1905 and its treasurer 1905–7.

BEESON, CHARLES HENRY, 1870–1949. Following study in Munich and a doctorate there, he returned to academic posts in America. After a captaincy in military intelligence 1918–19 he served for the balance of his active career as professor of Latin at Chicago. In 1930–31 he was annual professor of classical studies at the American Academy in Rome. He was managing editor of *Classical Philology* 1936–38, president of the Mediaeval Academy of America 1936–39, and the author or editor of several Latin texts.

BERENSON, BERNARD, 1865–1959. Born in Lithuania, he came in youth to America and graduated from Harvard in 1887. He was an advisor on art acquisitions to wealthy collectors and a recognized authority on Renaissance Italian painting, as nearly a score of publications give evidence. He established a home, a library, and a private collection of paintings at Villa I Tatti near Florence, which he bequeathed to Harvard.

BIDDLE, GEORGE, 1885– . A mural painter with works in many countries, he was president of the National Society of Mural Painters in
1935 and of the Mural Artists' Guild 1937–38 and was artist-in-
residence at the American Academy in Rome 1952–53. He is a member of the National Society of Arts and Letters, the author of three
volumes on art.

BIGELOW, ANNIE. The daughter of John William and Anna Barton
Bigelow of New York and an accomplished musician, she married
Charles McKim on October 1, 1874, but obtained a separation in 1877,
winning the chief custody of their daughter Margaret, who was born
in 1875. In 1887 Annie Bigelow McKim married as her second husband the Reverend John Williams, a pastor in Newport, R.I., and
elsewhere. They had three sons.

BIGELOW, WILLIAM B. Son of John William Bigelow and consequently a
brother-in-law of Charles McKim, he studied at the Paris Beaux Arts
and then worked in the office of Gambrill and Richardson, New York
architects, where were also McKim and Rutherford Mead. In 1878 the
three young men formed a partnership, from which Bigelow retired
in 1879 and was replaced by Stanford White.

BIGELOW, WILLIAM STURGIS, 1850–1926. A graduate of Harvard and an
M.D. in 1874, he was both a prominent Boston surgeon and a trustee
of the Boston Museum of Fine Arts. He became a fellow of the American Academy of Arts and Sciences.

BLACK, HENRY ST. FRANCIS, 1863–1929. He was president of the George
A. Fuller Company, a leading construction firm in New York.

BLAKE, MARION E., 1892–1961. She was a fellow in classical studies at
the American Academy in Rome 1924–25. After her death her friends
gave in her memory the Marion E. Blake Fund to the Academy. She
was a distinguished archaeologist who published widely.

BLASHFIELD, EDWIN ROWLAND, 1848–1936. He studied painting in Paris
in 1867, and his exhibitions there and at the Royal Academy won him
two gold medals. He was a member of the group that planned an
Academy in Rome while at the Shack at the Chicago World's Fair, a
trustee of that School when it was established, and in 1905 an incorporator of the American Academy. He was also president of the
National Institute of Arts and Letters 1915–16 and of the Society of
American Artists, as well as a member of the American Institute of
Architects and of the National Commission on the Fine Arts in 1912.

BLISS, CORNELIUS NEWTON, 1874–1949. An officer and director of the
Bankers' Trust Company and director of other financial institutions,
he was also a trustee of the Metropolitan Museum in New York. He
was an active officer of the Red Cross in Europe during World War I.

BLOCH, HERBERT, 1911–   . He was born in Berlin and became a Doctor of Letters at Rome in 1935. After an academic career which included authorship of books on classical subjects and membership in many scholarly organizations, he became professor of Greek and Latin at Harvard in 1953. He was professor in charge of classical studies at the American Academy in Rome 1957–59 and a special guest of the Academy in 1965.

BORING, WILLIAM ALCIPHRON, 1859–1937. He studied at the Paris Beaux Arts, practiced architecture in Los Angeles 1883–86, and then was employed in McKim, Mead, and White in New York. He was an intimate of Charles McKim and from its inception an active supporter of the American School and then the American Academy in Rome. He received several gold medal awards and was president of the Society of Beaux Arts Architects in America and of the Architectural League. He was a trustee of the American School and an incorporator of the American Academy in 1905. He served from 1908 until his death as treasurer of the Academy, and was professor and dean of the Columbia University Architectural School.

BOVIE, S. PALMER, 1917–   . He was fellow in classics at the American Academy in Rome 1949–50 and director of its summer session 1960–62. He has since served as chairman of the Department of Classics at Douglass College of Rutgers University.

BOWEN, ELIZABETH DOROTHEA COLE (Mrs. Alan Cameron), 1899–   . She has published many novels, short stories, and essays since 1923, and is a Commander of the Order of the British Empire. She has been on many lecture tours and academic appointments in America and is an honorary member of the American Academy of Arts and Letters. She was writer-in-residence 1959–60 at the American Academy in Rome and an occasional guest in later years.

BOYCE, GEORGE KENNETH, 1906–   . He was fellow in classics of the American Academy in Rome 1933–35, assistant in the library of the University of Michigan 1936–39, and librarian at the American Academy 1939–40, but returned to the University of Michigan when the war broke out and the Academy closed in 1940. He was an officer on the staff of the Morgan Library in New York 1946–54 and since then has been head of the Rare Book Department of the University of Michigan. In 1940 he published a monograph on Pompeii. His wife, also a classicist, was connected with the American Academy 1933–35.

BOYNTON, LOUIS H., was Rotch Travelling Fellow to the American School of Architecture in Rome 1896–97 and was married in 1897 in Hermon MacNeal's apartment there.

BRADFORD, LINDSAY, 1892–1959. He was president and later chairman of the Board of the City Bank Farmers' Trust Company 1936–56, as well as a director of various financial and manufacturing companies. His trusteeships included Barnard College, Bennington College, the Russell Sage Foundation, and the American Academy in Rome, of which he was also treasurer 1945–56.

BRADY, NICHOLAS FREDERIC, 1878–1930. He was a notable New York capitalist; an officer or director of many corporations. In 1925 he gave generously to the American Academy in Rome.

BRANDEGEE, MRS. EDWARD D. (Mary Bryant Pratt), 1871–1956. She inherited a substantial fortune and in 1891 married Charles Franklin Sprague, Harvard '79 and a Boston lawyer who was a member of the 56th and 57th Congresses. They built Faulkner Farm in Brookline, which after important additions she left to a Brandegee Foundation, and which has since 1957 been the home of the American Academy of Arts and Sciences. Charles Sprague died in 1902, and in 1904 she married Edward Deshon Brandegee, business man and from 1913 to 1918 regent of Harvard. Mrs. Brandegee was, with the help of Richard Norton, a collector. Her clay models by Bernini are now in the Fogg Museum; she gave early editions of classical authors to Harvard as well as to the American School of Classical Studies in Rome. Sargent painted her portrait.

BRECK, GEORGE WILLIAM, 1863–1920, was the first winner of a Lazarus Fellowship in Mural Painting to the American Academy in Rome 1897–1902. He was director of the Academy 1906–9 and supervised its move to the Villa Mirafiori.

BREWSTER, WALTER S., 1872–?. A banker and broker of Chicago and president of the Chicago Stock Exchange, he was a trustee of the American Academy in Rome, which he visited with his wife. Together they initiated the Kate Lancaster Brewster Fellowship in Landscape Architecture at the Academy. Before her death in September 1947 his wife established a trust agreement which brought $27,891.50 to the Academy, thus completing, with her previous gifts, the $50,000 endowment of that fellowship.

BRIMMER, MARTIN, 1829–1896. He was a prominent attorney, art patron, and philanthropist in Boston. He was president of the Boston Museum of Fine Arts 1870–95 and a fellow of the Harvard Corporation 1864–68 and 1877–96.

BROOKS, VAN WYCK, 1886–1963. After a few years with a publishing house, he retired to devote his entire career to writing. His publications include nearly thirty volumes of history, literary criticism, biography, etc. He was writer-in-residence at the American Academy in Rome 1955–56. A graduate of Harvard, he received many honorary degrees.

BROWN, FRANK EDWARD, 1908– . He was a fellow in classical studies at the American Academy in Rome 1931–33 and then held various posts at Yale, taking part in its archaeological expeditions to the Near East and heading its excavations at Dura Europus. He returned to the American Academy in Rome as professor in charge of classical studies and director of excavations 1947–52, when he went back to Yale as professor of Latin and master of Jonathan Edwards College 1952–63 and 1953–56 respectively. He was a trustee of the Academy and a member of its executive committee 1954–63, and chairman of the committee on the School of Classical Studies 1958–63. He was director of the Academy 1965–69 and has since been professor in charge of its School of Classical Studies.

BRUNNER, MRS. ARNOLD W. (Emma B.), d. 1938. She was the wife of Arnold William Brunner, architect, president of the Architectural League and member of the National Institute of Arts and Letters and of the National Academy of Design. His gifts to the American Academy in Rome made him one of its Patrons, and upon her death Mrs. Brunner made the Academy a further bequest of $20,000.

BRYAN, WILLIAM JENNINGS, 1860–1925. He began legal practice in Illinois in 1883 and was soon elected congressman. He was a candidate for senator or president in every election from 1894 to 1908, as nominee of the Democratic party. He served under Woodrow Wilson as secretary of state 1913–15.

BURNHAM, DANIEL HUDSON, 1846–1912. His notable architectural practice included the Union Station in Washington and the Flatiron Building in New York, as well as many other large buildings in many cities, especially Chicago. He was chief architect of the Chicago Exposition 1890–93 and president of the American Institute of Architects in 1894. He was one of the leaders in founding the American School of Architecture in Rome in 1894. In 1917 his daughter, Mrs. Margaret Burnham, gave the Academy $25,000 for the Daniel Burnham Fund for Fellows in Architecture.

BURTON, HARRY E., 1868–1944. He was professor of Latin at Dartmouth 1903–38 and annual professor of classical studies at the American Academy in Rome 1927–28.

BUTLER, NICHOLAS MURRAY, 1862–1947. In addition to having been president of Columbia University 1901–45, he was active in many academic, philanthropic, political, and public affairs, always with energy, intelligence, confidence, and influence. He was an incorporator of the American Academy in Rome in 1905 and thereafter a trustee.

CADWALADER, JOHN LAMBERT, 1837–1914. He was an attorney in New York, assistant secretary of state 1874–77, president of the New York Public Library and of the New York Bar Association, and trustee of the Carnegie Institution, the Carnegie Endowment for Peace, and the Metropolitan Museum. He was an incorporator of the American Academy in Rome in 1905, and his gift of $1,000 made him a life member.

CAIRNS, HUNTINGTON, 1904– . He began the practice of law in 1926 and was secretary of the American Commission for the Protection and Salvage of Artistic and Historic Monuments 1943–46. He was secretary and treasurer of the National Academy of Art 1943–65 and has published several volumes on legal, artistic, and social topics.

CANNON, HENRY WHITE, 1850–1934. He was U.S. Comptroller of the Currency 1884–86 and president and later chairman of the Chase National Bank 1886–1911. In 1920 he offered to give his villa in Florence to the American Academy in Rome.

CANNON, JOSEPH GURNEY, 1836–1927. He was a member of the House of Representatives from Illinois 1873–1921 and Speaker of the House 1903–11. He was known with affection or trepidation as "Uncle Joe."

CARLTON, NEWCOMB, 1869–1953. He was president and later chairman of the board of the Western Union Telegraph Company. In both world wars he was active in civilian war service and held decorations from the French and Italian governments. From 1929 he was a trustee of the American Academy in Rome and by a gift of $1,000 became its life member.

CARPENTER, RHYS, 1889– . After a Rhodes Scholarship at Oxford 1908–11, he was for many years professor of classics at Bryn Mawr. He was annual professor of classical studies at the American Academy in Rome 1926–27 and professor in charge of classical studies there 1939–40. He was director of the American School of Classical Studies in Athens 1927–32 and a visiting professor there 1957–58. He has published a dozen volumes and numerous articles, chiefly on Greek art. He has received many honors, including the gold medal of the American Institute of Archaeology in 1969 for "distinguished archaeological achievement."

CARTER, ELLIOTT COOK, JR., 1908– . He graduated from Harvard in 1930 and then devoted himself to the study and teaching of music at St. John's College, Annapolis, 1939–41, at the Peabody Conservatory in Baltimore 1946–48, and at Columbia 1948–50. Meanwhile he was twice awarded Guggenheim fellowships 1945–46 and 1950–51. He was a fellow and also artist-in-residence at the American Academy in Rome, and since 1960 has been professor of musical composition at Yale. His compositions have brought him honors in Europe and America.

CARTER, JESSE BENEDICT, 1872–1917. A brilliant undergraduate at Princeton and then a student in Germany for several years, he became professor of classics at Princeton 1898–1907. He went to Rome as director of the School of Classical Studies in 1907, and after its merger with the American Academy in Rome he served as director from January 1, 1913, to his death in 1917, when he was serving the American Red Cross on the Italian front. His widow gave the Academy library "his own carefully selected working library of 1,050 classical volumes."

CECERE, GAETANO, 1894– . Before World War I he was a student at the New York Beaux Arts Institute of Design. He was on active service in the U.S. Army in Europe 1916–19. He then went to Rome as fellow in sculpture at the American Academy 1920–23. He has since taught sculpture at the New York Beaux Arts Institute, the National Academy of Design, and several colleges and universities. His own sculptures have won him several medals and other awards.

CHANDLER, FRANCIS WARD, 1844–1926. He studied architecture in Paris 1867–69 and became a practicing architect in Boston and also professor of architecture at M.I.T. 1888–1911. He was a member of the Board of Art Commissioners in Boston 1898–1908. He was an incorporator of the American Academy in 1905 and thereafter a trustee.

CHANLER, MRS. WINTHROP (Margaret Terry), 1862–1952. She was born in Rome, became a musician and later an author, and in 1886 married Winthrop Chanler. She lived a great part of her life in Rome, where she was a leading figure in its musical, artistic, and social life. She spent her last years at Geneseo. N.Y.

CHASE, GEORGE DAVIS, 1867–1948. He studied at Leipzig 1897–98 and was professor of Latin at the University of Maine from 1905. In 1926 he became secretary of the Advisory Council on Classical Studies of the American Academy in Rome.

CHILD, RICHARD WASHBURN, 1881–1935. A lawyer, magazine editor, and a founder of the Council on Foreign Relations, he was ambassador to Italy 1921–24 and U.S. representative at several conferences of nations in Europe from 1922. He published a dozen volumes and was decorated by the Italian government.

CIARDI, JOHN, 1916– . A graduate of Tufts, he taught English at Harvard 1946–53 and at Rutgers 1954–61. Since 1940 he has published many volumes of his verse, and since 1956, as poetry editor of the *Saturday Review,* he has roundly praised or condemned the verse of others. He was a fellow of the American Academy in Rome in 1956 and has since been at the Academy as an artist-in-residence.

CLARK, CHARLES UPSON, 1875–1960. He was a fellow in the School of Classical Studies in Rome 1898–1900 and became a professor of classics at Yale. He returned to Rome as professor in classical studies 1912–1913, and when Carter was appointed director of the newly merged American Academy, Clark "looked after the activities" of the Classical School, though Carter remained its nominal head until Clark was appointed its director 1916–17. He lectured and published widely.

CLARK, MRS. HAROLD TERRY (Marie Odenkirk). In 1940 she married Harold Clark (1882–1965, an attorney in Cleveland, an author, a president of the Cleveland Museum of Art, and a trustee of schools and philanthropies). In 1965, the year of his death, she gave through President Rapuano $5,000 to the American Academy in Rome.

CLEWS, MRS. HENRY (Lucy Madison Worthington). She was the wife of Henry Clews (1840–1923, who served the U.S. government in financial matters from 1861 and headed a large financial interest from 1877). In late 1947 she offered to give her Château de la Napoule on the French Riviera to the American Academy in Rome as a memorial to her husband. She was a great-niece of President Madison.

COOK, WALTER, 1846–1916. In 1877 he studied in Munich and at the Beaux Arts in Paris contemporary with McKim. He then became an architect in New York and was president of the American Institute of Architects 1912–13.

COOLIDGE, MRS. FREDERICK SHURTLEFF (Elizabeth Sprague). Music patron and philanthropist, she made gifts to the Library of Congress, the Pittsfield Music Association, the Chicago Orchestra, and the Coolidge Foundation. She sponsored in 1923 a series of concerts held in the Villa Aurelia at the American Academy in Rome. She was given decorations in France, Belgium, London, and Frankfurt.

COPLAND, AARON, 1900– . He studied music largely under private tutors and began composing in 1920. He was a Guggenheim fellow 1925–26; won the Pulitzer Prize for Music in 1944 and was professor at Harvard 1951–52. He has received various medals and awards for his compositions.

CORTISSOZ, ROYAL, 1869–1948. He was art editor and later literary editor of the *New York Tribune* 1891–1913. He published extensively on the fine arts, including a biography of Saint-Gaudens in 1907 and of

John LaFarge in 1911. He was a trustee of the American Academy in Rome 1921–47.

COVELL, WILLIAM S., d. 1956. He was a Charles McKim Scholar from Columbia at the American School of Architecture in Rome for some eighteen months during 1897–98.

COWLES, RUSSELL, 1887– . Dartmouth '09 and a fellow of the American Academy in Rome 1915–21, with an interval of war service and an extension of his fellowship. He has exhibited his paintings in most leading national exhibitions over many years, and examples of them are in many important museums and galleries. He now lives chiefly in New York.

COWLEY, MALCOLM, 1898– . Harvard '20 and then a free-lance writer until 1929, when he became associate editor of the *New Republic* until 1944. He is the author of many volumes of fiction, biography, poetry, and criticism.

COX, ALLYN, 1896– . A son of Kenyon Cox, he studied at the National Academy of Design 1911–16 and was in Rome as fellow in mural painting at the American Academy 1916–20. His works include many murals in libraries, clubs, banks, and in the rotunda of the U.S. Capitol, and have won many awards. He is a trustee of the Abbey Fund and lives chiefly in New York.

COX, GARDNER, 1906– . He attended Harvard, M.I.T., and the Boston Music School 1924–31 and then embarked upon an impressive career as a painter, largely of portraits. He headed the Department of Painting at the Boston Museum of Fine Arts 1954–55 and was artist-in-residence at the American Academy in Rome 1960–61. His work is represented at the Boston Museum, the Fogg Museum, the National Gallery, and at colleges and universities. Since January 1963 he has been a trustee of the American Academy in Rome.

COX, KENYON, 1856–1919. Painter, author, and critic, he studied in Paris. His murals are in the Library of Congress and state capitols. He was president of the Mural Painters' Association.

CRESSON, MARGARET FRENCH (Mrs. William Penn Cresson). She is a daughter of Daniel Chester French and a sculptress of bronze busts, portrait heads, and memorial plaques. She has been very active in several art societies. In 1941 she offered to bequeath to the American Academy in Rome her estate in Stockbridge, Mass., with some 150 acres and a large house with its furnishing and art collection. The Academy replied that it would welcome the bequest.

CROWNINSHIELD, FREDERIC, 1845–1918. He studied art in France and Italy, especially mural painting and stained glass. He taught painting at the Boston Museum of Fine Arts 1879–85 and was the author of several volumes of poetry and a book on mural painting. He was a trustee of the American Academy and its director 1908–12, when he retired to a home at Capri, where he later died.

CURRIER, STEPHEN, 1930–1967. He was born in Santa Fe, N.M. Early in his thirties he became known, in spite of his great personal modesty, as an active and able philanthropist. He was president of Urban America and an officer or director of several industrial companies and foundations. He was elected a trustee of the American Academy, but a few weeks later he, his wife, and their pilot vanished on a plane flight between Puerto Rico and the Virgin Islands.

CURTIS, CHARLES DENSMORE, 1875–1925. He was a fellow in classics at the American Academy in Rome in 1915 and lecturer and professor of archaeology there between 1916 and 1924. He was also editor of Academy publications 1921–24.

CUYLER, ELEANOR DE GRAFF. She was a sister of Cornelius C. Cuyler, sometime treasurer of the School of Classical Studies in Rome, and in 1914 she gave $5,000 and pledged annual gifts to the Academy library in memory of her brother. The gifts came when they were most needed.

DALE, CHESTER, 1882–1962. He was a New York banker and broker and a director of various public utility companies. He became a notable collector of valuable paintings, a benefactor of the National Gallery and the Metropolitan Museum, and a trustee of both.

DAMROSCH, WALTER JOHANNES, 1862–1957. He organized and directed the New York Symphony Orchestra 1903–27 and was president of the American Academy of Arts and Letters. A leader in many musical undertakings and organizations, he was decorated by the Italian government while a guest in Rome of the American Academy in 1920. He was a trustee of the Academy 1928–45.

DAY, FRANK MILES, 1861–1918. He studied art in Europe for three years and was a practicing architect in Philadelphia from 1887. He was president of the American Institute of Architects and of the National Institute of Arts and Letters and a member of the Royal Institute. He was an incorporator and trustee of the American Academy.

DEDAEHN, COLONEL PETER, c. 1881–1971. After forty years of service to the American Academy in Rome, primarily as librarian, he retired on October 1, 1961, at the age of eighty and was awarded the Academy's Medal for the length, distinction, and devotion of his services. He died in January 1971.

DE FOREST, ROBERT WEEKS, 1848–1931. As a leading attorney in New

York he was general counsel of the Central Railroad of New Jersey and an officer or director of railroads and business enterprises. He was president of the New York Municipal Art Commission 1905–29 and the Russell Sage Foundation and vice-president of the American Red Cross. He was a trustee of the American Academy in Rome, its general counsel, and a member of its finance committee 1909–31.

DEISS, JOSEPH JAY, 1915–   . He graduated from the University of Texas and served in Washington during World War II. He then became a professional in industrial public relations in New York but from 1954 devoted himself to full-time writing and spent much time abroad, especially in Italy. He published six historical studies. On February 1, 1966, he became vice-director of the American Academy in Rome but resigned that office effective June 30, 1969.

DENISON, WILLIAM K. 1869–?. He was a graduate of Harvard and a member of the first trio of fellows of the School of Classical Studies in Rome 1895–96. From 1897 he served until retirement as assistant professor and then professor of classics at Tufts.

DENNISON, WALTER, 1869–1917. After a fellowship in classics at the American Academy in Rome 1895–97, he was successively professor of classics at Oberlin, Michigan, and Swarthmore 1899–1917. He was annual professor in the School of Classical Studies in Rome 1908–9.

DIETSCH, PERCIVAL CLARENCE, 1881–1961. He was Rinehart Fellow in Sculpture at the American Academy in Rome 1905–9 and left a bequest of $5,000 to the Academy.

DILL, JAMES BROOKS, 1854–1910. He graduated from Yale in 1876, was judge in the Court of Appeals in New York 1905–11, and was the author of three books on corporation law. He was, presumably as legal counsel, issued one of the ten shares of capital stock of the School of Architecture in Rome upon its incorporation May 18, 1895.

DINSMOOR, WILLIAM B., 1886–   . For most of his active career he was a professor of classical architecture at Columbia. He was a trustee of the American Academy in Rome 1932–56 and served for some years after 1938 as secretary to the trustees and then as second vice-president of the board. In July 1944 he was appointed acting director of the Academy but was unable to get a passport to Italy and resigned that titular office in April 1945. In 1960 he was awarded the Academy's Medal for Outstanding Service.

DUCKWORTH, GEORGE ECKEL, 1903–1972. He was professor of classics at Princeton from 1929 until his death; director of summer sessions at the American Academy in Rome 1951–55; trustee, 1948–59. He was the author of scholarly works on classical literary topics.

EASTMAN, GEORGE, 1854–1932. His development of film for photography resulted in his creation of the Eastman Kodak Company in 1882, over which he presided for fifty years. He also created and long financed alone the Eastman School of Music and gave away large sums to the University of Rochester, to medical and dental education and care, and to charities.

EDGELL, GEORGE HAROLD, 1887–1954. He was a fellow at the American School of Classical Studies in Rome in 1912 and returned to Rome as annual professor in classical studies at the American Academy 1918–19. In 1924 he was secretary of the American Academy's Advisory Committee on the Fine Arts. He was professor and dean of Harvard's School of Architecture 1925–35 and director of the Boston Museum of Fine Arts from 1935.

EGBERT, JAMES CHIDESTER, 1859–1948. Graduating from Columbia in 1881, he became adjunct professor of classics there from 1895 and professor of Latin from 1906. He wrote and edited a number of classical studies. He was annual professor at the Rome School of Classical Studies 1903–4, a trustee of the American Academy in Rome 1911–45, and vice-president of the Academy 1940–44.

EINSTEIN, LEWIS, 1877–1967. He served in several U.S. embassies 1903–30, meanwhile publishing a dozen volumes on history, politics, and poetry. He received decorations or other honors from several European countries and gave or bequeathed rare books as well as other gifts and large sums to the American Academy in Rome. He was a Patron of the Academy.

ELKINS, GEORGE W., 1858–1919. He inherited wealth and headed various industrial companies in the Philadelphia area, as well as holding directorships in various financial institutions. He collected oil paintings. In 1900 Thomas Waldo Story solicited his aid for the American Academy in Rome.

ELLSWORTH, JAMES WILLIAM, 1849–1925. He was owner or operator of various coal mines and a director of railroads and telegraph companies. His interest in the fine arts led to his membership in the board of directors of the Chicago Exposition and his decoration as Commander of the Order of the Crown of Italy. He was a connoisseur of books, Chinese porcelains, oriental rugs, and Greek statuary and in 1920 gave $5,000 to the American Academy in Rome.

ELWELL, GEORGE HERBERT, 1898– . He studied music in Paris 1922–24 and then in Rome 1924–27 as fellow in music at the American Academy. He has long been professor of composition at the Cleveland Institute of Music, as well as composer and music critic.

ELY, THEODORE NEWEL, 1846–1916. He was a railroad executive and a director of steel and other companies in the Philadelphia area. He was an incorporator, a benefactor, a trustee, and vice-president of the American Academy in Rome, for which he established a fellows' loan fund. He was made an honorary member of the American Institute of Architects.

FAIRBANKS, FRANK PERLEY, 1875–1939. He was a fellow in mural painting at the American Academy in Rome 1909–12 and a captain in the American Red Cross 1917–19, receiving two Italian decorations. He returned to the Academy as professor of fine arts 1919–21 and remained there until 1932. The Supreme Court building in Washington contains his mural decorations.

FAIRCLOUGH, HENRY RUSHTON, 1862–1938. He was a professor of classics at the University of Toronto 1897–1902 and again 1922–38 and an editor of several classical works. He was annual professor at the American School of Classical Studies in Rome 1910–11.

FAULKNER, BARRY, 1881–1966. He was a fellow in painting at the American Academy in Rome 1907–10, annual professor of fine arts there 1922–23, and from 1930 an Academy trustee. His sculpture is in many public buildings including the National Archives and several state capitols. In 1960 he was awarded the Academy's Medal for Outstanding Service.

FIELD, MARSHALL, 1835–1906. A leading merchant and capitalist of Chicago, he founded the Field Museum and made large gifts to the University of Chicago.

FINLEY, DAVID EDWARD, 1890– . Lawyer, financial expert, executive, diplomat, and authority on the fine arts, he practiced law in Philadelphia 1915–17 and was lieutenant in the U.S. Army 1917–18. He then returned to the law in Washington but interrupted that practice to serve in the Treasury and in the Foreign Service 1921–33. He was director of the National Gallery of Art 1938–56, president of the American Association of Museums 1945–49, and chairman of the National Commission of Fine Arts 1950–63, while also trustee of other art commissions.

FLAGLER, HARRY HARKNESS, 1870–1952. Sportsman, capitalist, and real estate developer, he offered in 1921 to secure $25,000 for a Walter Damrosch Fellowship in Music at the American Academy in Rome, and did so, giving the greater part himself. His wife was also a Benefactor of the Academy.

FLETCHER, HENRY PRATHER, 1873–1959. His diplomatic career from 1902 included ambassadorships to Chile in 1909, Mexico in 1916, Belgium in 1922, and Italy 1924–29.

FLEXNER, ABRAHAM, 1866–1959. He was director of medical education for the General Education Board 1925–28 and after further leadership of Rockefeller foundations served as director of the Institute of Advanced Study at Princeton 1930–39. He published several books on higher education and a report on medical training which resulted in a national reform of medical education.

FOLLEN, CHARLES F. C., 1796–1846. German by birth and a leader in the 1815 abortive liberal movement in Germany, he came to America to avoid likely imprisonment in 1824. Here he became a leader in the anti-slavery movement and the first professor of German language and literature at Harvard.

FRANK, TENNEY, 1876–1939. He studied at Göttingen and Berlin 1910–11 and was professor of Latin at Bryn Mawr and then at Johns Hopkins from 1919, publishing widely on subjects of classical scholarship. He was professor in charge of classical studies at the American Academy in Rome 1916–17 and 1922–25.

FRASER, LEON, 1889–1945. He was a director of leading banks, railroads, and industrial companies but was also active in government advice and service in international finance, at which he was considered a great expert. He was trustee and treasurer of the American Academy in Rome 1938–45.

FREER, CHARLES LANG, 1856–1919. A capitalist with large interests in railroads and industries in the Detroit area, he collected works of art and gave his collections, and a million-dollar building to house them, to the Smithsonian Institute. He was an incorporator and Benefactor of the American Academy in Rome.

FRENCH, DANIEL CHESTER, 1850–1931. He was a leading sculptor, with studios in Washington and New York and with examples of his work in the U.S. Capitol, the Boston Court House, and the Chicago Museum, as well as in the Lincoln Memorial in Washington. He was chairman of the National Commission on Fine Arts 1912–15, a trustee of the Metropolitan Museum, and an incorporator and trustee of the American Academy in Rome.

FRICK, HENRY CLAY, 1849–1919. From 1897 he was a powerful capitalist in coal and steel, an art collector, and a cautious but generous philanthropist. In 1905 he became an incorporator of the American Academy in Rome and visited the Academy in March 1912. A large gift made him one of the Academy's Founders.

FRIEDLANDER, LEO, 1888–1966. Having studied sculpture at the Brussells Beaux Arts, he was a fellow at the American Academy in Rome 1913–16. Later he was professor of sculpture at New York University. His colossal sculptures are at Valley Forge, Rockefeller Center, the Arlington Bridge in Washington, and the chamber of the House of Representatives.

FROTHINGHAM, ARTHUR LINCOLN, 1859–1923. Schooled in Rome 1868–71 and at Leipzig in 1883, he was professor of archaeology and the history of art at Princeton 1887–1906. He was for some time proprietor as well as editor of the *American Journal of Archaeology* and was the author of some ten books on the fine arts.

FRY, SHERRY EDMUNDSON, 1879–?. He studied at the Chicago Art Institute in 1900, in Paris including a year at the Beaux Arts 1902–3, and in Florence in 1904. In 1907 he received a gold medal for sculpture at the Paris Salon and in 1908 he was elected fellow in sculpture at the American Academy in Rome, where he remained until 1911. He was vice-president of the Academy's Alumni Association in 1920.

GARLAND, JAMES A. In 1880 McKim designed a house for him at Elberton, N.J. In 1894 he attended the trustees' dinner at the Metropolitan Museum. He left a trust fund of which his son James A. Garland, Jr. (1870–1906), was trustee.

GARNSEY, ELMER ELLSWORTH, 1862–1946. A mural painter, he was one of the designers of the Chicago Exposition in 1900. His mural works are in the Library of Congress, the Boston Public Library, the New York Stock Exchange, and other public buildings. He was an incorporator of the American Academy in Rome in 1905.

GARRETT, JOHN WORK, 1872–1942. He had large banking interests in Baltimore but was in the Foreign Service from 1901 and was ambassador to Italy 1929–33.

GARRISON, WENDELL PHILLIPS, 1840–1907. A son of William Lloyd Garrison, he married in 1865 Lucy McKim, sister of Charles McKim. He was long the editor of the *New York Nation* and was the author of several books.

GARRISON, WILLIAM LLOYD, 1805–1879. The most widely known abolitionist, he founded and edited the anti-slavery newspaper *The Liberator,* helped to found the New England and later the National Anti-Slavery Societies, and was president of the latter 1843–65.

GIBBONS, JAMES, 1834–1921. He was Bishop of the Roman Catholic Church from 1868, Archbishop of Baltimore from 1877, Cardinal and ranking prelate in America from 1886.

GILBERT, CASS, 1859–1934. The architect of many libraries and other public buildings and a leader in nearly every large organization concerned with architecture and the fine arts, he was president of the

American Institute of Architects in 1909 and of the National Academy of Design 1926–30 and a member of the Royal Academy. He was an incorporator of the American Academy in Rome in 1905, a contributor to the McKim Memorial Fund in 1914, and by his gifts a Benefactor of the Academy.

GOODWIN, WILLIAM WATSON, 1831–1912. After study at Göttingen, Berlin, and Bonn he became in 1856 a tutor at Harvard. He then advanced through the various academic ranks to professor of classics during service at Harvard until 1901. He was the first director of the American School of Classical Studies in Athens.

GORDON, GEORGE BYRON, 1866–1927. An anthropologist and also a man of affairs living chiefly in Pittsburgh, in 1927 he bequeathed $25,000 to the American Academy in Rome to establish, in memory of his daughter, the Katherine Edwards Gordon Fellowship in Landscape Architecture. In the same year his widow gave another $25,000 to that fellowship.

GREENE, JEROME DAVIS, 1874–1959. He was secretary to the Corporation at Harvard 1901–10, manager of the Rockefeller Institute for Medical Research 1910–12 and a trustee until 1932, secretary and trustee of the Rockefeller Foundation and its subsidiaries 1913–39, and secretary to the president and Corporation at Harvard 1934–43. He was widely active in philanthropies and was a trustee of the American Academy in Rome.

GREENE, WILLIAM C., 1890– . He was a Rhodes Scholar at Oxford from 1911, and then at Harvard, where he became professor of classics until his retirement. He was annual professor of classical studies at the American Academy in Rome 1931–32.

GRISWOLD, RALPH ESTY, 1894– . After three years as fellow in landscape architecture at the American Academy in Rome 1920–23, he settled to private practice in Pittsburgh, but was landscape architect-in-residence at the Academy in Rome 1949–50, when he advocated fellowships of longer duration and other changes. He is a consultant in Williamsburg, Va.

GROVER, JANET BUCHANAN, d. May 15, 1946. In 1947 it was found that she had bequeathed some $25,000 to the American Academy in Rome, to be used "for scholarships for American students in Rome."

GUÉRIN, JULES, 1866–1946. He was a mural painter whose work is seen in many public buildings. In October 1947 he bequeathed a legacy to the American Academy in Rome, which proved after settlements to approximate $200,000.

GUERNSEY, ROSCOE, 1872–1961. He took a doctorate in classics at Johns Hopkins in 1901, then taught classics at Columbia University, and in 1918 became executive secretary in New York of the American Academy in Rome, a post from which he retired, after 26 years of service, in 1945.

GUGLER, ERIC, c. 1890– . He was a fellow at the American Academy in Rome 1911–14 and became a practicing architect in New York. He held a commission at the San Francisco Exposition in 1939 and was a trustee of the American Academy in Rome 1938–67.

HADZITTS, GEORGE DEPUE, 1873–1954. He studied at the American School of Classical Studies in Rome 1900–01 and was a member of the faculty of the University of Pennsylvania 1903–43 and professor there 1923–43. He was annual professor in classical studies at the American Academy in Rome 1929–30, president of the American Philological Association in 1945, and published widely on classical subjects.

HAFNER, VICTOR. He was a fellow in architecture at the American Academy in Rome 1923–25, but the trustees declined to award him a diploma because he had not met its standards of scholarship and his "conduct violated the regulations of the Academy."

HALE, WILLIAM GARDNER, 1849–1928. After study at Leipzig and Göttingen 1876–77, he was successively professor of Latin at Harvard, Cornell, and Chicago and the first director of the American School of Classical Studies in Rome 1895–96. He edited classical and archaeological periodicals and was the author of four books on the Latin language. He was a member of the managing committee of the American School in Athens 1885–1922.

HAMILL, ALFRED ERNEST, 1883–1953. A banker in Chicago; a scholar and collector of books and paintings, he was president of the Newberry Library from 1930 and a trustee of the American Academy in Rome.

HAMMOND, MASON, 1903– . Rhodes Scholar at Oxford 1925–28, he has been associate or full professor at Harvard since 1939, and was master of Kirkland House there 1945–55. He has been closely associated with the American Academy in Rome on several occasions and in several capacities: as professor in charge of classical studies 1937–39 and 1955–57, as director of its 1949 summer session, and since 1941 as a trustee. He was awarded the Academy Medal for Outstanding Service.

HANCOCK, WALKER KIRTLAND, 1901– . He studied the fine arts at Washington University, St. Louis, at the University of Wisconsin, and at the Pennsylvania Academy of Fine Arts. He was a fellow in sculpture at the American Academy in Rome 1925–28 and artist-in-residence 1956–57 and 1962–63, and is a trustee. He was a captain in World War II, has won many honors and awards for his sculpture, and lives chiefly at Gloucester, Massachusetts.

HANSON, HOWARD, 1896– . He was the first candidate to be awarded a fellowship in music at the American Academy in Rome, but left before his fellowship ended to become director of the Eastman School of Music in Rochester 1924–64, which he developed into an outstanding institution, meanwhile becoming himself a leader in music education. He has conducted most leading American and European orchestras; his own symphonic and other compositions have received many awards and honors. Retired, he lives in Rochester and in summer on a private island on the Maine coast.

HARKNESS, ALBERT GRANGER, 1856–1923. From 1883 until 1923 he was a professor of classics, first at Colgate and then at Brown. He was annual professor at the American School of Classical Studies in Rome 1902–3.

HARRIS, DAVID T., 1923– . An investment banker attached to the United States Trust Company of New York, he became a trustee of the Academy in 1967 and a member of its executive committee in 1970.

HARRISON, WALLACE KIRKMAN, 1895– . He was a fellow in architecture at the American Academy in Rome 1922–23 and is regarded as one of the leading architects in New York. Among buildings designed by his firm are those of Rockefeller Center, Lincoln Center, and La Guardia airport. He is a Benefactor of the American Academy and since 1953 a trustee. In 1964 he was elected trustee emeritus.

HAY, JOHN, 1838–1905. Lawyer and statesman, he was private secretary to President Abraham Lincoln, ambassador to the Court of St. James 1897–98, and secretary of state in 1898.

HAYES, BARTLETT H., JR., 1904– . Long the director of the Addison Gallery of American Art at Phillips Andover Academy and a fellow of the American Academy of Arts and Sciences, he is the author of several volumes on the fine arts and of a television series on the arts. He assumed the directorship of the American Academy in Rome on March 1, 1970.

HAZELTINE, WILLIAM STANLEY, 1835–1900. He and his sculptor brother James Henry Hazeltine (1833–1907) lived in Rome and died there. William was a landscape painter and in 1897 became what McKim called a "local trustee" of the American Academy in Rome.

HELFER, WALTER, 1896–1958. He was fellow in musical composition at the American Academy in Rome 1925–28 and then served for many years as professor of music at Hunter College, New York.

HENDRICKSON, GEORGE LINCOLN, 1865–1963. He studied at Bonn and Berlin and then became professor of Latin at Colorado College 1889–91, the University of Wisconsin 1891–96, the University of Chicago 1897–1907, and Yale 1907–33. He was acting director of the American School of Classical Studies in Rome 1913–14 and director of that School after its merger with the American Academy 1919–20. He was president of the American Philological Association in 1936.

HENRY, BARKLIE MCKEE, 1902–66. Vigorous, genial, and able, he was a trustee and director of banks, foundations, and philanthropies, including the Carnegie Institution, the Institute for Advanced Studies at Princeton, the Morgan Library, the Rockefeller Institute and the John Hay Whitney Fund. As a trustee of the American Academy in Rome 1960–66 he closely studied at first hand its current program and standing and made stimulating suggestions for its improvement.

HERRIMAN, WILLIAM H., c. 1827–1918. Himself a painter, he was a collector of books, prints, and paintings. In his later years he lived in Rome and from 1897 was a trustee of the original American School in Rome, and an incorporator of the American Academy in 1905. He bequeathed to the Academy about 60 paintings by American artists and some 3,000 volumes which authorities said could not even then have been purchased for less than $50,000.

HEWLETT, JAMES MONROE, 1868–1941. An architect by profession, he also was by avocation a painter of murals of some distinction. As a young man he was with the firm of McKim, Mead, and White 1890–94 but afterward set up his own firm in New York and was successful, and was president of the Architectural League of New York 1919–21 and president of the Society of Mural Painters 1921–26, as well as vice-president of the American Institute of Architects. In 1932 he began a three-year appointment as director of the American Academy in Rome, but for reasons not wholly clear, he left in 1934 on leave from its trustees, on the agreement that he would not return to the Academy.

HEYLAND, MRS. CLARA JESSUP (Mrs. Alexander S. Heyland), d. 1909. She was a daughter of Alfred Jessup of Philadelphia.

HIGGINSON, HENRY LEE, 1834–1919. A graduate of Harvard, he studied music in Vienna but returned to volunteer as a private in the Civil War. He emerged, having been severely wounded, as a major. He recovered, became a partner in the leading financial firm of Lee, Higginson, and Company in Boston, member of the Harvard Corporation, president for many years of the Boston Music Hall, and trustee of the Carnegie Institution and the New England Conservatory of Music. He was one of the founders of the original American School in Rome by a gift, in the name of Harvard College, of $100,000, and was a trustee of the American Academy 1905–9.

HIGHET, GILBERT ARTHUR, 1906– . He has been professor of Greek and Latin at Columbia University since 1938 and is a noted author, critic, and teacher. He was a trustee of the American Academy in Rome 1960–65.

HILLES, MRS. FREDERICK WHILEY, 1900– . Her husband was long a professor of English at Yale and published scholarly studies of Reynolds and Johnson. In 1966 she gave $50,000 to the American Academy in Rome to establish, in memory of her cousin, the Marjorie Morse Dawson Fund for the purchase of books for the library. She is a Patron of the Academy and was elected trustee in 1971.

HOLLAND, LOUISE ADAMS (Mrs. Leicester B. Holland) 1893– . She taught Latin at Smith College 1918–23; took a doctorate at Bryn Mawr in 1920, and was a fellow in classical studies at the American Academy in Rome 1922–23. She taught classics at Vassar 1925–27 and at Bryn Mawr and Haverford 1928–49. She was visiting professor in classical studies 1959–60 at the Academy. She was a Guggenheim fellow 1948–49 and published several monographs. Her husband, an architect, was professor of fine arts at Vassar and the University of Pennsylvania 1925–46 and at the American School in Athens 1922–23.

HOWARD, MISS NICEA, 1899– . Perhaps a sister of Charles Howard the artist, she gave in 1953, in memory of her brother Jesse Howard, Jr., $3,000 to the American Academy in Rome. In 1958 she gave another $3,000 to support a fellowship in memory of her friend Frances Barker Tracy. By 1962 she had given a total of some $45,000 to the Academy. She also established a Howard Fellowship at Brown University.

HOWE, GEORGE, 1886–1955. He graduated from Harvard in 1908 and from the Paris Beaux Arts Institute in 1912. He began the practice of architecture in Philadelphia in 1913 and with occasional interruptions continued it until 1942. One such interruption was his lieutenancy in the U.S. Army overseas 1917–18. He was architect-in-residence at the American Academy in Rome 1947–48 and chairman of the department of architecture at Yale 1950–54.

HOWLAND, CHARLES P., 1869–1932. Lawyer and director of financial institutions in New York from 1894; trustee of the Rockefeller Foundation, the General Education Board, and Johns Hopkins University.

HUNT, MYRON, 1868–1952. He studied architecture in Europe 1894–96 and became a leading architect in Chicago and from 1903 in Los Angeles.

HUNT, RICHARD HOWLAND, 1862–1931. After study at the Paris Beaux Arts he established himself as an architect in New York, where he was immensely successful. His designs included the new wing at the Metropolitan Museum, buildings for several universities, and residences for members of the Vanderbilt family and for Mrs. O. H. P. Belmont.

HUNT, RICHARD M., d. 1895. He was one of the original organizers of the American School in Rome 1893–95.

HUTCHINSON, CHARLES LAWRENCE, 1854–1924. He was a banker and grain merchant in Chicago; also chairman of the Fine Arts Commission, treasurer of the University of Chicago, honorary member of the American Institute of Architects, and in 1905 an incorporator of the American Academy in Rome.

HYDE, JAMES HAZEN, 1876–1959. A Harvard graduate in 1898, he inherited a fortune and took a successful part in financial affairs in his middle years, but lived thereafter chiefly in France. He was a noted Francophile, heading various organizations and movements in support of French arts and literature, and received honors and decorations in France. He gave generously to causes that interested him, including a sum to the American Academy in Rome in 1925.

JACOBS, HENRY ALLEN. He was McKim Scholar in Architecture from Columbia University to the American School in Rome in 1898.

JAMES, ARTHUR CURTIS, 1867–1941. He was a capitalist in railroads and a trustee of various philanthropies. His gift of $10,000 to the American Academy in Rome in 1917 made him a Benefactor.

JENNEWEIN, CARL PAUL, 1890– . He was a fellow in sculpture at the American Academy in Rome 1916–18 and again 1919–20. Examples of his sculpture are now in the White House, in leading museums and art galleries, and were shown at the San Francisco Exposition in 1939. He was president of the National Sculpture Society 1960–63.

JEROME, THOMAS SPENCER, d. 1914. Long a resident of Capri, he bequeathed to the American Academy in Rome one third of his extensive library and funds of about $40,000 to establish the distinguished lectureship bearing his name.

JOHNSON, ALLAN CHESTER, 1881–1955. He was an assistant professor and professor of the classics at Princeton 1912–49. He was a trustee of the American Academy in Rome 1929–46, and professor of classical studies there 1933–34. He was chairman of its committee on classical studies 1940–45. An eclectic classicist, he was also a trustee of the American School in Athens.

JOHNSON, DORA. She was a Carnegie Fellow in Archaeology at the American School of Classical Studies in Rome in 1910.

JOHNSON, MISS HELEN R., d. 1936. Of Bennington, Vermont, in 1936 she left a bequest of $12,000 to the American Academy in Rome.

JOHNSON, ROBERT UNDERWOOD, 1853–1935. Editor, author, diplomat, he was a leader in securing war relief for Italy 1917–19 and was ambassador to Italy 1920–21. He received several European decorations. He also published several volumes of his poems.

JOHNSTONE, WILLIAM HARCOURT, 1899– . A graduate of the University of Michigan, with a law degree from Harvard, he served the Bethlehem Steel Company in various capacities from 1924 until his retirement as a vice-president and director in 1967.

JONES, JOHN WESLEY, 1907– . He has been with the U.S. Foreign Service since 1930 and served successively in consular posts in Mexico, India, and Rome 1931–41. He was then an officer in the State Department 1941–45, but went to Rome as first secretary of embassy 1945–48. Later he served in the embassies in Nanking and Madrid and was ambassador to Libya and Peru 1958–69.

JONES, THOMAS HUDSON, 1892–1969. He studied sculpture at the Albright Art School, the Boston Museum Art School, and the Carnegie Institute of Technology 1906–14. He was a fellow in sculpture at the American Academy in Rome 1919–22 after having served with the U.S. Medical Corps in World War I. He returned to the American Academy 1932–33 as professor of fine arts. Several of his sculptural works are in the New York Hall of Fame. He was visiting sculptor at the Academy in Rome 1932–33.

JUILLIARD, AUGUSTUS D., d. 1917. In 1913 he gave $1,000 a year for three years through Breck Trowbridge "toward the running expenses" of the American Academy in Rome. In June 1916 he became a Patron of the Academy with a further gift of $25,000.

JUILLIARD, FREDERICK A., d. 1937. He was a nephew of Augustus Juilliard and with part of his inherited wealth he founded the Juilliard Foundation for Music. He was a merchant, a philanthropist, and a director of banks, industrial companies, and the Metropolitan Opera Company. In 1921 he joined the advisory committee on music of the American Academy in Rome and made a gift of $25,000 which was later increased to $50,000 as endowment for music at the Academy. He was a Patron of the Academy.

JUSSERAND, JEAN ADRIEN ANTOINE JULES, 1855–1932. Diplomat, author, and historian, ambassador of France to Washington from 1902, president of the American Historical Association in 1921, and recipient of many honorary degrees, he attended the dinner in 1905 to celebrate the incorporation of the American Academy in Rome.

KAHN, OTTO HERMAN, 1867–1934. He learned banking in Germany and London and traveled extensively in Europe; he then headed the financial firm of Kuhn, Loeb, and Company from 1897. He was sometime president and sometime chairman of the board of the Metropolitan Opera Company from 1931 and a trustee of the Philharmonic Orchestra of New York, the American Federation of Arts, and the American Shakespeare Foundation. About 1910 he became a Benefactor of the American Academy in Rome by a considerable gift.

KANE, JOHN. He was an affluent New Yorker and a friend of Charles McKim, who met him in London in 1904. His house at 610 Fifth Avenue was designed by McKim, Meade, and White in 1907. He was a director of the Metropolitan Museum, and in 1910 he gave $5,000 to the American Academy in Rome and became one of its Benefactors.

KECK, CHARLES, 1875–1951. After study at the National Academy of Design and the Art Students' League in New York, he was a fellow in sculpture at the American Academy in Rome 1900–1904. Examples of his sculpture include a bust of President Truman in the Senate building and several others in the New York Hall of Fame.

KECK, TRACY, d. November 1921. He was head of the American School of Classical Studies 1898–99 and is buried in the Protestant Cemetery in Rome.

KELSEY, FRANCIS WILLEY, 1858–1927. After study in Europe 1883–85, he became in 1889 professor of Latin at the University of Michigan. He was annual professor in the School of Classical Studies in Rome 1900–1 and a trustee of the Academy from 1911. He directed four excavations in the Near East and was the editor of a number of Latin texts and handbooks.

KENDALL, WILLIAM MITCHELL, 1856–1941. He studied architecture for several years in Italy and France and became a partner in McKim, Mead, and White in 1906. In 1905 he was an incorporator and trustee of the American Academy in Rome, and he bequeathed $100,000 to the Academy. He was chairman of the National Commission on the Fine Arts from 1916.

KIMBALL, RICHARD ARTHUR, 1899– . After graduating from Yale in 1922 and then the Yale School of Architecture, he began practice in

New York in 1927, and with his partners was outstandingly successful in domestic architecture as well as public buildings and memorials. He was director of the American Academy in Rome 1960–65;
on retiring he was awarded its Medal for Outstanding Service and
induced to remain in close contact with the Academy. He now lives in
Salisbury, Conn., and occasionally cannot resist returning to the
practice of architecture.

KRAUTHEIMER, RICHARD, 1897– . He was born in Bavaria and came to
the United States in 1935. He was professor of the history of art at
Vassar 1937–52 and at the Institute of Fine Arts of New York University 1952–71. He was a Guggenheim fellow in 1950 and 1963 and
has published volumes on Ghiberti and on early Christian and By-
zantine art. He was awarded the Medal for Outstanding Service of
the American Academy in Rome.

KUBLY, HERBERT, 1915– . Writer, editor, and reporter including assignments with the *New York Herald Tribune* and *Time Magazine*
1942–44, he has since 1969 been professor of English at the Kenosha
branch of the University of Wisconsin. He was a Fulbright scholar
in Italy 1950–51 and a visitor to Rome in 1966.

LABATUT, JEAN, 1899– . He was born in France and studied art at
Toulouse and then at the Paris Beaux Arts Institute. He went to
Princeton in 1928 and became a U.S. citizen in 1939. He was professor of architecture at Princeton until his retirement in 1968, but
from 1924 was also a leading spirit in urban planning and landscape
architecture. He was artist-in-residence at the American Academy in
Rome in 1953, 1964, and 1968.

LAFARGE, CHRISTOPHER GRANT, 1862–1938. He studied architecture at
M.I.T. and then under H. H. Richardson. From 1886 he was a practicing architect in New York, of always mounting repute. His designs
included those for the Cathedral of St. John the Divine in New York
and for many other churches. He was vice-president of the American
Institute of Architects and from 1909 trustee and from 1912 secretary
to the Board of the American Academy in Rome.

LAFARGE, JOHN, 1835–1910. He studied architectural decoration and
painting in Paris and then with William M. Hunt, later concentrating
on religious mural painting and glass staining. He was president of
the Society of American Artists and one of the original creators of
the American School in Rome. In 1905 he was one of the incorporators of its successor, the American Academy.

LAING, GORDON JENNINGS, 1869–1945. He was a fellow of the School of
Classical Studies in Rome in 1897. He then went to the University of

Chicago, where from 1899 to 1943 he went through the academic ranks from instructor to professor of classics and dean. He published extensively on classical subjects and returned to Rome as professor of classical studies at the American Academy 1911–12.

LAIRD, WARREN POWERS, 1861–1948. He was a practicing architect in Boston and New York 1882–90, with a year of study in Europe. He then became professor of architecture at the University of Pennsylvania 1891–1932 and dean of its School of Fine Arts 1920–32.

LAMOND, FELIX, 1863–1940. He studied music in London, his birthplace, but came to America and became a citizen in 1892. He lectured at Columbia on music literature and taught organ music, while also organist and choirmaster of Trinity Chapel in West 26th Street, 1898–1921. He was music critic for the *New York Herald* 1909–15. He was said to have "distinguished himself in various fields" including great administrative ability displayed in his work for the Red Cross in World War I. In 1925 he was awarded the Order of the Crown of Italy for his leadership in initiating the fellowships in music at the American Academy in Rome. He was professor of music at the Academy from 1920 and left to it a bequest in 1940. In 1929 he developed his plan for a center of relaxed musical composition at the villa of Roquebrune, between Mentone and Monte Carlo, to which Myron Taylor contributed. Its managing committee consisted of Lamond, Sowerby, Hanson, a French musician, and the director of the American Academy in Rome. Roquebrune was independent of the Academy but open to its music fellows.

LANIER, CHARLES, 1837–1926. He was a New York banker, the president of two mid-eastern railroads, and a director of the Southern Railway Company. A friend of J. P. Morgan, Senior, he was an incorporator of the American Academy in Rome in 1905.

LAWSON, EDWARD, 1886–1968. He was the first fellow in landscape architecture at the American Academy in Rome in 1915. He then served in World War I and returned to the Academy in 1921 to complete his three-year fellowship. He returned again in 1928 as professor of landscape architecture.

LAZARUS, JACOB H. The scholarships in his name were given, with endowment, to the Metropolitan Museum by his widow, Amelia B. Lazarus, in 1893.

LEE, RENSSELAER WRIGHT, 1898– . He graduated from Princeton in 1920 and was successively professor of fine arts at Northwestern, Smith, Columbia, and New York University, until he became professor at Princeton 1955–66. He is a very active leader in international as well as national art and educational circles. He was elected a trustee of the American Academy in 1958 and became its president in 1969. He was awarded the Academy's Medal for Outstanding Service.

LEIGHTON, GEORGE E., 1840–1901. He was a capitalist and prominent attorney of St. Louis and chairman of trustees at Washington University.

LEITER, LEVI, 1834–1904. He was a leading capitalist of Chicago. His daughter Mary Victoria married Lord Curzon of Kedleston and was a famous beauty and society leader in Britain.

LOCKWOOD, DEAN PUTNAM, 1883– . He was an instructor in classics at Harvard 1899–1910 and took his doctorate there in 1907. He then taught at Columbia 1911–18, when he took appointment at Haverford College, where he was associate, full, and emeritus professor for the balance of his career. He was professor in charge of classical studies at the American Academy in Rome 1927–28 and an incorporator of the American Philological Society.

LOCKWOOD, NORMAND, 1906– . He was a fellow in musical composition at the American Academy in Rome 1929–32, having studied music in Paris and Rome 1924–28. He served from 1945 as professor of music at Union Theological Seminary in New York and more recently as composer-in-residence at the University of Denver. His compositions are highly regarded.

LODGE, HENRY CABOT, 1850–1924. After leaving Harvard in 1871 he went rapidly and successfully into Massachusetts and then national politics and was a very influential senator from Massachusetts 1893–1923, as well as the author of several volumes of history. He attended the large dinner in Washington in celebration of the incorporation of the American Academy in Rome.

LORD, AUSTIN WILLARD, 1860–1922. He held the first Rotch Scholarship 1888–90 and then worked in the architectural firm of McKim, Mead, and White in New York until in 1894 he went to Rome as the first director of the new American School in Rome. He returned to New York to become an incorporator of the American Academy in Rome in 1905 and a practicing architect. He also served as professor of architecture at Columbia.

LORD, MILTON EDWARD, 1898– . He studied in Paris 1925–26 and was librarian at the American Academy in Rome 1926–30. He was at the Boston Public Library 1932–65 and became its director.

LOTHROP, STANLEY B. In June 1913 he was appointed assistant librarian "without encumbrance on the budget" at the American Academy in Rome, but in 1914 he was voted compensation for services at $500 a year. In 1914 he was officially recorded as "a regular member of the School of Classical Studies" and was lecturer on the history of art at the Academy in 1915, 1916, and 1917. He was a major in the American Red Cross in the district near Rimini 1918–19 and in 1920 returned to the Academy, where he collaborated with Van Dusen in the preparation of the 1920–21 brochure on the Academy library.

Low, SETH, 1850–1916. He was mayor of Brooklyn 1881–85, president of Columbia 1890–1901, mayor of New York City 1902–3, and a member of the Managing Committee of the American School 1890–96.

LOWRIE, WALTER, 1868–1959. A Princeton graduate, he was one of the first fellows (in Christian architecture) at the School of Classical Studies in Rome in 1895. He succeeded Robert J. Nevin as rector of St. Paul's American Church in Rome in 1907.

LUENING, OTTO, 1900– . Flutist and composer, he studied at Munich 1915–17 and at Zurich 1917–20. He was director and conductor of the Rochester Opera Company 1925–28. He was professor of music at Bennington College and has been chairman of the Department of Music at Columbia University. He served as a trustee of the American Academy in Rome 1950–64 and again 1967–1971 and was its composer-in-residence in 1958 and 1965.

McCLELLAN, GEORGE B., 1865–1940. He began as a journalist in New York, was president of the New York Board of Aldermen 1893–94, a member of the 54th to 58th Congresses, mayor of New York 1903–9, professor of economics at Princeton 1912–31, and chairman of the executive committee of the Smithsonian Institution. He was an incorporator of the American Academy in Rome in 1905 and a trustee from 1911.

McCORMICK, CYRUS HALL, 1859–1936. He graduated from Princeton in 1879 and became president and then chairman of the International Harvester Company 1884–1935. For half a century he was a leading and politically controversial figure in Chicago.

McCREA, NELSON GLENN, 1863–1944. He served in ranks from tutor to professor in Latin at Columbia 1889–1942, and was professor of classical studies at the American Academy in Rome 1921–22.

McDANIEL, WALTON BROOKS, 1871– . After graduation from Harvard in 1893 he studied in Paris and Rome 1897–98 and served as professor of classics at the University of Pennsylvania 1909–37. He was annual professor of classical studies at the American Academy in

Rome 1919–21 and president of the American Philosophical Association in 1921.

MACDOWELL, EDWARD ALEXANDER, 1861–1908. He studied piano and composition in Paris and Frankfort 1876–81 and taught piano at Darmstadt and Wiesbaden 1881–88, when he returned to America and became professor of music at Cornell until 1904. Meanwhile he had served as president of the American Society of Composers 1897–98. He was elected a trustee of the American Academy in Rome at the first meeting of its incorporators in April 1905 but was forced by illness to withdraw from the board in February 1906. The Macdowell Art Colony in Vermont bears his name.

MCILHENNY, HENRY PLUMER, 1910– . Harvard '33, he became curator of decorative arts at the Philadelphia Museum of Art 1935–64 and trustee 1964. He was a member of the Smithsonian Art Commission and of the Arts Commission for the White House. He was art historian in residence at the American Academy in Rome 1947–48 and has been a director of the Philadelphia Orchestra Association and of the Metropolitan Opera Association in New York.

MACKAY, CLARENCE HUNGERFORD, 1874–1938. Capitalist and head of a large telegraphy company, he commissioned the firm of McKim, Mead, and White for the erection of his homes and other structures in 1902, 1905, and 1907. He was chairman of the board of the New York Philharmonic Society and a director of the Metropolitan Opera Company. He was an incorporator of the American Academy in Rome in 1905 and in 1906 gave the Academy $10,000 for physical improvements in the Villa Mirafiori.

MCKIM, CHARLES FOLLEN, 1847–1909. At Harvard 1866–67, he then studied at the Paris Deaux Arts Institute and traveled in Europe, from London to Rome, 1867–70. He returned to New York and an architect's office, and in 1879 formed a partnership with Rutherford Mead and Stanford White. Stimulated by his associations at the Chicago Exposition in 1893, he led in formulating and bringing into being the American School in Rome 1894–95 and in its subsequent transition into the American Academy in 1905. He continued to dominate that undertaking until his death in 1909.

MACLEISH, ARCHIBALD, 1892– . Yale '15. By 1924 he had begun to publish volumes of poetry and prose, which have continued to appear until at least 1968. In a varied and ubiquitous career he has been winner of the Pulitzer Prize in Poetry in 1932 and of the Pulitzer Prize in Drama in 1951. During the interval he served as librarian of Congress 1939–44 and as assistant secretary of state 1944–45. He was writer-in-residence at the American Academy in Rome, president of the American Academy of Arts and Letters, and from 1949–62 Boylston Professor at Harvard. He holds many foreign decorations.

McMILLAN, JAMES, 1838–1902. A business and financial leader in Detroit, he was senator from Michigan 1889–1902 and became in 1897 a trustee of the American School in Rome.

MacNEIL, HERMON ATKINS, 1866–1947. He studied two years at the Paris Beaux Arts Institute and in 1895 became the first Rinehart Fellow in Sculpture at the American Academy in Rome 1896–99. Examples of his sculptural work are in the Metropolitan Museum, the Chicago Art Institute, the U.S. Supreme Court, and the Hall of Fame in New York University.

MacVEAGH, MRS. CHARLES (Fanny Davenport Rogers). In 1887 she married Charles MacVeagh (1860–1931), who practiced law in New York from 1883 and later in Washington; he headed relief to Italy after World War I and was ambassador to Japan 1925–29. In 1914 she gave funds for trees in the new courtyard to the American Academy in Rome.

MacVEAGH, FRANKLIN, c. 1840–1934. A prosperous merchant and banker of Chicago and active in Chicago civic affairs, he was secretary of the treasury under President Taft 1909–13.

MAGOFFIN, RALPH VAN DEMAN, 1874–1942. He was a fellow in the School of Classical Studies in Rome in 1907 and professor in charge of classical studies at the American Academy in Rome 1922. He was president of the Archaeological Institute of America 1921–31 and professor of classics at New York University 1923–39.

MAGONIGLE, HAROLD VAN BUREN, 1867–1935. He was an apprentice in architecture with McKim, Mead, and White 1888–94, when he won a Rotch Travelling Fellowship and became one of the first fellows at the American School in Rome 1894–95. He had already received a gold medal from the Architectural League in 1889 and indulged in sculpture as well as architecture. Upon his return to America he practiced in partnership until 1924 and then alone. He was architect for many public buildings including the U.S. embassy at Tokyo. He published several books on the arts.

MANSHIP, PAUL, 1886–1966. He was a fellow in sculpture at the American Academy in Rome 1909–12 and served as professor there 1922–23, having meanwhile made himself a notable figure in sculpture in America. At various times he was honorary president of the National Sculpture Society and a corresponding member of the Institute of France, the Academy des Beaux Arts, the National Argentine Academy of Fine Arts, and the National Academy of St. Luke, Italy. He was a trustee of the American Academy in Rome 1942–66 and long a very influential figure in its juries for the selection of sculptors for the Rome Prize.

MARQUAND, ALLAN, 1853–1924. He was professor of the history of art and archaeology at Princeton 1883–1924 and professor in the School of Classical Studies in Rome 1896–97. He was a recognized doyen of the fine arts academicians.

MARTINELLI, EZIO, 1913– . A sculptor, he has been a leading member of the staff of Sarah Lawrence College from 1947 and was sculptor-in-residence at the American Academy in Rome in 1965.

MAUGHAM, SOMERSET, 1874–1965. Few modern British writers have been his equal in novels, plays, and short stories published, in popularity, and in sales.

MEAD, WILLIAM RUTHERFORD, 1846–1928. He studied architecture in Europe for two years and in 1879 went into partnership with McKim, and a year later also with Stanford White. He was an incorporator of the American Academy in Rome in 1905 and for the rest of his life a devoted and effective supporter of that Academy and of McKim's ideas concerning it. He was its president 1910–28 and continuously a trustee. In 1916 he gave the Academy $25,000 to support a fellowship in architecture. He was made Knight Commander of the Crown of Italy in 1922 and held a gold medal from the National Institute of Arts and Letters.

MEEKS, EVERETT VICTOR, 1879–1954. He studied at the Paris Beaux Arts Institute for four years and then practiced architecture with Carrère and Hastings in New York 1908–14. He then became professor of architecture at Cornell and from 1916 was at Yale as professor and dean of the School of Fine Arts. In 1920 he began a service of more than twenty years as a trustee of the American Academy in Rome.

MELLON, EDWARD P., 1875–1953. He was a nephew of Andrew Mellon (secretary of the treasury, who gave $10,000 to the American Academy in Rome in 1916). He became an architect and designed the tomb of President Harding in Marion, Ohio, a large hospital in Pittsburgh, and a church in East Orange. He was a trustee of the American Academy and acting secretary of its board of trustees 1917–18. In his later years he lived near Wilmington, Del.

MELLON, PAUL, 1907– . Yale '29, he inherited a fortune and has used it in great part to collect valuable works of art; to give them away generously, and to create new foundations for the wise distribution of his wealth. In addition to directorships in business and finance, he is or has been chairman of the boards of the A. W. Mellon Educational and Charitable Trust, the Bollingen Fund, the Old Dominion Fund, and the Avalon Fund. He holds various honors and awards.

MENDELL, CLARENCE WHITTLESLEY, 1893– . He was professor of Latin and notable dean of Yale College from 1919 until his retirement. He was a member of the managing committee of the American School in Athens 1922–40, a longtime active trustee of the American Academy in Rome 1928–53, and professor of classical studies there 1932–33. He was awarded the Academy Medal for Outstanding Service.

MERRILL, ELMER TRUESDELL, 1860–1936. He was successively a professor of Latin at Wesleyan, Trinity, and the University of Chicago 1888–1925. He was professor of classical studies at the American School of Classical Studies in Rome 1898–99 and at the American Academy in Rome 1924–25.

MESTROVIC, IVAN, 1883–1962. Born in Croatia, he studied fine arts in Vienna 1900–1907, came to the U.S. in 1947, and became an American citizen in 1954. A sculptor, he was professor of fine arts at Syracuse University 1947–55 and artist-in-residence at the American Academy in Rome in 1900. He received medals and honors for his work in sculpture.

MEYER, GEORGE VAN LENGERKE, 1858–1918. He was a merchant and financier in Boston 1879–99 and married a sister of Charles McKim's second wife in 1885. He was ambassador to Italy 1900–1905 and to Russia 1905–07, postmaster general 1907–09, and secretary of the navy 1909–13.

MIDDLETON, JOHN IZARD, 1785–1849. He inherited a fortune from his South Carolina parents, attended Cambridge University, and settled in Italy, where he became a painter, an amateur archaeologist, and a leader of international society. He was the author of *Greek Remains in Italy . . . and Picturesque Views of Ancient Latium.*

MILLES, CARL WILHELM EMIL, 1875–1955. He was born in Sweden and studied art in Stockholm, at the Paris Beaux Arts Institute, and in Munich. He came to the States in 1929, rapidly won high esteem as a sculptor, and became an American citizen in 1945. He won many honors and was artist-in-residence at the American Academy in Rome in 1900. His work is represented in Stockholm, London, Brussels, Zurich, Chicago, St. Louis, and Philadelphia.

MILLET, FRANCIS DAVIS, 1846–1912. He was a drummer boy in Grant's army in 1864, an A.B. from Harvard in 1869, and a student at the Royal Academy of Fine Arts in Antwerp 1871–72. He then became a successful journalist in Europe and Asia and received decorations from Russia, Rumania, France, and Japan 1873–1898. During intervals in America he was active in fine arts organizations and was with Burnham, McKim, and LaFarge at the Chicago Exposition 1892–93. He was an incorporator of the American Academy in Rome in 1905, a trustee of the Academy from that time, executive secretary of the Academy and its chief administrator from February 1911 to April 1912, when he went down with the *Titanic*.

Moe, Henry Allen, 1894– . A Rhodes Scholar at Oxford 1919–22, and then a teacher of law at Oxford and in New York, he gave up legal practice to become trustee and executive of foundations. He was long president of the John Simon Guggenheim Memorial Fund and Fellowship, president for many years of the American Philosophical Society, and also a trustee of the American Academy in Rome since 1942. He was awarded the Academy's Medal for Outstanding Service.

Mongan, Agnes, 1905– . A graduate of Bryn Mawr in 1927, she served at the Fogg Museum from 1928, in varied capacities including curator, assistant and associate director, and full director in 1969. In 1950 she was art historian-in-residence at the American Academy in Rome. She is a member of many national and international commissions on the fine arts and the author or co-author of several books on the arts.

Moore, Charles, 1855–1942. He was active in banking and journalism in Detroit, Washington, and Boston 1878–1914. He became chairman of the National Commission on the Fine Arts and an honorary member of the American Institute of Architects. He knew McKim, Burnham, and Olmsted in the days of the Shack at the Chicago Exposition and traveled with all three of them in Europe in 1901. He was an incorporator of the American Academy in Rome in 1905 and served as a trustee. He published biographies of Burnham in 1921 and of McKim in 1929.

Moore, Clifford Herschel, 1866–1931. He was successively professor of Latin at Chicago and Harvard and was professor at the School of Classical Studies in Rome 1905–6.

Moore, Edward C., Jr. He was a trustee 1921–31 and patron of the American Academy in Rome, to which he gave substantial gifts.

Moore, Lamont, 1909– . He graduated from Lafayette College and was briefly on the staff of the National Gallery before serving as assistant director of the American Academy in Rome 1947–48. He was associate director of the Yale University Art Gallery 1948–53, when he succeeded John Phillips as director.

MOREY, CHARLES RUFUS, 1877–1965. He was a fellow in the American School of Classical Studies in Rome in 1903 and served as professor of art and archaeology at Princeton from 1918. He returned to Rome as professor of classical studies at the American Academy 1925–26. During World War II he was cultural attaché at the Embassy in Rome and remained there as the war ended in the capacity of head of the Office of War Information in Italy. He served also as acting director of the Academy and then director 1945–47. He received decorations from four European nations.

MORGAN, EDWIN D., 1837–1913. In 1891 McKim, Mead, and White were architects for his home in Newport, R.I., and in 1900 for his handsome residence at Wheatley Hills, Long Island. In 1895 he gave $3,000 to the American School of Classical Studies in Rome, and in 1905 he was an incorporator of the American Academy.

MORGAN, JOHN PIERPONT, SENIOR, 1837–1913. Financier, collector, and philanthropist, he made repeated large gifts and loans that became gifts to the American School and then the American Academy in Rome. He was an incorporator of the Academy in 1905 and a trustee 1905–13.

MORGAN, JOHN PIERPONT, JUNIOR, 1867–1943. He emulated his father not only in ability as a leading banker and philanthropist but also in his own gifts to the American Academy in Rome. He declined with good reason an invitation to succeed his father as a trustee of the Academy, since it was then largely in his debt for renewed loans (which also became gifts), but later joined its Advisory Council.

MORRIS, MRS. PAUL. Her husband was a sculptor (1865–1916) who had studied with Saint-Gaudens and Daniel Chester French, and her offer to endow a sculptor's studio in the New York office of the American Academy in Rome was in her husband's name.

MOWBRAY, HENRY SIDDONS, 1858–1928. He studied art in Paris and Spain for eight years and then established himself as a mural painter in New York in 1886. He worked with McKim on the murals in the new University Club. He was an incorporator of the American Academy in Rome and a trustee. He became secretary to that board, then went to Rome to work on murals, and was persuaded by McKim to accept on a temporary basis the directorship of the Academy, which he held through 1904.

MUNSEY, FRANK ANDREW, 1854–1925. He was a large publisher of magazines in New York, the author of several novels, and a well-known and highly influential journalist and editor. His gift of $5,000 in 1910 made him one of the Benefactors of the American Academy in Rome.

NEVIN, ROBERT JENKINS, 1839–1906. He began his career as a lieutenant of Pennsylvania troops in the Civil War, gaining promotion to captain and major. He then graduated from the General Theological Seminary in New York and served as rector of St. Paul's Church in Rome, of which he had supervised the building, from 1869 until his death in 1906.

NEWBOLD, THOMAS. He was a friend of McKim with a house at 15 East 79th Street and a home in Perthshire, Scotland, where McKim visited him in 1903. His gift to the American Academy in Rome about 1910 made him one of its Benefactors.

NICOLL, JOHN RAMSAY ALLARDYCE, 1894– . He is a British authority on the drama and its history and was chairman of the Drama School at Yale 1932–45. He was professor of English at Birmingham University, England, 1945–61.

NOLAND, WILLIAM CHURCHILL, 1865–1951. An architect in practice in Richmond, Va., 1896–1940, he was a friend of George Bispham Page and with him at the American School of Architecture in Rome from November 1894.

NORTON, CHARLES DYER, 1871–1922. He graduated from Amherst in 1893 and was in Chicago with the Northwestern Mutual Life Insurance Company 1895–1908, when he became assistant secretary of the treasury and then private secretary to President Taft 1908–11. He was vice president of the First National Bank in New York and a director of several companies. During World War I he was second in command of American Red Cross services in Europe and one of its trustees. He returned to his banking activities after the war and was a trustee of the Metropolitan Museum of Art, the American Federation of Arts, and Russell Sage College. In 1913 he had been elected a trustee of the American Academy in Rome in succession to J. P. Morgan. He was a member of its executive committee from 1913, of its finance committee from 1916, and by his gifts became a Benefactor of the Academy.

NORTON, CHARLES ELIOT, 1827–1908. He traveled and studied in Europe from 1849 and was in Germany 1867–72. He was professor of fine arts at Harvard 1873–97.

NORTON, RICHARD, 1872–1918. A son of Charles Eliot Norton and an archaeologist, he studied in Germany and at the American School in Athens. He was professor at the American School of Classical Studies in Rome 1897–98 and director of the school 1899–1907. During

World War I he organized the American Volunteer Ambulance Corps and served with the French army.

OENSLAGER, DONALD MITCHELL, 1902– . After graduating from Harvard he studied theater design in Europe on a Sachs Fellowship. He became a leading designer of stage settings for plays, operas, and ballets. During World War II he was a combat intelligence officer. He has been a professor of scenic design at Yale and has lectured in many foreign countries on several continents. In 1953 he was artist-in-residence at the American Academy in Rome.

OGLE, MARBURY BLADEN, 1879– . He was professor of classics at the University of Minnesota and at Ohio State University. In 1931 he succeeded Henry Sanders as professor in charge of classical studies at the American Academy in Rome for two years.

OLIVER, JAMES HENRY, JR., 1905– . He was a fellow in classics and archaeology at the American Academy in Rome 1928–30, professor of classics at Johns Hopkins from 1946, and recently professor of classics at the American Academy in Rome. He has been a member of the executive committee of the American School in Athens since 1952 and has published many learned articles.

OLMSTED, FREDERICK LAW, 1822–1903. After farming for seven years he studied and practiced landscape architecture when it was still a new profession. As superintendent of Central Park in New York from 1857 he demonstrated his principles of landscaping and designed upon request public parks in other major cities, as well as the grounds and terraces of the capital in Washington, D.C. He was an official advisor at the Chicago Exposition in 1903 and there worked with the architects and artists of the Shack.

OLMSTED, FREDERICK LAW, JR., 1870–1957. After Harvard he followed his father in leading the development of landscape gardening in America (from 1895). In 1901, as a member of the new Senate Park Commission, he traveled in Europe with fellow members Burnham, McKim, and Charles Moore. He was professor of landscape architecture at Harvard 1903–14 and in 1905 was an incorporator of the American Academy in Rome and a member of its advisory council until 1947. He was active in the National Commission on Fine Arts 1910–18.

OSBORNE, MRS. HENRY FAIRFIELD (Lucretia Thatcher Perry). She was the wife of Henry Fairfield Osborne, capitalist and paleontologist. In 1922 she sent to the trustees of the American Academy in Rome about $10,500 raised for its program of music studies at a Gala Concert in New York which she and other ladies had organized. In

December 1924 she sent in another $8,000 they had also raised for that purpose.

OWINGS, NATHANIEL ALEXANDER, 1903– . A lively and brilliant partner in the noted architectural firm of Skidmore, Owings, and Merrill in Boston from 1936, he has been chairman of planning commissions in Chicago and California. He was architect-in-residence at the American Academy in Rome 1958–59 and has been a trustee 1967–71 and a generous supporter of the Academy.

PAGE, GEORGE BISPHAM. He studied and traveled in Europe as a fellow in architecture of the University of Pennsylvania 1893–94, and then came as fellow to the American School of Architecture in Rome in its first year, from November 1894. He later practiced architecture in Philadelphia and from 1899 was a member of the American Institute of Architects.

PAGE, THOMAS NELSON, 1853–1922. Lawyer, lecturer, and author of some twenty popular volumes, he was ambassador to Italy 1913–19. McKim, Mead, and White were the architects for his home in Washington in 1897.

PARKER, HORATIO WILLIAM, 1863–1919. He was educated partly in Europe and graduated from the Royal Conservatory in Munich in 1885. He was professor of music at Yale from 1894 and received honors and awards for his compositions.

PARRISH, SAMUEL L., d. 1932. McKim designed his new home in Southampton, Long Island, in 1889. There Parrish was president and chief benefactor of the art museum, and he established and annually supported the Parrish Art Museum Fellowship at the American Academy in Rome until 1931.

PEABODY, ROBERT SWAIN, 1845–1917. A Boston architect who had studied at the Paris Beaux Arts Institute 1868–69, he was a close friend of Francis Ward Chandler and Charles F. McKim. He was an overseer of Harvard from 1888 and an incorporator of the American Academy in Rome in 1905.

PEEBLES, BERNARD MANN, 1906– . He was a fellow in classical studies at the American Academy in Rome 1932–34. He has been professor of classics at Fordham University and at the Catholic University in Washington, as well as a director of the American Philological Association 1968–69.

PERKINS, ROBERT PATTERSON, 1861–1924. From 1914 he was president of the Bigelow-Hartford Carpet Company. During World War I he was lieutenant colonel in the American Red Cross, commanding in

Rome under Charles Norton, and living in 1917–18 at the American Academy in Rome.

PHELAN, JAMES DUVAL, 1861–1930. Attorney, three times mayor of San Francisco 1897–1902, and president of the commission that procured Daniel Burnham to make the Burnham Plan for San Francisco, he was senator from California 1915–21. In 1922 he made a world tour and in 1923 offered to secure funds in California for the American Academy in Rome if he were made one of its trustees. The offer was not acted upon.

PHILLIPS, WILLIAM, 1878–1968. He graduated from Harvard in 1900 and was in the Foreign Service or the State Department from 1903 until his retirement from active service in 1944. He was first secretary in the embassy in London 1909–12, assistant secretary of state 1917–20, undersecretary of state 1922–24 and again in 1933, ambassador to Belgium 1924–27, to Canada 1927–29, and to Italy 1936–41. He resigned the last post when Italy declared war on the United States and was ambassador to India 1942–44.

PINE, JOHN B., 1857–1922. An attorney in New York, he was a member of the New York Commission on the Arts 1907–9, a trustee of Columbia University from 1890, a trustee of the American Academy in Rome from 1910, and its legal counsel in 1917.

PLATNER, SAMUEL BALL, 1863–1921. He was successively instructor, assistant professor, and professor of Latin at Western Reserve University 1885–1921. He was a member of the managing and executive committees of the School of Classical Studies in Rome 1895–1911 and was annual professor at the school 1899–1900.

PLATT, CHARLES ADAMS, 1861–1933. He studied art and architecture in Paris and became a distinguished architect in New York. He was a trustee of the American Academy in Rome and its president 1928–33.

PLATT, WILLIAM, 1897– . A distinguished New York architect, he has been a valued trustee of the American Academy in Rome since 1942, serving on various occasions as chairman of the architectural juries and chairman of the Committee on the School of Fine Arts. He is a member of the executive committee and was awarded the Academy's Medal for Outstanding Service.

POLASEK, ALBIN, 1879–1965. He was a fellow in sculpture at the American Academy in Rome 1910–13 and a visiting professor there 1930–31. He received various honors and awards for his work in sculpture.

POPE, JOHN RUSSELL, 1874–1937. He was the first fellow to hold the new Rome Prize in Architecture at the American School in Rome

1895–97 and gave further study to the arts in Paris. In 1900 he established his practice in New York, where his work was pre-eminent. It included many large private homes, as well as additions or alterations to the British Museum, the Tate Gallery, the Frick Museum, new construction of the Washington National Gallery and many collegiate buildings at Yale and elsewhere. He was a trustee of the American Academy from 1926 and its president 1933–37.

PORTER, HENRY KIRKE, 1840–1921. He was in business in Pittsburgh from 1866 and became president of the Porter Company, which manufactured locomotives. He was elected to the House of Representatives 1903–5, became a trustee of various educational and charitable institutions, and was an incorporator in 1905 of the American Academy in Rome.

POST, CHANDLER RATHFON, 1881–1959. He studied at the American School in Athens and from 1905 was professor of Greek and fine arts at Harvard.

PRATT, FREDERICK BAYLEY, 1865–1945. Of the Pratt family of Standard Oil, with a handsome home at Glen Cove, Long Island, he was a generous benefactor of many educational and charitable institutions, including the American Academy in Rome.

PRATT, RICHARDSON, 1894–1959. From 1919 he was a financial authority and a director of companies, a trustee of Amherst and of St. Luke's Hospital. He was trustee 1940–59 and secretary to the board of the American Academy in Rome, to which he bequeathed $25,000. In 1963 his wife gave the Academy another $5,000.

PROCTOR, ALEXANDER PHIMINISTER, 1862–1950. He was Rinehart Fellow at the American School in Rome 1896–97 and later settled in Seattle, where he lived for many years. In 1900 he was awarded a gold medal for sculpture at the Paris Exposition. Examples of his work are in the Metropolitan Museum, the Corcoran Gallery, and in many public buildings and parks.

PUVIS DE CHAVANNES, PIERRE, 1824–98. He was a well-known French painter, muralist, and illustrator, whose early popularity has stood the test of nearly a century.

RAND, EDWARD KENNARD, 1871–1945. He took a doctorate in Munich in 1900, having taught Latin at the University of Chicago 1895–98. He then went to Harvard where he was professor 1909–42. He was sometime president of the American Philological Society and of the Mediaeval Academy of America. He was a trustee of the American Academy in Rome from 1911 but resigned from that office in 1929 due to the pressure of other work. He was later induced to rejoin the board. He was professor at the School of Classical Studies in Rome 1912–13.

RAPUANO, MICHAEL, 1904– . After study at Cornell he was a fellow in landscape architecture at the American Academy in Rome and has since practiced in New York. He held a commission at the San Francisco Exposition in 1939. From 1947 he was a trustee of the American Academy and its president 1958–69. His generous gifts have made him one of its Patrons. He was awarded the Academy's Medal for Outstanding Service.

REINHARDT, GEORGE FREDERICK, 1911– . After holding various posts in the federal government and its foreign service he became ambassador to Vietnam 1955–56, to the United Arab Republic 1960–61, and to Italy 1961–68.

RICE, MRS. WINTHROP MERTON (Helen Swift Jones). She was a landscape architect in her own right and through Michael Rapuano gave $1,000 to the American Academy in 1966.

RICHARDSON, HENRY HOBSON, 1838–1886. He studied architecture at the Paris Beaux Arts Institute and then became a partner in the New York architectural firm of Gambrill and Richardson. He was architect for Trinity Church in Boston, several buildings at Harvard, the Albany Senate chamber, and many libraries.

RICHARDSON, LAWRENCE, JR., 1920– . After training as an archaeologist, he held a fellowship at the American Academy in Rome 1948–50 and returned there as field archaeologist 1952–53. He was elected a trustee of the Academy in 1969. He is chairman of the Department of Classics at Duke University. His wife, Emeline Hill Richardson, was also a fellow in classics at the American Academy in Rome 1949–52, worked with him at the Academy's excavations, and is now teaching at the University of North Carolina.

RICHARDSON, WILLIAM SYMMES, 1873–1931. He studied at the Beaux Arts Institute in Paris, took employment with McKim, Mead, and White in 1895, and became a partner in 1906. He served in Italy with the American Red Cross 1917–18 and afterward settled in a house across the street from the Academy in Rome. He was professor of fine arts there 1925–26, and his house is now the property of the Academy through the bequest of his sister, Miss Ethel Richardson, in 1963.

RICHTER, GISELA, 1882– . During many years at the Metropolitan Museum in New York she acquired a reputation as a very distinguished scholar of classical art. She was Jerome Lecturer at the American Academy in Rome 1952–53 and in recent years has lived mostly in an apartment in Rome and been a close friend of the Academy, which in 1964 awarded her a medal for Outstanding Service to the Academy.

RICKER, NATHAN CLIFFORD, 1843–1924. At the University of Illinois he ascended from instructor to professor of architecture between 1873 and 1911, and also served until 1905 as dean of engineering. He was president of the Board of Examiners in Architecture 1897–1917.

RINEHART, WILLIAM HENRY, 1825–74. While apprenticed to a stone cutter in Baltimore he won a gold medal in 1851 for a stone copy of Tenier's *Smokers*. This secured help for him to go to Florence and then to Rome as sculptor 1854–58. On his return to America he executed commissions for sculpture in the Capitol in Washington; his work is also in the Metropolitan Museum. His estate established the Rinehart School of Sculpture at the Maryland Institute, and the Rinehart Scholarships, assigned to the American Academy in Rome.

ROBERTS, LAURANCE PAGE, 1907– . After graduation from Princeton in 1929 he became a distinguished scholar of Far Eastern art and was long director of the Brooklyn Museum before service as a captain in the U.S. Army in World War II. He was director of the American Academy in Rome 1946–60 and was awarded the Academy's Medal for Outstanding Service.

ROBINSON, DOUGLAS, d. 1918. He was an officer and director of various financial institutions in and about New York, including the Bankers' Trust Company. He married Corinne Roosevelt.

ROBINSON, EDWARD, 1858–1931. After studying the fine arts for five years in Europe, including fifteen months in Greece, he became in 1885 a curator in the Boston Museum of Fine Arts and from 1902 was its director. He was director of the Metropolitan Museum 1910–31. He was an incorporator of the American Academy in Rome in 1905 and one of its trustees 1906–31.

ROBINSON, RODNEY POTTER, 1890–1950. He was at the University of Cincinnati 1927–1950, becoming professor of classics and philology and later dean. He was professor in charge of classical studies at the American Academy in Rome 1935–37.

ROBINSON, THOMAS L., 1880–1940. A lawyer and banker, he was with the American Red Cross 1917–19 and with the Dawes Commission in 1924. From 1926 he was vice-president of the Guaranty Trust Company in New York.

ROCKEFELLER, JOHN D., JR., 1874–1960. Financier and philanthropist, he gave $200,000 to the American Academy in Rome in 1922, and foundations which he headed also helped substantially.

ROLFE, JOHN CAREW, 1859–1943. He was professor of Latin at the University of Pennsylvania from 1902; also professor in the American School of Classical Studies in Rome 1907–8 and at the American Academy in Rome 1923–24.

ROOSEVELT, NICHOLAS, 1893– . He has been a newspaper correspondent and editor, an author, a diplomat, and an ardent active conservationist. He was minister to Hungary 1930–33 and c. 1966 became a life member of the American Academy in Rome by a gift to its endowment.

ROOT, ELIHU, 1845–1937. He was a prominent attorney in New York from 1867 and headed a large law firm. He was secretary of war 1899–1904 and secretary of state 1905–9; then senator from New York 1909–15. He was an incorporator of the American Academy in Rome in 1905.

ROSENWALD, JULIUS, 1862–1932. Philadelphia merchant and philanthropist, creator of the Rosenwald Foundation, he was chairman of the board of Sears Roebuck and Company from 1925; trustee of the Rockefeller Foundation, the University of Chicago, Tuskegee Institute, and Hull House; and especially active and generous in support of efforts to benefit the American negro. In 1926 he gave a sum to the American Academy in Rome.

ROSPIGLIOSI, MARGHERITA, 1909– . On October 1, 1968, she completed twenty years of valuable service in Rome as secretary of the American Academy.

ROTCH, BENJAMIN S., 1850–94. Harvard '71, he then studied architecture at M.I.T. and the Paris Beaux Arts Institute. He returned to practice architecture in Boston and was a trustee of the Boston Museum of Fine Arts. He had planned to create a scholarship in the fine arts, and after his death his family, led by his son Arthur Rotch, did so in his name.

ROWELL, HENRY THOMPSON, 1904– . He studied and then taught classics at Yale, and also directed with notable success the summer sessions of the American Academy in Rome 1937–39, 1947–48, and 1950–51. He became professor of Latin at Johns Hopkins in 1940 and a trustee of the American Academy in 1946. He was professor in charge of classical studies at the Academy 1961–63 and became president of the Academy in 1972.

SAGE, MRS. RUSSELL (Margaret Olivia Slocum), 1828–1918. She was born in Syracuse and in 1869 married Russell Sage, capitalist. He died in 1906, leaving her a large fortune, to the generous distribution of which she devoted the rest of her life. She created the Russell

Sage Foundation with an initial gift of $10,000,000, and in 1916 she founded the Russell Sage College of Practical Arts in Troy, N.Y. She made many other gifts to charities and education.

SAINT-GAUDENS, AUGUSTUS, 1848–1907. He studied at the National Academy of Design, the Beaux Arts Institute in Paris, and in Rome 1870–72 and then established himself as a sculptor in New York. His work won medals of honor at the Paris and Buffalo expositions and he was perhaps the best-known and most-admired sculptor of his time in America. He was an instigator and in 1905 an incorporator of the American Academy in Rome.

SANDERS, HENRY A., 1868–1956. He was a member of the managing committee of the American School in Athens 1902–6; professor of Latin at the University of Michigan from 1911; annual professor of classical studies at the American Academy in Rome 1915–16, and professor in charge of classical studies there 1928–31. He was president of the American Philological Association 1936–37 and the author of many scholarly publications.

SANDERS, ROBERT L., 1906– . After studying music at the Bush Conservatory in Chicago he was a fellow in music at the American Academy in Rome 1925–29. He returned to Chicago as professor at the Chicago Conservatory 1929–38 and then went to the University of Indiana in 1938 as professor and dean. He was a Guggenheim fellow 1954–55 and composed symphonies and concertos. He is now in the Music Department of Brooklyn College.

SARGENT, JOHN SINGER, 1856–1925. He was born in Florence and educated largely in Italy and Germany. He continued with the study of painting in Florence and Paris and after 1884 lived in London. He was a leading English portrait painter of his day and won many honors.

SAVAGE, EUGENE FRANCIS, 1883– . He studied painting at the Corcoran Art School in Washington, the Art Institute in Chicago, and privately in Munich. He was a fellow at the American Academy in Rome 1912–15 and professor of painting at Yale 1923–42. He was a member of the National Commission of Fine Arts 1933–41. His landscapes and portraits won several awards and medals and are represented at the Chicago Art Institute and at Yale. He was trustee of the American Academy 1928–47.

SCHERMERHORN, FREDERICK AUGUSTUS, 1844–1919. After serving in the Union Army 1864–65, he settled in New York and became a financial figure there. As a trustee of Columbia his leadership as well as his gifts made possible the creation of a department of architecture. He shared in the beginnings of the American Academy, as an organizer and a donor, and was one of its incorporators in 1905.

SCHIFF, MORTIMER L., 1877–1931. A partner and sometime head of the leading financial house of Kuhn, Loeb, and Company, he gave $10,000 to the American Academy in Rome in 1923.

SCHMIDLAPP, MRS. CARL JACOB. She was the wife of Carl Jacob Schmidlapp of Cincinnati, director of industrial companies and a vice-president of the Chase National Bank. In 1914 she gave funds to the American Academy to furnish the dining room of its new main building in Rome.

SCHNACKE, MAHLON K., d. November 1948. He replaced Wyllis E. Wright in 1933 as librarian of the American Academy in Rome, serving until his death.

SCHWARTZ, ANDREW THOMAS, 1867–1942. He was Lazarus Fellow in Mural Painting at the American Academy in Rome 1900–1902 and returned to America for a lifetime career in mural painting. Examples of his work are in the New York County Court House and the Kansas City Museum.

SESSIONS, ROGER HUNTINGTON, 1896– . Though known to be married at the time, he was awarded a fellowship in musical composition at the American Academy in Rome 1928–31, after previous study in Berlin and Italy. He became professor of music at Princeton 1935–45 and later at the Juilliard School of Music in New York. His compositions have won honors and awards. He was later professor of music at Berkeley, Calif., and returned to Princeton as professor in 1953. Since 1965 he has been on the faculty of the Juilliard School.

SHEPARDSON, WHITNEY HART, 1890–1966. Colgate '10, Rhodes Scholar at Oxford 1910–13, attorney, railroad president from 1917, and author of books on world affairs, he was trustee 1946–66, donor, and first vice-president of the American Academy in Rome.

SHOE, LUCY T. (later Lucy Shoe Meritt), 1906– . A graduate of Bryn Mawr in 1927, she took her master's degree there in 1928 and a doctorate in 1935. She was long a professor of classics at Mount Holyoke. In 1937 she was a fellow in classical studies at the American Academy in Rome, and from that year was also a member of the managing committee of the American School in Athens. She was a fellow at the Institute for Advanced Study at Princeton in 1946, and in later years; in 1950–51 she returned as fellow to the Academy, which has published two volumes of her work on Greek and Roman architecture.

SHOWERMAN, GRANT, 1870–1935. He was a fellow in the School of Classical Studies in Rome 1898–1900 and then went to the University of Wisconsin as professor of classics. He served also as professor of classical studies at the American Academy in Rome 1922–23 and as director of its summer sessions 1923–32. He published charming essays as well as several volumes on Roman letters and history.

SIMMONS, EDWARD, 1852–1931. Harvard '74, he then studied painting in Paris. His work later won prizes and important commissions for mural decorations such as those in the Library of Congress, various state capitols, and the homes of John D. Rockefeller and Frederick Vanderbilt. In 1922 he published an autobiography. He was a trustee of the American School in Rome in 1896.

SJÖQVIST, ERIC, 1903– . He was a member of several Swedish archaeological excavations in Greece and director of the Swedish excavation in Cyprus 1927–31. He then became librarian of the Royal Library at Stockholm until he left in 1940 to head the Swedish Archaeological Institute in Rome until 1948, during which period he was well known at the American Academy. He then took appointment as professor of classical archaeology at Princeton 1948–69. He was archaeologist-in-residence at the Academy 1962–63 and Jerome Lecturer in 1966.

SLAUGHTER, MOSES STEPHEN, 1860–1923. He studied at Berlin and Munich 1893–94 and from 1906 was professor of Latin at the University of Wisconsin. He was professor at the American School of Classical Studies in Rome 1909–10 and was again in Italy 1918–19 as a captain in the American Red Cross, when he was decorated by the Italian government.

SMITH, CLEMENT LAWRENCE, 1844–1909. He was professor of Latin and later dean at Harvard 1873–1902 and sometime president of the American Philological Association. He served as director of the School of Classical Studies in Rome 1897–98.

SMITH, JAMES KELLUM, 1893–1961. He was Stewardson Fellow in Architecture of the University of Pennsylvania at the American Academy in Rome 1920–23; then a member from 1924 and a partner from 1929 of McKim, Mead, and White. He held a commission at the San Francisco Exposition in 1939, was a major in the Air Force in 1942, a trustee of the American Academy in Rome from 1933, and its president 1937–58. In 1961 he was awarded the Academy's Medal for Outstanding Service.

SMITH, JAMES KELLUM, JR., 1927– . Secretary of the Rockefeller Foundation, he has been a trustee of the Academy since 1965 and was treasurer 1966 and second vice-president 1967–72. He is a member of the Executive Committee.

SMITH, JOSEPH LINDON, 1863–1950. A mural painter, he worked with Charles McKim in the decoration of the new Boston Public Library and held other commissions in Boston. Later resident in New York, he was frequently in Europe, was with the American Red Cross in Italy, and did archaeological excavation and pictorial description on an expedition in Egypt by the Metropolitan Museum.

SMITH, KIRBY FLOWER, 1862–1918. He was professor of Latin at the Johns Hopkins University 1889–1918 and professor of classics and acting director of the American School of Classical Studies and of the American Academy in Rome 1914–15.

SORCHAN, MRS. VICTOR (Charlotte Hunnewell). In the early years of the American School and Academy in Rome she organized women in New York to join her in giving select evening affairs to raise money for their support and gave generously herself. Widowed in 1921, she married Dr. Walton Martin (1869–1949), a surgeon and professor of surgery at Columbia University.

SOWERBY, LEO, 1895–1968. He was the first fellow in music to attend the American Academy 1921–24. He devoted his career to musical composition, at which he was notable. He was director of the College of Church Musicians in Washington from 1962 until his death.

STEINERT, ALEXANDER L. 1900–   . He was a fellow in musical composition at the American Academy in Rome 1927–30 and is currently resident in New York.

STEVENS, GORHAM PHILLIPS, 1876–1963. He studied at M.I.T. and then, 1901–2, at the Beaux Arts Institute in Paris. He was with McKim, Mead, and White in New York 1902–3 and then a fellow of the American School in Athens 1903–5. He returned to McKim, Mead, and White until he went to Rome in 1912 as director of the American Academy until January 1, 1913. He then served as acting director, in the frequent absences of Jesse Benedict Carter, until he again became director 1917–32 after the death of Carter. He was director of the American School in Athens 1939–41. He was a captain in the American Red Cross 1917–18. In 1960 he was awarded the Academy's Medal for Outstanding Service. He bequeathed $100,000 to the Academy in Rome.

STILLMAN, JAMES, 1850–1918. He began in New York as a cotton merchant but became president and later chairman of the board of the National City Bank 1891–1909, as well as a director of many companies. His town house in New York was designed by McKim,

Mead, and White in 1904, as was a house built for him at Pocantico Hills in 1907. He was an incorporator of the American Academy in Rome in 1905, and its benefactor, though his gifts were reduced as a result of the 1907 panic.

STOKES, ANSON PHELPS, 1874–1958. A devoted graduate of Yale and from 1899–1921 a Yale Corporation member and its secretary, he took orders in the Episcopal church and was also active in its service, including his years as canon of Washington Cathedral 1924–39. Tireless in pursuit of his philanthropies, he was a trustee of the American Academy in Rome 1911–1919.

STORER, MRS. BELLAMY (Maria Longworth), 1849–1932. She was a friend of Charles McKim's daughter and offered to bequeath her estate to the American Academy in Rome. She founded the Rockwood Pottery and won gold medals for her own pottery at the Paris exhibitions of 1889 and 1900. Bellamy Storer was a lawyer and diplomat who died in 1922.

STORY, THOMAS WALDO. He was the son of William Wetmore Story (1819–95), a lawyer and sculptor who lived in Rome from 1856. The son, also an artist, became a trustee of the American Academy in early 1898 and was one of its incorporators in 1905.

STUART, MERIWETHER, 1905–   . In 1941 he was a professor of classics at Hunter College in New York and editor of the *Bulletin* of the Archaeological Institute of America. During the emergency immediately following World War II he served as executive secretary *pro tem* of the American Academy in Rome from October 1945 to November 1946.

STYRON, WILLIAM, 1925–   . He took his degree at Duke University in 1947 and embarked on a career as a writer. He was a fellow in writing at the American Academy in Rome 1952–53 and later, and has been a member of the Yale faculty since 1964. He won a Pulitzer Prize in 1968 for the *Confessions of Nat Turner,* widely regarded as a modern classic.

SULLIVAN, LEWIS HENRY, 1856–1924. He studied architecture at M.I.T. and then at the Beaux Arts Institute in Paris. He practiced architecture in Chicago from 1880 and did work for the Chicago Exposition in 1893. He received a gold medal in Paris in 1894 and wrote many magazine articles on architecture and allied topics. Both his style and his personality left their mark upon American architects and architecture.

TATE, ALLEN, 1899–   . Vanderbilt University '22; professor of English at the College for Women of the University of North Carolina

1938–39; at Princeton 1939–42 and at the Library of Congress 1943–44; professor of humanities at the University of Chicago 1949; professor of English, University of Minnesota 1951–68; and Fulbright Professor at Oxford University 1958–59. He was a Guggenheim fellow 1928–30 and writer-in-residence at the American Academy in Rome 1953–54. He has published several volumes of poetry and about poetry, and many articles on literary topics.

TAYLOR, FRANCIS HENRY, 1903–57. A student of the history of art, he was a visiting fellow at the American Academy in Rome 1925–26, Carnegie fellow at Princeton 1926–27, and Guggenheim fellow in 1931. He was director of the Worcester, Mass., Art Museum 1931–40, of the Metropolitan Museum of Art of New York 1940–55, and again of the Worcester Museum 1955–57. He was awarded many honors and several decorations in Europe and was a trustee of the American Academy in Rome.

TAYLOR, JOSEPH DEEMS, 1885–1966. Composer and critic, a leading spirit in music in New York, he was a trustee of the American Academy in Rome from 1929.

TAYLOR, LILY ROSS, 1886–1969. She was a Bryn Mawr Scholar at the School of Classical Studies in Rome 1909–10 and fellow in archaeology at the American Academy 1917–22, but during the latter part of World War I she was with the American Red Cross in Italy and the Balkans. She was professor of Latin at Bryn Mawr 1927–52; twice professor in charge of classical studies at the American Academy in Rome 1934–35 and 1952–53 and Jerome Lecturer at the Academy 1964–65. In 1964 the Academy gave her its Medal for Outstanding Service.

TAYLOR, MYRON CHARLES, 1874–1959. Legal counsel of the United States Steel Corporation, he became its chief executive officer 1932–38. He served on various federal commissions until in 1939 he accepted appointment as personal representative, with the rank of ambassador, of President Roosevelt and then President Truman, at the Vatican. He held that appointment until 1950 and received many European decorations, honors, and citations. In 1930 he provided funds for Felix Lamond to acquire the Villa Roquebrune on the French Riviera for musicians. He was a trustee of the American Academy in Rome 1930–53.

TEMPLE, SETH JUSTIN, 1867–1949. He was the first Charles McKim Fellow in Architecture from Columbia to the American School of Architecture in Rome in November 1894. After 1904 he was an architect at Davenport, Iowa.

THOMAS, M. CAREY, 1857–1935. She studied at Leipzig, Zurich, and the Sorbonne and took a doctorate at Zurich 1879–82. She was president of Bryn Mawr College 1894–1922.

THOMPSON, RANDALL, 1899– . He was a fellow in music at the American Academy in Rome 1922–25, professor of music at the University of California at Berkeley 1937–39, director of the Curtis Institute in Philadelphia 1939–41, and professor of music at the University of Virginia 1941–45, at Princeton 1945–48, and Harvard 1948–65. He was a trustee of the American Academy 1946–69.

TROWBRIDGE, SAMUEL BRECK PARKMAN, 1862–1925. He studied at the American School in Athens and at the Beaux Arts Institute in Paris after taking a degree in architecture at Columbia in 1886. He then became an architect in New York, an incorporator of the American Academy in Rome in 1905, one of its trustees from 1906, and its vice-president from 1917. His work in architecture received honors and decorations from France, Greece, Serbia, and Rumania.

ULLMAN, BERTHOLD L., 1882–1965. He was a fellow of the American School of Classical Studies 1906–8 and professor of Latin at the University of Chicago 1925–44 and at North Carolina 1944–59. He was a brilliant scholar in the fields of classical and Renaissance Latin.

VAN BUREN, ALBERT WILLIAM, 1878–1968. A graduate of Yale in 1900, fellow of the Archaeological Institute 1903–5, and at the American School of Classical Studies 1902–6, he remained there as librarian and as an assistant professor of archaeology in 1908. He took his Ph.D. at Yale in 1915, and after the merger of the School of Classical Studies with the American Academy in Rome he became librarian of the latter until 1925, and thereafter remained there as curator of its museum, editor of its publications, and professor of archaeology. He retired in 1945. In 1962 he was awarded the Academy's Medal for Outstanding Service. He bequeathed half his estate to Yale and half to the American Academy in Rome, which received some $172,000.

VAN DEMAN, ESTHER BOISE, 1862–1945. An archaeologist, she was a fellow of Bryn Mawr College 1892–93 and of the School of Classical Studies in Rome 1901–3. She was again at that School as Carnegie Institution fellow 1906–10, and once again as Carnegie Institution research professor 1925–30. During the intervals between these appointments she lived much in Rome. She left a legacy to the Academy.

VANDERBILT, MRS. FREDERICK WILLIAM. Her husband (1856–1938) had houses in New York and in Hyde Park designed in 1896 and

1899 by McKim, Mead, and White. She was a sister-in-law of William Kissam Vanderbilt (1849–1920).

VANDERBILT, WILLIAM KISSAM, 1849–1920. Capitalist and director of railroads, he was also a director of the Metropolitan Opera Company and founder and president of the New Theater. In 1905 he became an incorporator of the American Academy in Rome, to which he gave $100,000.

VAN DOREN, MARK, 1894– . He graduated from the University of Illinois in 1914 and was at Columbia from 1920 to 1959 with ranks from instructor to full professor. He was literary editor of *The Nation* 1924–28, and won a Pulitzer Prize for poetry in 1931. He is the author of many volumes on poetry, drama, and literary criticism.

VEDDER, ELIHU, 1836–1923. Mural painter, he studied in Paris in 1856, in Italy 1857–61, in America 1861–65, and again in Paris in 1866. He resided in Rome, though with occasional visits to America, from 1867, and was affiliated with McKim, Mead, and White 1897–98. His decorative panels are in the Library of Congress and Bowdoin College. He published his autobiography in 1910 and a volume of verse in 1914.

VONNOH, MRS. ROBERT WILLIAM (Bessie Potter), 1872–1955. Her sculpture won several medals. She gave a generous sum to the American Academy in Rome in 1926. From 1938, by remarriage, she was Mrs. Edward L. Keyes.

WALKER, CHARLES HOWARD, 1857–1936. An architect of Boston, he led in establishing a Department of Design in the Boston Museum of Fine Arts in 1884. In 1896 the trustees of the new American School of Architecture in Rome sounded him out regarding becoming its director, but he remained at the Department of Design in Boston and continued as its director after it had become a school.

WALKER, JOHN, III, 1906– . Harvard '30, associate in charge of the School of Fine Arts at the American Academy in Rome 1935–39, chief curator and then director of the National Gallery in Washington 1939–56, he is the author of several volumes on the fine arts. A recipient of many honors, he has been a trustee of the American Academy in Rome since 1940.

WALTERS, HENRY, 1848–1931. Capitalist and director of railroads and financial institutions, yachtsman, art collector, and philanthropist, he was a trustee of the Metropolitan Museum of Art, the New York Public Library, and the Peabody Museum in Baltimore. He was the first large Founder donor of the American Academy in Rome, an incorporator, and a trustee. He was an officer in the French Legion of Honor.

WARD, JOHN QUINCY ADAMS, 1830–1910. He was a sculptor, examples of whose statues are in New York, Boston, Washington, and Brooklyn; president of the National Academy of Design in 1872 and of the National Sculpture Society in 1896. He was a founder and trustee of the Metropolitan Museum of Art and an incorporator of the American Academy in Rome in 1905.

WARE, WILLIAM ROBERT, 1832–1915. He practiced architecture in Boston 1860–81 and was also professor of architecture at M.I.T. 1865–81. In the latter year he went to New York as professor of architecture at Columbia. He was a member of the managing committee of the American School in Athens 1885–1915 and was one of the founders of the American School of Architecture in Rome 1893–95.

WARREN, MINTON, 1850–1907. Professor of Latin at Johns Hopkins and then at Harvard, he was president of the American Philological Association 1897–98 and director of the American School of Classical Studies in Rome 1896–98.

WASSON, GORDON, 1898– . He was a financial reporter for the *New York Herald Tribune* 1925–28 and then with the Guaranty Trust Company 1928–34. He then served with J. P. Morgan and Company, of which he became a director. He was a trustee of the American Academy in Rome 1957–63 and secretary of the Board 1960–63.

WATKINS, FRANKLIN CHENAULT, 1894– . From 1914–20 he studied painting at the Pennsylvania Academy of Fine Arts, where he was later medallist, instructor, and director. A painter of distinction, he was artist in-residence at the American Academy in Rome 1953–54 and is an honorary life fellow of the Academy.

WAUGH, SIDNEY, 1904–63. He studied at the School of Fine Arts in Rome in 1924 and in Paris 1925–28 and then as a fellow in sculpture at the American Academy in Rome 1929–32. A captaincy in the U.S. Air Force interrupted his later career but examples of his sculpture are in the Metropolitan Museum, the Chicago Art Institute, the Victoria and Albert Museum, and in several government buildings in Washington. He was director of the Rinehart School of Sculpture in Baltimore and held two Croix de Guerre and also Italian decorations from the war.

WEBEL, RICHARD KARL, 1900– . Born in Germany, he came with his parents to America and graduated from Harvard in 1923. He was a fellow in landscape architecture at the American Academy in Rome

1926–29 and then served on the faculty of the Harvard School of Design 1929–39. Meanwhile he also engaged from 1931 in private practice in Boston. He later moved to Glen Head, Long Island. His gifts to the American Academy have made him a life member. He was landscape architect-in-residence, 1963.

WESCOTT, GLENWAY, 1901– . He has been writing books since the age of twenty, is a member of the American Academy of Arts and Letters, and has been vice-president of the National Institute of Arts and Letters. He is a leading contemporary novelist.

WEST, ANDREW FLEMING, 1853–1943. He was professor of Latin at Princeton 1883–1928 and dean of the Princeton Graduate School 1901–28. He was chairman of the managing committee of the American School in Athens 1901–13, a trustee of the American Academy in Rome 1911–28, and chairman of its advisory committee on classical studies from 1917. He published some ten volumes on various subjects.

WESTERMAN, WILLIAM LINN, 1873–1954. He studied at Berlin in 1902 and after the usual academic initiations was professor of history at the University of Wisconsin 1914–20, at Cornell 1920–23, and at Columbia 1923–48. He was president of the American Historical Association in 1944 and professor in charge of classical studies at the American Academy in Rome 1926–27. He was a trustee of the Academy 1921–32.

WETMORE, GEORGE PEABODY, 1846–1921. He was governor of Rhode Island 1885–87 and senator from Rhode Island 1895–1913.

WHARTON, EDITH NEWBOLD JONES (Mrs. Edward Wharton), 1862–1937. She was the author of some forty books, chiefly fiction, and a leader of conservative New York society. She received decorations from France and Belgium.

WHICHER, GEORGE MASON, 1860–1937. He was professor of Greek and Latin at Hunter College 1899–1924, secretary of the Archaelogical Institute of America 1919–21, professor in charge of classical studies at the American Academy in Rome 1921–22, and the author or joint author of several volumes, including verse.

WHITE, HENRY, 1850–1927. His diplomatic career from 1883 included posts in Vienna, London, Rome, and Algeciras. He was ambassador to Italy 1905–7, to France 1907–9, and to Chile in 1910. He was a trustee of the Carnegie Institution, the Corcoran Gallery of Art in Washington, the Smithsonian Institution, and George Washington University. He was an incorporator of the American Academy in

Rome in 1905 and acted for its trustees in the purchase of the Villa Mirafiore.

WHITE, STANFORD, 1853–1906. He traveled and studied in Europe 1878–80 and upon his return joined in the partnership of McKim, Mead, and White. He was an incorporator of the American Academy in Rome in 1905 and visited the Academy in its new home on the Janiculum Hill in January 1914.

WHITNEY, MRS. HARRY PAYNE (Gertrude Vanderbilt). Mrs. Whitney studied sculpture in Paris, and her work was highly praised. In 1910 she gave generously to the American Academy in Rome and in 1922 she made a bronze plaque for the Academy in connection with its acquisition of funds to create the Walter Damrosch Fellowship for Music at the Academy.

WHITNEY, WILLIAM COLLINS, 1841–1904. A graduate of Yale in 1863 and of the Harvard Law School, he practiced law in New York and was secretary of the navy 1885–89. He built three homes designed for him by McKim, Mead, and White in 1890, 1900, and 1902. His gifts made him a benefactor of the American School and Academy in Rome, of which he was a trustee from 1897.

WIDENER, PETER A. B., 1834–1915. A Philadelphia coal, railroad and utilities magnate and a prominent political conservative, he was also a collector and a philanthropist. He built and endowed the Widener Memorial School for Crippled Children and gave a free public library to Philadelphia. His collection of valuable paintings is now in the National Gallery, Washington.

WILDER, THORNTON NIVEN, 1897– . He was a visiting student and writer at the American Academy in Rome 1920–21. As distinguished author and playwright he has received medals and awards in Britain, France, and West Germany as well as in America.

WILKINS, H. BLAKISTON. He was executive secretary of the American Academy in Rome 1917–21 and was made a Commander of the Order of the Crown of Italy in 1920.

WILLIAMS, MARY, 1907– . She held various posts at the Brooklyn Museum, including editor of publications, 1942–46. Since 1946 she has been the invaluable executive secretary of the American Academy in Rome.

WILSON, HARRY LANGFORD, 1867–1913. He was professor of archaeology at Johns Hopkins University 1906–13, and annual professor of classical studies at the American School of Classical Studies in Rome 1906–7.

WIND, EDGAR, 1900–1971. He was born in Berlin and studied at the Universities of Berlin, Freiburg, Vienna, and Hamburg 1918–22. He served in various capacities at the Warburg Institute in London 1927–42, when he came to America as professor at the University of Chicago 1942–44 and Smith College 1944–55. He became a U.S. citizen in 1948 and was art historian in residence at the American Academy in Rome 1950–51. In 1955 he became professor of the history of art at Oxford. He was an eloquent lecturer and a writer of distinction on many topics, notably Italian Renaissance art in its relation to ancient philosophies.

WINLOCK, HERBERT EUSTIS, 1884–1950. Harvard '06 and then almost constantly engaged in archaeological excavations in the Near East 1906–37, including the highly important discoveries at Luxor, Lisht, and Kharga. He was director of the Metropolitan Museum of Art 1932–39, the author of a dozen books on archaeology, and the holder of several European decorations and many honorary degrees. He was a trustee of the American Academy in Rome from February 1934. He was a major in World War II.

WINTER, EZRA, 1886–1949. He was a fellow in mural painting at the American Academy in Rome 1911–14. Afterward he came to be regarded as a leading American muralist; he held a commission at the San Francisco Exposition in 1939, and his murals are in the Library of Congress and many universities and schools.

WINTER, JOHN GARRETT, 1881–1956. He was a member of the faculty of the University of Michigan at ranks from instructor to professor 1906–56, while also director of the University Museum of Archaeology 1928–51 and of its Institute of Fine Arts 1928–48. In 1929 he was the first lecturer of the Thomas Spencer Jerome Foundation at the American Academy in Rome. He was a member of the managing committee of the American School in Athens and the advisory committee of the American Academy in Rome, as well as sometime president of the American Philological Association and author or editor of a dozen volumes on the classics.

WOODBRIDGE, FREDERICK JAMES, 1900– . He graduated from the Columbia School of Architecture in 1923 and studied at the American Academy in Rome 1923–25. He was the architect at the excavations at Antioch and Carthage 1924–25 and a practicing architect in New York from 1929. During World War II he was in naval aviation as an observer with the rank of lieutenant commander. In 1951–52 he was architect-in-residence at the American Academy in Rome while a Fulbright fellow.

WRIGHT, WYLLIS EATON, 1903– . Williams College '25. He joined the staff of the New York Public Library but in 1930 succeeded Milton Lord as librarian of the American Academy in Rome. In 1933 he returned to the New York Public Library and since 1945 has been librarian of Williams College.

ZELLERBACH, JAMES DAVID, 1892–1963. He graduated from the University of California in 1913 and later became president and then chairman of the board of the Crown Zellerbach Company of San Francisco. He was the first head of the Economic Cooperation Administration (Marshall Plan) in Italy 1948–50 and ambassador to Italy 1956–60. When he left Italy his company gave funds to support a fellowship at the American Academy in Rome.

Fellows of the Academy

(Original Name of the Academy, 1894–1897)

*Wm. S. Covell, '98   *John Russell Pope, '97

SCHOOL OF FINE ARTS

1897–1972

Architecture

Joseph Amisano, '52
Richard W. Ayers, '38
C. Dale Badgeley, '29
Gregory S. Baldwin, '71
Richard E. Baringer, '53
Richard Bartholomew, '72
Charles G. Brickbauer, '57
Cecil C. Briggs, '31
Dale C. Byrd, '52
Walker O. Cain, '48
Kenneth E. Carpenter, '15
James Chillman, Jr., '22
Frederic S. Coolidge, '48
Thomas V. Czarnowski, '68
Royston T. Daley, '62
Spero P. Daltas, '51
Thomas L. Dawson, Jr., '52
Arthur F. Deam, '26
Ronald L. Dirsmith, '60
*William Douglas, '28
Bernard Evanbar, '63

*George Fraser, '28
Robert M. Golder, '63
Michael Graves, '62
James A. Gresham, '56
Olindo Grossi, '36
Myron A. Guran, '72
Richard G. Hartshorne, Jr., '39
John D. Heimbaugh, '70
Wm. J. H. Hough, '17
Erling F. Iversen, '40
David J. Jacob, '58
James Jarrett, '59
B. Kenneth Johnstone, '32
Henri V. Jova, '51
Raymond M. Kennedy, '19
George S. Koyl, '14
James R. Lamantia, Jr., '49
Thomas N. Larson, '64
David L. Leavitt, '50
*Ernest F. Lewis, '11
George T. Licht, '37

* Deceased

Theodore Liebman, '66
John H. MacFadyen, '54
Henri Marceau, '25
Tallie B. Maule, '52
Henry D. Mirick, '33
Robert J. Mittelstadt, '66
Theodore J. Musho, '61
Robert L. Myers, '54
George H. Nelson, '34
Stanley H. Pansky, '53
William E. Pedersen, Jr., '66
Charles O. Perry, '66
Warren A. Peterson, '55
Homer F. Pfeiffer, '30
Warren Platner, '56
Walter L. Reichardt, '33
Peter Miller Schmitt, '72
Thomas L. Schumacher, '69
Jon Michael Schwarting, '70

Stuart M. Shaw, '28
Philip T. Shutze, '20
*James Kellum Smith, '23
Peter F. Smith, '69
*Richard H. Smythe, '13
Dan R. Stewart, '57
Charles T. Stifter, '63
John J. Stonehill, '60
Wayne Taylor, '62
Milo H. Thompson, '65
Duane E. Thorbeck, '64
Robert Venturi, '56
Austris J. Vitols, '67
*Walter L. Ward, '16
Harry E. Warren, '09
Robert A. Weppner, Jr., '36
Charles D. Wiley, '48
Edgar I. Williams, '12
Astra Zarina, '63

Environmental Design

Gerald D. Adams, '68
Robert R. Dvorak, '72
June Meyer Jordan, '71
J. Michael Kirkland, '70

R. Alan Melting, '70
William Reed, '68
Will Shaw, '68

Landscape Architecture

Eric Armstrong, '61
E. Bruce Baetjer, '54
Richard C. Bell, '53
Stephen F. Bochkor, '57
Robert T. Buchanan, '59
Vincent C. Cerasi, '50
*Henri E. Chabanne, '34
Charles A. Currier, '48
Frederick W. Edmondson, Jr., '48
Jon S. Emerson, '67
Ralph E. Griswold, '23
Dale H. Hawkins, '52
*Alden Hopkins, '36
Frank D. James, '68
Dean A. Johnson, '66

John F. Kirkpatrick, '39
Robert S. Kitchen, '38
Albert R. Lamb III, '70
*Edward Lawson, '21
James M. Lister, '37
Roger B. Martin, '64
Stuart M. Mertz, '40
Richard C. Murdock, '33
Norman T. Newton, '26
Don H. Olson, '62
Neil H. Park, '33
George E. Patton, '51
Paul R. V. Pawlowski, '69
Peter M. Pollack, '71
Thomas D. Price, '32

* Deceased

Charles A. Rapp, '72
Michael Rapuano, '30
R. T. Schnadelbach, '66
Seth H. Seablom, '68
*Charles R. Sutton, '32

Erik A. Svenson, '58
Morris E. Trotter, '35
Richard K. Webel, '29
Brooks E. Wigginton, '50
Ervin H. Zube, '61

Literature

Robert E. Bagg, '59
Harold Brodkey, '61
John Ciardi, '57
Walter Clemons, Jr., '62
Alan Dugan, '63
Ralph Ellison, '57
Robert Francis, '58
George P. Garrett, '59

Anthony E. Hecht, '52
Edmund Keeley, '60
Sigrid de Lima, '54
Louis Simpson, '58
George Starbuck, '63
William Styron, '53
Richard Wilbur, '55

Musical Composition

Stephen Albert, '67
Samuel Barber, '37
Leslie R. Bassett, '63
Jack H. Beeson, '50
Elliott Carter, '54
Morris Cotel, '68
William D. Denny, '41
John C. Eaton, '62
Herbert Elwell, '27
Jack R. Fortner, '68
Lukas Foss, '52
Vincent S. Frohne, '66
*Vittorio Giannini, '36
Alexei Haieff, '49
Howard H. Hanson, '24
Higo H. Harada, '60
John Heineman, '69
James L. Heinke, '72
*Walter Helfer, '28
Stanley Hollingsworth, '58
Andrew W. Imbrie, '49
Herbert R. Inch, '34
Werner Janssen, '33
Hunter Johnson, '35
Ulysses Kay, '52

Kent W. Kennan, '39
Barbara Kolb, '71
Arthur R. Kreutz, '42
Gail T. Kubik, '52
Ezra Laderman, '64
Billy Jim Layton, '57
Marvin D. Levy, '64
Normand Lockwood, '32
Salvatore J. Martirano, '59
Robert W. Moevs, '55
*Charles Naginski, '40
Paul E. Nelson, '63
Daniel Perlongo, '72
George Rochberg, '51
Loren Rush, '71
Robert L. Sanders, '29
Roger H. Sessions, '31
Harold S. Shapero, '51
William O. Smith, '58
*Leo Sowerby, '24
Alexander L. Steinert, '30
Randall Thompson, '25
Richard A. Trythall, '67
Henry Weinberg, '70
Louis Weingarden, '70

* Deceased

Charles Whittenberg, '66
Frank Wigglesworth, '54
Richard M. Willis, Jr., '57
George B. Wilson, '61

Philip G. Winsor, '67
Frederick Woltmann, '39
Yehudi Wyner, '56

Painting

Harry G. Ackerman, '34
Lennart Anderson, '61
John A. Annus, '61
Donald Aquilino, '60
Jack L. Bailey, '72
Gilbert Banever, '36
Dunbar D. Beck, '30
Wayne Begley, '61
Ronald C. Binks, '62
A. Robert Birmelin, '64
Alfred H. Blaustein, '57
Matthew W. Boyhan, '39
*Daniel Boza, '35
*Francis Scott Bradford, '27
*George W. Breck, '99
Paul Chalfin, '09
*F. Tolles Chamberlin, '11
Carlo A. Ciampaglia, '23
John Civitello, '70
Russell Cowles, '20
Allyn Cox, '20
Thomas H. Dahill, Jr., '57
*George Davidson, '16
Harry A. Davis, Jr., '41
*Salvatore De Maio, '33
Peter Devries, '67
Seymour Drumlevitch, '52
*Frank P. Fairbanks, '12
*Barry Faulkner, '10
Alan E. Feltus, '72
A. Clemens Finley, '27
Loren R. Fisher, '42
Alfred E. Floegel, '25
Gregory Gillespie, '67
Leon Goldin, '58
Robert B. Green, '38
Stephen Greene, '54
Alan M. Gussow, '55

Philip Guston, '49
Walter H. Hahn, '57
James A. Hanes, '53
John E. Heliker, '49
Jack Henderson, '65
James J. Hennessey, '64
*James J. Hoffman, '56
Walter K. Hood, '55
Robert J. Jergens, '63
Richard A. Johnson, '68
Clifford E. Jones, '39
Zubel Kachadoorian, '59
Deane Keller, '29
Marjorie E. Kreilick, '63
*Salvatore Lascari, '22
Joseph Lasker, '52
John C. Leavey, '70
Kenneth R. Lithgow, '71
Robert McCloskey, '49
James Owen Mahoney, '35
John R. Manning, '59
John L. Massey, Jr., '61
Eugene E. Matthews, '60
Donald M. Mattison, '31
*Michael J. Mueller, '28
Arthur Osver, '54
William Ouellette, '65
Charles A. Owens, '48
William J. Patterson, '67
Bernard Perlin, '51
Steve Raffo, '55
Roger Ricco, '65
Norman J. Rubington, '53
*Robert K. Ryland, '06
Karen Saler, '68
Raymond Saunders, '66
Eugene Savage, '15
*Andrew T. Schwartz, '02

* Deceased

*Frank H. Schwarz, '24
Ronald Schwerin, '64
Mitchell Siporin, '50
John M. Sitton, '32
Michael C. Spafford, '69
*Frederick C. Stahr, '14
*Harry I. Stickroth, '17
Gilbert L. Stone, '67

William Thon, '48
John H. Wenger, '72
*Ezra Winter, '14
*Hy. Lawrence Wolfe, '11
Kenneth R. Worley, '70
Christopher Wray, '69
Jack Zajac, '58

Sculpture

Peter Abate, '51
Edmond R. Amateis, '24
Robert F. P. Amendola, '35
John Amore, '40
*Harry P. Camden, '27
Aldo J. Casanova, '61
Gaetano Cecere, '23
Lewis C. Cohen, '70
*Percival Dietsch, '09
Linda Dauw Dries, '69
Edward E. Dron, '71
Richard Howard Ellis, '65
Lawrence S. Fane, '63
Gilbert A. Franklin, '49
*Leo Friedlander, '16
Angelo W. Frudakis, '52
Sherry E. Fry, '11
*Harrison Gibbs, '38
Philip Grausman, '65
*John Gregory, '15
John Gulias, '49
Walker Hancock, '28
*Allen Harris, '61
*Charles Y. Harvey, '10
Milton Hebald, '58
Alexander Hunenko, '68
C. Paul Jennewein, '20
*Thomas H. Jones, '22
Luise Kaish, '72
Herbert L. Kammerer, '51
Jerry B. Kearns, '70
*Charles Keck, '04
Paul J. Kirchmer, '58
Joseph Kiselewski, '29

George M. Koren, '41
Reuben R. Kramer, '36
*Hermon A. MacNeil, '99
Robert J. McKnight, '35
*Paul Manship, '12
John Matt, '72
Ira C. Matteson, '55
Alvin Meyer, '26
Warren T. Mosman, '34
*Berthold Nebel, '17
Anthony J. Padovano, '62
John Nick Pappas, '67
Robert Pippenger, '42
*Albin Polasek, '13
Gifford M. Proctor, '37
*Joseph E. Renier, '20
John W. Rhoden, '54
Henry C. Rollins, '66
David K. Rubins, '31
Concetta Scaravaglione, '50
*William M. Simpson, '33
Susan V. Smyly, '67
George H. Snowden, '30
Lawrence T. Stevens, '25
Paul R. Suttman, '68
*Harry D. Thrasher, '14
*Sidney B. Waugh, '32
Albert W. Wein, '49
Elbert Weinberg, '53
Charles A. Wells, Jr., '66
Stephen G. Werlick, '64
Robert W. White, '55
James N. Wines, '57

* Deceased

American School of Classical Studies in Rome

(Original Name of the School of Classical Studies, 1895–1913)

*George Henry Allen, '02
*Henry Herbert Armstrong, '03
*Susan Helen Ballou, '06
William Warner Bishop, '99
*Joseph Granger Brandt, '12
*Howard Crosby Butler, '98
*Charles Upson Clark, '01
Guy B. Colburn, '10
William Kendall Denison, '96
*Walter Dennison, '97
*Norman Wentworth DeWitt, '04
*Albert F. Earnshaw, '97
*George H. Edgell, '12
Frank R. Elder, '12
*Herbert Edward Everett, '06
*Philip J. Gentner, '07
*Austin M. Harmon, '07
*Dora Johnson, '11
*George D. Kellogg, '00
*Gordon J. Laing, '97

Clark D. Lamberton, '08
*Dean P. Lockwood, '09
*Elias A. Lowe, '11
*Walter Lowrie, '96
*Ralph V. Magoffin, '07
Clarence L. Meader, '98
*Charles Rufus Morey, '03
*Richard Offner, '13
*George N. Olcott, '99
Thomas J. Preston, Jr., '09
Mabel Douglas Reid, '01
John Shapley, '13
*Grant Showerman, '00
Clara L. Thompson, '09
*Albert William Van Buren, '06
*Esther B. Van Deman, '09
*Henry B. Van Hoesen, '08
Anthony Pelzer Wagener, '11
*Arthur Harold Weston, '12
Philip B. Whitehead, '13

School of Classical Studies

1913–1972

*Freeman W. Adams, '51
Hubert L. Allen III, '67
William S. Anderson, '55
James I. Armstrong, '56
William A. Arrowsmith, '57
H. Ess Askew, '32
William T. Avery, '39
Eric C. Baade, '57
Charles L. Babcock, '55
Mary Taylor Babcock, '54
Claude W. Barlow, '38
Malcolm Bell III, '70
Bertram I. Berman, '49
Harold L. Bisbee, '36
*Doris Taylor Bishop, '49

*Marion L. Blake, '25
Frances Gertrude Blank, '40
S. Palmer Bovie, '50
Aline Abaercherli Boyce, '35
George K. Boyce, '35
Otto J. Brendel, '51
Richard Brilliant, '62
Dericksen M. Brinkerhoff, '61
Donald F. Brown, '41
Donald Freeman Brown, '53
Frank E. Brown, '33
Virginia Brown, '68
*Walter R. Bryan, '22
Anne Burnett, '59
Joseph C. Carter, '71

* Deceased

Michael Cheilik, '64
Ethel L. Chubb, '21
Wendell V. Clausen, '53
Emily Wadsworth Cleland, '21
Jacquelyn Collins Clinton, '69
Howard Comfort, '29
*John R. Crawford, '14
*John S. Creaghan, S.J., '48
James J. M. Curry, '63
*C. Densmore Curtis, '15
*John Day, '27
Mario A. Del Chiaro, '60
Susan B. Downey, '65
Miriam Friedman Drabkin, '40
Margaret H. DuBois, '72
Elizabeth Cornelia Evans, '32
Kenneth S. Falk, '54
J. Rufus Fears, '71
Joseph Fontenrose, '52
Bettie Forte, '60
Richard I. Frank, '64
Alfred K. Frazer, '61
Bruce W. Frier, '68
Mildred McConnell Gardner, '28
Katherine A. Geffcken, '55
Alfred Gelstharp, Jr., '33
Frank D. Gilliard, '65
Robert F. Goheen, '53
*Charlotte E. Goodfellow, '48
Arthur E. Gordon, '49
Harold C. Gotoff, '59
*Chester Carr Greene, Jr., '34
Richard E. Grimm, '56
Martha Leeb Hadzi, '55
John Arthur Hanson, '55
Raymond D. Harriman, '16
Robert E. Hecht, Jr., '49
Ursula Heibges, '66
Herbert Hoffmann, '58
Richard J. Hoffman, '72
Louise Adams Holland, '23
R. Ross Holloway, '62
Lester C. Houck, '40
George W. Houston, '69
Michael H. Jameson, '59
Franklin W. Jones, '31

Dawson Kiang, '71
Adele Jeanne Kibre, '32
Anne Laidlaw, '61
Richmond Lattimore, '35
Lillian B. Lawler, '26
John O. Lenaghan, '59
*Ernestine Franklin Leon, '23
Brooks Emmons Levy, '56
Martha Hoffman Lewis, '53
Naphtali Lewis, '36
Elaine P. Loeffler, '53
Anna Marguerite McCann, '66
*Eugene S. McCartney, '16
George McCracken, '31
William L. MacDonald, '56
William T. McKibben, '51
Berthe M. Marti, '51
Lucy Shoe Meritt, '37
*William Stuart Messer, '22
Ann Freeman Meyvaert, '58
Agnes Kirsopp Lake Michels, '33
Mariateresa Marabini Moevs, '64
John A. Moore, '56
Floyd C. Moreland, '69
Charles T. Murphy, '54
Chester F. Natunewicz, '59
Norman Neuerburg, '57
Raymond T. Ohl, '30
James H. Oliver, Jr., '30
*Erling S. Olsen, '39
Mary-Kay Gamel Orlandi, '69
James E. Packer, '64
Thalia A. Pandiri, '67
Paul Pascal, '52
Bernard Mann Peebles, '34
*Roy M. Peterson, '17
Collice Henry Portnoff, '30
Michael C. J. Putnam, '64
*John T. Reardon, '17
Homer F. Rebert, '24
Meyer Reinhold, '35
Emeline Hill Richardson, '52
Lawrence Richardson, Jr., '50
Dorothy M. Robathan, '49
*Charles A. Robinson, Jr., '26
Florence H. Robinson, '25

* Deceased

*Robert S. Rogers, '24
Ruskin R. Rosborough, '24
Irene Rosenzweig, '30
David O. Ross, Jr., '66
Inez Scott Ryberg, '26
Frederick LaMotte Santee, '27
*Susan M. Savage, '38
Dorothy M. Schullian, '34
Ann Reynolds Scott, '67
Russell T. Scott, Jr., '66
Charles P. Segal, '63
George J. Siefert, Jr., '36
Edmund T. Silk, '31
William G. Sinnigen, '54
Walter F. Snyder, '38
Edward W. Spofford, '64
Chester G. Starr, Jr., '40

*Lillian Starr, '27
Arthur R. Steinberg, '64
*Gilbert H. Taylor, '20
*Lily Ross Taylor, '22
William R. Tongue, '48
Myra Uhlfelder, '50
*Margaret C. Waites, '13
Francis R. Walton, '37
Helen Russell White, '52
Michael Wigodsky, '61
Lois V. Williams, '48
Charles Witke, '62
Philip F. Wooby, '53
*Horace W. Wright, '16
John Wright, '68
John W. Zarker, '60

Alumni Scholars

Robert A. Brooks, '42
Herbert S. Long, '42

Carl R. Trahman, '42

Post-Classical Humanistic Studies

Robert A. Blazis, '65
Denis J. M. Bradley, '72
Paul M. Clogan, '67
Thomas Culley, S.J., '67
Frank A. D'Accone, '64
Linda L. Fowler, '65
Frederick F. Hammond, '66
Richard G. Kenworthy, '70

Julius Kirshner, '69
Benjamin G. Kohl, '71
Janet Martin, '72
John Monfasani, '71
John W. O'Malley, S.J., '65
Emil J. Polak, '63
Kenneth J. Pratt, '63
Eyvind Ronquist, '70

Art History

James S. Ackerman, '52
Glenn M. Andres, '69
Eugene A. Carroll, '61
Hereward Lester Cooke, Jr., '54
Horst de la Croix, '63
Charles G. Dempsey, '65
Joachim E. Gaehde, '57

B. Howard Hibbard, '58
Patrick J. Kelleher, '49
Dale Kinney, '72
Milton J. Lewine, '62
C. Douglas Lewis, Jr., '65
Richard B. K. McLanathan, '49
Margaret Koons Miller, '51

* Deceased

William B. Miller, '51
Henry A. Millon, '60
Charles I. Minott, '64
Loren W. Partridge, '68

Donald Posner, '61
Susan Saward, '71
Richard W. Stapleford, '67
Patricia Waddy, '70

Artists and Scholars in Residence, 1947–1972

Max Abramovitz, architect
James S. Ackerman, art historian
Mark Adams, painter
Nelson W. Aldrich, architect
Helen H. Bacon, classicist
J. B. Bakema, architect
Samuel Barber, composer
Edward L. Barnes, architect
Charles Edward Bassett, architect
Jack H. Beeson, composer
Pietro Belluschi, architect
Eugene Berman, painter
George Biddle, painter
Herbert Bloch, classicist
Peter Blume, painter
Varujan Bohosian, sculptor
Henry C. Boren, historian
Louis Bouché, painter
Elizabeth Bowen, writer
James Brooks, painter
Van Wyck Brooks, writer
T. Robert S. Broughton, classicist
Frank E. Brown, archaeologist
Elliott Carter, composer
Thomas D. Church, landscape architect
Francis F. A. Comstock, architect
Aaron Copland, composer
Malcolm Cowley, writer
Gardner Cox, painter
John H. D'Arms, classicist
David Diamond, composer
Seymour Drumlevitch, painter
Philipp Fehl, art historian
Ross Lee Finney, composer
Gilbert A. Franklin, sculptor

Siegfried Giedion, architectural historian
Ralph E. Griswold, landscape architect
Philip Guston, painter
Alexei Haieff, composer
Mason Hammond, classicist
Walker Hancock, sculptor
John Arthur Hanson, classicist
Adlai S. Hardin, sculptor
Bartlett H. Hayes, Jr., art historian
Anthony E. Hecht, poet
Philip Hofer, art historian
Louise Adams Holland, classicist
R. Ross Holloway, classicist
George Howe, architect
Harry Hubbell, classicist
James M. Hunter, architect
Andrew W. Imbrie, composer
David J. Jacob, architect
H. W. Janson, art historian
Matthew Josephson, writer
Louis I. Kahn, architect
Clarence Kennedy, art historian
Ruth Wedgewood Kennedy, art historian
Richard Krautheimer, art historian
Jean Labatut, architect
John La Montaine, composer
Roy F. Larson, architect
Robert Laurent, sculptor
Irving Lavin, art historian
Rico Lebrun, painter
Rensselaer W. Lee, art historian
Julian Levi, painter
Milton E. Lord, librarian

Jeanne R. Lowe, writer
Otto Luening, composer
Henry C. McIlhenny, art historian
Archibald MacLeish, writer
Louis A. McMillen, architect
Berthe M. Marti, classicist
Ezio Martinelli, sculptor
Bohuslav Martinu, composer
C. W. Mendell, classicist
Henry A. Millon, art historian
Charles Mitchell, art historian
Robert W. Moevs, composer
Alfred Moir, art historian
Agnes Mongan, art historian
Douglas Moore, composer
Nicolas Nabokov, composer
Norman T. Newton, landscape architect
Costantino Nivola, sculptor
Donald M. Oenslager, stage designer
Arthur Osver, painter
Nathaniel A. Owings, architect
William L. Pereira, architect
Charles O. Perry, sculptor
Henry Varnum Poor, painter
Donald Posner, art historian
Kathleen Garris Posner, art historian
Gregorio Prestopino, painter
Jesse Reichek, painter
Philip H. Rhinelander, philosopher

Lawrence Richardson, Jr., classicist
Colin Rowe, architect
Henry T. Rowell, classicist
Harold Shapero, composer
Edmund T. Silk, classicist
Sidney Simon, sculptor
Mitchell Siporin, painter
Erik Sjöqvist, archaeologist
Craig Hugh Smyth, art historian
Wallace Stegner, writer
Edward Durell Stone, architect
Cecil L. Striker, art historian
Allen Tate, poet
Lily Ross Taylor, classicist
Paul Thiry, architect
Randall Thompson, composer
William Thon, painter
Harold Tovish, sculptor
Aldo Van Eyck, architect
Robert Venturi, architect
Robert Penn Warren, writer
Franklin C. Watkins, painter
Richard K. Webel, landscape architect
Hugo Weisgall, composer
Robert W. White, sculptor
Frank Wigglesworth, composer
*Edgar Wind, art historian
Rudolf Wittkower, art historian
Frederick J. Woodbridge, architect
Jack Zajac, sculptor

Trustees of the Academy
1973

Index

Index of Persons

And Some Places